INSIDE THE CROSSTOWN SHOOTOUT

Cincinnati vs. Xavier

The Rivalry That Captivates a City

INSIDE THE

Crosstown

SHOOTOUT

Bill Koch

Inside the Crosstown Shootout

Cincinnati vs. Xavier: The Rivalry That Captivates a City

Copyright ©2016 Bill Koch, Cincinnati, Ohio, U.S.A.

ISBN-13: Softcover 978-0-9982771-0-3

Covert artwork copyright ©2016 by T.L. Price
Composition by T.L. Price

Produced and published by Dennis Tuttle, 5editorial, Silver Spring, Md.

This book was printed in the United States of America.

10 9 8 7 6 5 4 3 2 1

To Doug Henry, my former sports editor at the Cincinnati Post who first gave me the chance to cover college basketball when he assigned me to the Xavier beat in 1983. In addition to being a master at improving stories through the editing process, Doug cared as much about his employees' careers as he did his own.

TABLE OF CONTENTS

INTRODUCTION
A 12-Minute Drive, But Worlds Apart

I've always thought it odd that the college basketball rivalry between the University of Cincinnati and Xavier University is called the Crosstown Shootout.

If one school were located on the west side of Cincinnati and the other on the east side, it would make more sense because you'd actually have to travel across town to get from one to the other. But that's not the case. The drive from Fifth Third Arena on UC's campus to Cintas Center on Xavier's campus takes 12 minutes, depending on traffic. I clocked it at 3.5 miles, hardly a crosstown excursion.

But such close proximity is one element of the rivalry that makes it distinctive. So is the fact that UC is a large state school with an undergraduate enrollment of 33,218 while Xavier is a small Catholic Jesuit school with an undergraduate enrollment of 4,066.

Still, it wouldn't be much of a rivalry if one school dominated the other. That was the case before 1980 when the Bearcats had won 22 of the last 24 games and held an overall series advantage of 34-12. That all changed on Feb. 4 of that year when Bob Staak, in his first season as Xavier's head coach, guided the Musketeers to a 77-69 upset of UC at Riverfront Coliseum. Since then, Xavier has won 22 games to UC's 15, including three in a row and eight of the last 11. Four of Xavier's victories during that time have been in overtime. Twice the Musketeers have knocked off UC when the Bearcats were ranked No. 1 in the country.

As the years have passed, the vitriol between the teams – and especially their fans – has grown to the point where a fight broke out among the players in 2011 at Cintas Center. This wasn't a typical sports skirmish that includes pushing and shoving and not much else. Punches were thrown, blood flowed, and the game was stopped with 9.4 seconds remaining. Xavier led at the time, 76-53, and was declared the victor. Players from both teams were suspended, the fight became national news, and there was talk of suspending the series until calm could be returned to the rivalry. Instead, it was moved to a neutral court for two years before it was moved back to the schools' home courts with both sides promising to be on their best behavior.

That wasn't the first time tempers flared or punches were thrown. This game has always been played with an edge that sometimes spilled over into fights on the court and rowdiness among fans. UC great Oscar Robertson remembers an incident from his sophomore year in 1958 when he scored 29 points in the Bearcats' 80-68 win at Cincinnati Gardens.

"During a timeout, I'm standing there in the huddle and all of a sudden a whiskey bottle lands on the floor right beside our huddle," Robertson said. "I thought, 'What is going on?'"

One published account from that time described the bottle in question as a wine bottle that was clearly thrown at Robertson, but the Big O says he's not sure he was the target.

"I hope not," he said. "But it missed, so it doesn't really matter. We kept on playing."

Robertson averaged 30.7 points, 16 rebounds and seven assists in three games against the Musketeers. As a junior he scored 38 points with 23 rebounds and eight assists in a 92-66 UC victory at the Gardens. The Bearcats won all three of their games against the Musketeers during the Robertson era by an average score of 83-67. Still, he remembers the Xavier games as highly competitive and intense.

"It was always a tough game," he said, "with both teams being in the same city. It was very intense. I don't think that's ever going to change. Guys were emotional. They wanted to win the game."

Xavier's Steve Thomas scored 45 points against UC in the 1964 game but the Bearcats still won, 94-92, after Thomas was called for traveling in the final five seconds. Late in that game, UC's Ron Bonham took a swing at Xavier's Bryan Williams. Three years later, in UC's 79-69 overtime win, UC's Raleigh Wynn and Xavier's Joe Pangrazio got into a scuffle during which Pangrazio grabbed a crutch from the stands and threw it at Wynn. In the early 1980s, UC's Keith Starks took a swing at Xavier's Dexter Campbell because he thought Campbell had intentionally elbowed him in the face. In 1985, UC's Myron Hughes punched Xavier's Eddie Johnson and knocked him to the ground after Johnson had elbowed him.

The rivalry has included one game where UC coach Bob Huggins refused to shake hands with Xavier coach Pete Gillen after a Musketeer victory and one where a UC player predicted in the newspaper that the Bearcats would blow out Xavier, which is exactly what happened.

UC has long dominated the series and still holds a commanding 49-34 lead. The Bearcats won 12 in a row against Xavier from Dec. 13, 1957 through March 3, 1967. Xavier stopped that UC winning streak with a 72-71 win on Mar. 5, 1968, but the Bearcats responded by winning 10 of the next 11. Lately, though, the Musketeers have taken charge.

"It's going in X's favor," Robertson said. "Is it a rivalry or not? You've got to be able to compete, that's the key. No doubt about it. They've got the upper hand."

Xavier usually wins the close games. The Musketeers are 5-1 in overtime games, 13-5 in games decided by three points or fewer. UC is 30-8 in games decided by 10 points or more.

For most of the rivalry, UC not only dominated on the court, but was a nationally respected program while Xavier floundered in relative obscurity. The Bearcats played in a better conference. Xavier had no league affiliation until 1979 when it became a charter member of the Midwestern City Conference along with Evansville, Oklahoma City, Oral Roberts, Detroit, Butler and Loyola (Ill.). At the time, UC was a member of the Metro Conference with such national powers as Louisville and Memphis State.

The Musketeers left the MCC in 1995 for the Atlantic 10 Conference, which was definitely an upgrade, but still not as highly regarded as UC's Conference USA. In 2005, UC moved to the Big East Conference, which then was widely considered the most competitive league in the country. So even when the Musketeers were regularly going to the NCAA Tournament and advancing to the Sweet 16 in 2009, 2010 and 2012, UC fans still disparaged the quality of play in their conference. But that advantage slipped away for the Bearcats when the Big East collapsed after the 2012-'13 season because of the departure of Syracuse, Pittsburgh, Notre Dame, and West Virginia for other conferences. Louisville and Rutgers left the following year.

UC then joined Big East holdovers Connecticut and South Florida to piece together the American Athletic Conference. At the same time, Xavier left the A-10 and partnered with the remaining members of the Big East-Villanova, Georgetown, Marquette, DePaul, St. John's, Providence and Seton Hall-to form a new league that kept the Big East name the Bearcats once were so proud of. In 2015-'16 the new Big East was the fourth highest rated league in the country, according to RealTimeRPI. com; the AAC was eighth.

So now the Musketeers not only dominate the Crosstown Shootout, they play in a better league. They also outdraw the Bearcats in home attendance averaging 10,281 in 2015-'16 to UC's 9,415. The Musketeers play in Cintas Center, a 10,250-seat arena that opened in 2000. The Bearcats play in 13,176-seat Fifth Third Arena, which opened in 1989 and is scheduled for a major renovation beginning in 2017. Put it all together and Xavier is no longer the little brother in this rivalry. The tables have clearly turned, so that it's now difficult to continue to think of a Xavier victory over UC as a case of David slaying Goliath. But few would claim the rivalry has lost its edge due to the Musketeers' recent success. If anything, it has grown more intense and even more compelling.

The series began on March 7, 1928 when it christened the new Schmidt Fieldhouse on the Musketeers' campus. St. Xavier College, as it was known at the time, won, 29-25. Here's how Ben Dahlman of the Cincinnati Enquirer described the game: "They played before a wondrous crowd in the wondrous fieldhouse at Winding Way and Marion Ave. Nine thousand persons looked upon the two as they played, and played hard. It is a splendid fieldhouse, this home of the Musketeer, and a very representative crowd watched the two scamper about. The wonderful behavior of the crowd struck everyone as forcibly as did the victory of the Musketeer over the Bearcat, the proud champion of the Buckeye Association. The Bearcat played well, the Musketeer played better.

"But that crowd – tier upon tier of human faces looking down upon the playful Musketeer and the even more playful Bearcat. Professors, deans, financial wizards, bankers, editors, business men, clubmen, with their wives, sisters, mothers or the girl friend, all sat in perfect calm. Then at times they would join in the songs and yells of their alma mater, then shriek in ecstasy as the Bearcat shot a goal or the Musketeer made a basket. All fine and orderly."

The reference to 9,000 fans is puzzling considering that Schmidt Fieldhouse currently accommodates only 2,900 fans and never could hold more than 4,250. As for the "fine and orderly" comportment of the fans, we'll have to take Dahlman at his word. It was a different time, after all. But such delicate comportment has not been seen at a UC-Xavier game in many years.

UC and Xavier didn't play again until March 3, 1943, with the Musketeers winning again, 51-37. On Feb. 27, 1946, the Bearcats won for the first time, 53-39, the first of three straight wins for UC. The first five games of the rivalry were played at Schmidt before it was moved in March 1949 to Cincinnati Gardens, which has hosted more UC-Xavier games than any other venue, with UC holding a 27-15 edge there.

From 1948 through 1958, the game was played twice a year until settling into its current one-game-a-year format. It remained strictly a local affair until Jan. 28, 1998 when it went national for the first time and was televised on ESPN.

There have been 26 Shootouts in which UC was ranked in the Associated Press Top 25 and the Musketeers were not. The Bearcats are 20-6 in those games. Xavier has been ranked six times when UC was not and has won all six of those games. There have been two games where both teams were ranked at the time of the Shootout and Xavier won both times.

Covering the Crosstown Shootout nearly every year since 1983 has been one of the treats of my career as a sportswriter for the Cincinnati Post and the Cincinnati Enquirer. I always thought it deserved to have a book written about it, but was never able to come up with a workable approach. I didn't want to do the Top 25 games or Top 50 players. That seemed trite for such a captivating rivalry.

And then I remembered that before every Shootout I covered I would watch the players warm up and wonder what was going through their minds. Were they nervous? What did this game mean to them? How did the coaches approach it? What would the players remember years from now? And most importantly, what was it like to play in a rivalry of such magnitude?

So I decided to do an oral history in the tradition of the late Studs Terkel, who used that approach to write bestselling books such as "Working" and "Race." I thought, why not talk to the players and coaches in the same way and let them tell us what it's like to play in the Shootout?

I started with the 1980 game that changed the nature of the rivalry. I succeeded in talking to every UC and Xavier coach from 1980 until now, with the exception of Xavier's Skip Prosser, who died of a heart attack in 2007. In his place, I talked to Dino Gaudio, one of Prosser's closest friends and his former assistant coach. I wanted to talk to players who enjoyed big moments in the Shootout, and some who had played in the most compelling games. But I also talked to some players simply because I knew they would do a good job of explaining their feelings about the rivalry.

In search of a different perspective, about halfway through the process I decided to talk to the radio announcers from the two schools and to Mike DeCourcy, the nationally respected college basketball columnist for the Sporting News. DeCourcy knows about the rivalry first-hand, having covered it for the Cincinnati Enquirer from 1997 to 2000.

As I made my way through the interviews, I found that most of the participants enjoyed talking about their experience in the Shootout and almost all of them knew their record against their rival. But not everyone I contacted was eager or willing to share his story. Several players initially agreed to be interviewed but never followed through. When I had trouble reaching one high-profile Xavier player, coach Chris Mack intervened and the player told him that he would call me. But he never did, nor did he ever respond to my phone calls or text messages. And still another player politely declined to be part of the book, saying in effect that his experience playing in the Shootout was a good one, but he preferred not to talk about it. Fair enough.

A few thanked me for including them in the book. Several others-most notably Xavier's Brian Grant and Darnell Williams-asked me to let them know when the book came out so they could buy a copy. And several apologized for taking so long to get back to me.

And then there was former UC coach Bob Huggins. I knew that no Crosstown Shootout book would be complete without Huggins, but I also knew from experience that trying to get him to discuss anything in depth on the phone is a difficult proposition at best. So I called him and asked if he would agree to be interviewed in person if I drove to Morgantown, where he's the head coach at West Virginia. We set up a time and I made the five-hour-plus drive.

When I pulled up in front of the basketball building at the appointed time, I noticed there was no car in his designated parking space and wondered if he had forgotten. When I walked inside, I was told by the receptionist that he was not there. Soon a member of the basketball staff came out and told me the same thing. He said I was welcome to wait if I wanted to, so I settled into a chair in the lobby and hoped for the best.

Within a few minutes, Huggins came striding purposefully through the door. We walked back to his office and talked for about an hour. He repeatedly told me that he couldn't remember a lot of specifics about the games against Xavier and at the end of the interview, after I tried every approach I could think of, I ran out of questions. He then apologized. "I'm sorry I wasn't able to help you more," he said.

I thanked him for talking to me and as I walked outside to begin the long drive to Cincinnati, I wondered if I had wasted my time. But when I got back to Cincinnati and transcribed the interview, I found that Huggins had given me much more than he realized. In fact, his interview turned out to be, in my opinion, some of the best stuff in the book.

Eventually many of the interviews centered in four areas, sometimes by design, sometimes simply because that's where the player or coach led me. The four areas were: the 1980 game that changed the rivalry and the impact it had in making Xavier the program it is today; the November 1996 game in which Xavier's Lenny Brown made a buzzer-beating shot to upset the No. 1-ranked Bearcats; the love and respect that players and coaches from both sides had for Prosser; and the fight that left an indelible mark on the rivalry in 2011.

I discovered that until recently the players from both teams knew each other well and many remain friends today. I also discovered how much the game still means to the players many years later, even to those who went on to successful NBA careers or who play professionally overseas.

My thanks to all the coaches, players and media representatives who took the time to share their experiences and insights with me. Thanks especially to former UC player Terry Nelson, who runs UC's Legends program; Xavier associate athletic director Tom Eiser; and Shannon Russell, the former Xavier beat writer for the Cincinnati Enquirer. All of them helped me get in touch with interview subjects, as did Paul Keels, the play-by-play voice of the Ohio State Buckeyes who helped me reach Thad Matta; Doug Tammaro, the sports information director at Arizona State, who helped me get in touch with his old friend Sean Miller; Lenny Stokes, who went out of his way to put me in touch with 2000 National Player of the Year Kenyon Martin; and Connecticut assistant athletic director Phil Chardis, who helped me reach Bob Staak.

Thanks also to my friend and former colleague Steve Kemme for his editing expertise; to Cliff Radel and John Erardi, my former colleagues and current weekly lunch companions for their patience in listening to me talk about this project during the past 10 months and for their valued advice along the way; to former Cincinnati Enquirer publisher Rick Green for his generosity with Enquirer photos; and to Jeff Suess, the Enquirer librarian who assisted us in finding the photos we needed; to UC athletic director Mike Bohn, associate athletic director Ryan Koslen and assistant athletic director Andre Foushee; to Dennis Tuttle of 5editorial for his assistance in publishing this book; and, as always, to my wife, Rose, and daughter, Heather, for their encouragement, advice and invaluable help along the way.

COACHES

*Bob Staak used a victory over UC in 1980 to help Xavier
gain credibility after he took over as head coach.*

BOB STAAK

Xavier head coach, 1979-'85

"That turned the corner for us."

*D*uring his first season as the head basketball coach at Xavier, Bob Staak led the Musketeers to an 8-18 record. At most schools, a season like that would be buried in the small type of the media guide and forgotten. But at Xavier the 1979-'80 season might have been the most important in the history of the program because of one game-the Musketeers' 77-69 victory over UC in the Crosstown Shootout.

Staak's first head coaching job was at a school where the basketball program was referred to as "a mom and pop operation" by a former XU player. The Musketeers played as an independent and had endured 10 losing seasons in the last 12 when Staak arrived. A former star player at Connecticut, Staak was hired to replace Tay Baker after he had helped future Naismith Memorial Basketball Hall of Fame coach Chuck Daly lead the Ivy League Penn Quakers to the Final Four in 1979.

Baker was the head coach at UC from 1965 to 1972 and an assistant coach on the Bearcats' 1961 and 1962 national championship teams. He had gone 70-89 in six seasons at Xavier and resigned at the end of the 1978-'79 season after the Musketeers went 14-13.

On June 16, 1979, Xavier became a charter member of the Midwestern City Conference, which has evolved into the Horizon League. The Musketeers went 0-5 during their first season in the MCC, but one of their eight non-conference victories was an upset of UC.

Staak arrived on Victory Parkway with no knowledge of a rivalry with UC–if you could even call it a rivalry. The Bearcats had won their last eight games against

Xavier, 22 of their last 24, and owned a 34-12 advantage in the series overall.

"I remember some alumni and some followers of the program who told me, 'I don't care what you do, just beat UC, just beat UC,'" Staak said. "That's all I heard. I think part of that was the pent-up frustration of some of the people. They hadn't beaten UC in (eight years) prior so it was something very much on their mind and it became something that was a big goal as far as I was concerned. I don't think I had that sense when I first got there, but the longer I spent leading up to the (UC) game the more I developed a sense of how important the game was to people."

At the time, the Musketeers' non-conference schedule included such basketball non-entities as Kenyon, Thomas More, Ohio Wesleyan and Union but also Indiana, West Virginia, Marquette and Notre Dame.

"(UC) always tried to look down their nose at Xavier's team like the stepbrother," Staak said. "It was a little bit annoying. You'd get shots from people that your schedule wasn't what UC's was. I inherited the schedule that I had that first year so I'm really taking the criticism for something I had no control over. (Former UC coach) Ed Badger and I still joke about it to this day. We played Union College and he used to say, 'You're playing Onion.' And then I'd say we're playing Thomas More and he'd say, 'You're playing one guy.'"

Once he better understood the sports terrain in Cincinnati, Staak figured out that the best way for him to gain credibility in a town dominated by baseball's Reds, the NFL Bengals and UC basketball was to beat the Bearcats.

"I knew that we could make some impact in terms of what people thought about us if we were able to beat them," Staak said. "As it turned out, that kind of turned the corner for us for what we were trying to do overall."

Staak got his first crack at Badger and the Bearcats on Feb. 4, 1980, at Riverfront Coliseum. The Musketeers were 6-11 and had lost seven of their last nine games. UC was 10-9, hardly the power it once was, and had lost four of its last five. Still, the Bearcats were expected to beat Xavier, as they seemingly always did, although they had won by only two points the previous year.

The game had become so one-sided that attendance had fallen off in recent years. Only 7,051 fans showed up for the game in Baker's final season, 5,382 the year before that. But a big crowd of 11,237 was on hand for Staak's first game against the Bearcats.

Because he wanted to build excitement around his program, Staak decided to juice up the XU offense by having the Musketeers play what he hoped would be an entertaining, up-tempo style. That style paid dividends against UC.

"We got off to a great start," Staak said. "We got a lot of baskets in transition. I think we were ahead by double figures (37-21) at halftime. A lot of that came from transition.

I think we kind of caught them by surprise when we got it up and down the floor. As I recall, they came back on us, but we never lost the lead. We played a lot of zone and we mixed up defenses. We were playing a 1-3 and a chaser. It was like a box-and-one but it was out of our 2-3 zone where we would take one guy and we'd play him on (UC point guard) Eddie Lee. I think we confused them with that a little bit as well."

UC led, 12-11, with 14 minutes left in the first half when Xavier went on a run that gave the Musketeers a 29-16 advantage. The Bearcats shot just 24 percent in the first half while Xavier made 52 percent of its shots. Lee finished with 26 points for UC but scored only five in the first half when the Musketeers built their big lead. The Bearcats trimmed the XU lead to five with 14:30 remaining, but got no closer. When it became apparent that the Musketeers had pulled the upset, guard Keith Walker punctuated the victory with an emphatic dunk.

The unthinkable had occurred. Xavier had beaten UC. The rivalry was on.

"None of the (Xavier) players had ever experienced (a win over UC), particularly guys like Gary Massa and Steve Wolf, who was sitting out that year," Staak said, "and Joe Schoenfeld and some of the local guys.

> **It was kind of an underdog mentality that we had, so from that standpoint it was a little bit emotional because we had done something that people really didn't believe we could do.**

They really appreciated it. I remember one guy, he came up to me after the game on the court, and he just grabbed me and he opened his mouth but nothing came out. He was virtually speechless. I think in the huddle right at the end of the game when I felt that we had the game won, we emphasized to our players that we own the city. That was kind of an exaggeration, but at least we had established ourselves as something that was going to be reckoned with in the future.

"It was kind of an underdog mentality that we had, so from that standpoint it was a little bit emotional because we had done something that people really didn't believe we could do. We made some strides in terms of the interest level of our program and the backing that the school gave us in terms of building what we were starting to build. I think that kind of rejuvenated people, got them a little more excited about seeing us play.

"As we moved on, there got to be a little bit more pressure because in my mind we were expected to win now. That's how I felt. When we had the good teams, I just felt like we were the team that should win and UC is now the underdog.

"I watch (the Crosstown Shootout) every year. I have invested in that (Xavier) program a lot of blood, sweat and tears that went into getting it to the point where it's matured into the program that it is now. After the first one, it was almost like, well it was a fluke, you know, yeah, you won one game. Well, while I was there we won four out of six.

"It was always a big game as far as I was concerned because it was kind of my mentality from the Philadelphia Big Five. When we were (at Penn) it was a city series and you had a mythical Big Five champion every year, not that they really gave you anything for it. Whatever team had the best record against the other four (Villanova, Temple, St. Joseph's and LaSalle) was the Big Five champion. (In Cincinnati) there was only UC and us so it was like this is our city championship. That's how I took it."

Staak, who left Xavier for Wake Forest after the 1984-'85 season, never experienced another rivalry to match the intensity or the emotion of the Crosstown Shootout.

"(At Wake Forest) our in-state rival was NC State and that was a little bit more important to me because my best friend in the business, Jim Valvano, coached NC State," he said. "He had coached me as a senior at UConn, so there was a special meaning to that game. But in terms of the intensity, I think the UC game was much more."

ED BADGER
UC head coach, 1978-'83

"I didn't realize it was going to be like a Civil War."

When Gale Catlett left UC in 1978 after six years to become the head coach at West Virginia, the Bearcats replaced him with Ed Badger, who had spent the previous two seasons as the head coach of the NBA Chicago Bulls.

The Bulls went 84-80 in two seasons under Badger, who was runner-up for the NBA Coach of the Year Award when he led the Bulls to the playoffs in his first season. But in his second year the Bulls missed the playoffs. A long-time junior college coach, Badger became disenchanted with coaching professional athletes and had a difference in philosophy with Bulls ownership. So when he had the chance to leave and take over a UC program that had had 25 straight winning seasons, he jumped at the chance.

But in December, 1978, eight months after he was hired, the Bearcats were slapped with a two-year NCAA probation for infractions committed during Catlett's tenure. Badger, who had never coached at the Division I collegiate level, lasted five seasons at UC and posted a 68-71 record with two winning seasons. He was unable to take the Bearcats to the NCAA Tournament and was fired at the end of the 1982-'83 season. UC went 11-17 in his final season-its worst record in 37 years-and was 1-11 in the Metro Conference.

Badger won three of his five games against Xavier. One of the two he lost was the 1980 game that ended the Bearcats' dominance over the Musketeers and changed the complexion of the rivalry.

"To tell you the truth, when I came from Chicago, I didn't realize it was going to be like a Civil War," Badger said. "The fans were so damn loud I couldn't believe it, all the fans, both sides. They used to have floor seats at the Coliseum. They were throwing beer bottles made of glass at me."

There was never any animosity between Badger and Staak. They got along well then and still do and appeared together at a downtown luncheon every year before the Shootout.

"I had a lot of fun with him," Badger said. "He's a real good guy. The first year I'd talk first at the luncheon and I needled him all the way through it. Then he says, 'I'm speaking first next year.' I said, 'That's okay with me.' Then he spoke first and I ripped everything he talked about.' Oh, we were good friends.

"I remember when he took the Wake Forest job he called me and said, 'I'm going to Wake. I think it's a good opportunity.' I said, 'I think you're crazy. X is in a league that they can win and you've had great success. You're going over there to play teams coached by Norm Sloan and those schools up and down there.' The grass looks greener but it's not at a lot of places.

> ## The fans were so damn loud I couldn't believe it, all the fans, both sides.

"I thought he was a real good basketball guy. I thought his teams were well-prepared. He replaced Tay Baker, who was an old-time coach, and he didn't get too many kids from outside (the city). With Staak coming in, they started getting kids. He was very aggressive. I thought he did a good job with them."

After Staak and the Musketeers knocked off the Bearcats in 1980, Badger jokingly told Staak that he had saved his job. No one suspected at the time that one victory would have such a major impact on the Xavier program or that the Musketeers would have so much success against the Bearcats in the future. It was just one game, an unexpected loss for UC and a shot in the arm for Xavier. The way Badger tells it the expectation was that things would quickly return to normal and the Bearcats would resume their mastery over the Musketeers.

"Actually, it wasn't that big a deal at UC in relation to what we were trying to do in the conference," Badger said. "If we were going to become a good team and get back in the NCAA after those three years were up, we had to beat teams like Louisville and Memphis and Virginia Tech and all that. I didn't downplay (the Xavier game) but I thought it was much more important than it should be if you're going to do anything in the conference and in the NCAA. It was like they won the Civil War. You couldn't cross the Mason-Dixon line in Cincinnati."

Badger doesn't specifically remember that Staak used a chaser to slow Lee, but

*Ed Badger was the UC head coach in 1980 when Xavier
ended UC's dominance in the Crosstown Shootout.*

he said the tactic would have made sense.

"Lee was my point guard," he said. "(Normally) if you were playing a team that did that, you could put the guy who was being guarded on the baseline and just run (the chaser) into screens and bang the hell out of him. But when (Lee) is out front, it's a lot tougher. We didn't have a lot of what you would call Division I players. Probation hurt us.

"Eddie Lee was really a good player. He thought he was going to be a pro but he wasn't that good. He was a con man, but kind of a nice con man. I had dealt with con men before.

"He told our PR guy, 'I need more touches.' I used to tell him, 'Just play and shut the hell up.' He was getting enough touches. He was my point guard."

Lee, who scored 1,068 points at UC and ranks 41st on the Bearcats' career scoring list, was selected by the Denver Nuggets in the third round of the 1980 NBA draft, but never played in the league.

After Badger was fired by UC, he returned to the NBA where he worked for many years as an assistant coach and as a scout for a number of teams. He remembers the Crosstown Shootout fondly, but stops short of saying it was the best rivalry he's ever been associated with, citing NBA rivalries such as Bulls-Pistons or Celtics-Lakers.

"It's a different level," Badger said. "It wasn't like you were going to play Tulane on a Saturday afternoon. The town and the players and the radio and TV and everything…it was fun, really."

TONY YATES

UC player, 1960-'63
Head coach, 1983-'89

"We won all the time."

Tony Yates has the distinction of having played and coached in the Crosstown Shootout, but his playing days occurred in a much different era, during a time when UC won two national championships and narrowly missed a third when it lost in overtime to Loyola of Chicago in the 1963 national title game.

The UC teams that Yates played on from 1960 to 1963 were vastly superior to Xavier's. But even though the Bearcats were a national power, Yates said, and were heavily favored to beat the Musketeers every year, the game was still special.

"It was very intense," Yates said. "Back in my day, you got to know the guys on the other team. Some of the guys I had gone to school with or played against in high school, so we knew each other. One of the things that existed was if they could have knocked us off, what a great win that would have been for them. So they played very, very hard and tried to do that. We won out all the time, thank goodness. We had a much more talented team during those times than they did."

With Yates running the show for the Bearcats at point guard, UC beat the Musketeers, 89-53, during his sophomore year, squeaked by with a 61-58 victory his junior year, and won, 72-61, his senior year. That was the eighth straight win for UC in the rivalry, which was played every year back then at Cincinnati Gardens.

Playing under head coach Ed Jucker, the Bearcats employed a deliberate offensive approach and relied on a strong defense. Most opponents tried to speed them up on offense, Yates said, to try to get them out of their comfort zone, but they didn't have much success.

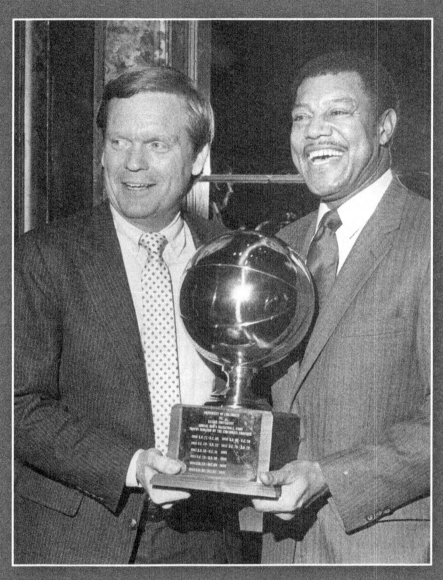

*Tony Yates, right, posing with Xavier coach Pete Gillen,
was 2-4 against Xavier as UC's head coach.*

"Fortunately we were more talented than most teams so we set the tone for the game and they had to follow that pattern even though they tried not to," Yates said. "They had to live with that."

Yates was the main reason opponents had so much trouble achieving the quicker tempo they desired. He ran the offense almost flawlessly, rarely turned the ball over, and was a direct link to Jucker, whose instructions he carried out to the letter. That's why Jucker referred to him as his coach on the floor.

"Coach set up a game plan and we followed and executed the game plan," Yates said. "That's how we won. Personally (Jucker and I) got along really well. If you weren't doing what you were supposed to be doing, he'd get after you big time. I knew what was supposed to be done and worked hard to carry it out.

> **If you don't win, you're going to have to live with it every day as you see people around the city. They'll let you know, especially the Xavier fans.**

"I had to get on some of (my teammates). My situation was kind of special because I had been out of school for five years before I came down there. I served four years in the Air Force and played basketball in there. When I came to UC I was married. I was kind of a mature guy and understood what you're supposed to do where a lot of the other guys were young guys just out of high school and they didn't understand. So you had to work with them to teach them so that they would understand. That was part of my job.

"They listened to me. Because if they didn't listen to me and do what was right, then I'd tell Juck, 'Take so-and-so out. He's not doing what he's supposed to do.' We worked together on that. If a guy wasn't playing defense right or doing his coverage like he was supposed to-and defense was very important-if a guy wasn't doing his job, I let Juck know."

When Yates became the head coach at UC – he was hired to replace Badger in 1983 – he did his best to impress upon his players, especially the ones who weren't from Cincinnati, how important the Xavier game was.

"You go out and play your heart out and get that victory for us," Yates told them, "because if you don't win, you're going to have to live with it every day as you see people around the city. They'll let you know, especially the Xavier fans."

Yates inherited a team that was essentially starting over after Badger was fired. He didn't have the talent to compete with Xavier, which was getting better every year under first under Staak and then Pete Gillen. It wasn't until Gillen's second year at Xavier that Yates recorded his first win as a coach over the Musketeers in 1987, a 75-73 victory at Riverfront Coliseum. He was 2-4 against Xavier as a coach.

"It didn't bother me," Yates said of his losses to the Musketeers. "If you have the talent, you'll win your share of the games. If you don't have the talent that you need, you won't. You have to live with that until you get the proper amount of talent so that you can be competitive."

Yates now spends six months in Florida every year and six months in Cincinnati. He still watches the Shootout when he can and says he's not particularly bothered by Xavier's recent success against UC because he knows those things are cyclical.

"It varies," he said. "People get different talented kids, develop them, and then other people maybe don't have the talent in particular years and the other team the next year, maybe they have more talent than you and then they win. I always rooted for the local teams, you know, Xavier and Miami, I'd root for them except when we played them. I wanted them to be successful."

PETE GILLEN

Xavier head coach, 1985-'94

"It wasn't fun for the coaches."

Pete Gillen's face was a deep crimson as he stalked off the court at Cincinnati Gardens, practically spitting out his anger at UC coach Bob Huggins, who had just refused to shake his hand after Gillen's Xavier team had beaten the Bearcats in overtime.

Animosity had been simmering between the two coaches ever since Huggins arrived at UC in 1989 and now it had reached its peak on Jan. 19, 1994 after the Musketeers turned back the Bearcats, 82-76, in what would be Gillen's final experience in the Shootout.

"Both benches were talking to each other (during the game)," Gillen said. "It wasn't good. I don't like talking about it. I don't know what happened. They had beaten us three years in a row, so we were antsy too. At the end, the refs called us together and we said some things and then after the game I went up to shake hands with (Huggins) and he didn't shake hands. We talked a few days later. We said we can't let that happen again. He said, 'Hey, sorry,' but I was wrong too. It's a two-edged sword. I was upset. He said things. I said things. But you shake hands. You know, it happens and you move on. They lost a tough game. When I lose a tough game, I'm no fun."

Gillen, who now does color commentary for CBS Sports Network, was the head coach at Xavier from 1985 through 1994. After five years as an assistant coach at Notre Dame, he was hired to replace Staak, who had taken the head coaching job at Wake Forest. Gillen was 202-75, with more wins than any coach in Xavier history, but he was 4-5 in the Crosstown Shootout.

His first game against UC was an 80-76 victory on Jan. 23, 1986, when Yates was still the Bearcats' head coach.

"It was the most intense game I was ever in as a coach," Gillen said. "We were fortunate to win. Every play was unbelievable. As a coach, I didn't have much control. Once the game started, it was a players' game because there was so much emotion. There wasn't a lot of X's O's. It was more which team wanted it the most and which team made the fewest mistakes."

Back in Gillen's day, both coaches appeared at the traditional downtown luncheon the day before the game with several hundred fans from both schools, mostly businessmen, who showed up to donate money and hear the two coaches give brief remarks. The athletic directors and other administrators from both schools also attended. The luncheon was just one part of the buildup that surrounded the game.

"The bakeries had different cookies, red and white for UC cookies, and blue and white for Xavier cookies," Gillen said. "And Skyline Chili, of course, if you wanted a 4-way or you wanted a 3-way, whatever. The buildup four, five, six days before was amazing. That game always took a lot out of us when we played the Bearcats. It was always tough. It was so draining, win or lose, physically, psychologically, emotionally. (For) the game afterwards, we were usually flat because we didn't have much gas left in the tank.

"It wasn't on TV that much at that time. It wasn't on ESPN or CBS or any of those networks. It was big in the city but I had not heard of it (before arriving at Xavier). We won (the first game) by four or something. How about that? I don't know who the freaking vice-president is but I can get close to that score. I know it was a great game. It was close, super intense, every play. It was just unbelievable. It was fun for the fans, the players, the media. It wasn't fun for the coaches because there was such an importance on winning the game. There was such stress to win.

"I learned (that you shouldn't) do too much the day before, just get them ready, just be positive and let the players from outside the city know how important the game was. At least from our point, if you beat Cincinnati you had a successful year because they were the king for so long, with Oscar (Robertson) and Ron Bonham and all the great teams they had. It was a big deal for Xavier winning that. My first game, when we won, I think we had won three in a row. I remember Ralph Lee putting three fingers in the air because we had won three straight.

"It's as big or bigger than a league game in a lot of ways. If we win or lose, we've still got our next game, the season's not over. But I didn't downplay it. I said, 'This is big, it's fun, just give it your best shot.' It's exciting and everybody's watching. We used to have some of the Bengals players come in, some of the Reds players that were in town.

*Pete Gillen's 202 wins in nine seasons
are the most for any coach in Xavier history.*

"I had seen a lot of rivalries, the Big Five with Villanova when I was at St. Joe's. At that time, UCLA and Notre Dame was real big. They played twice a year. But (the Shootout) was as intense or more intense than any of the ones I had been involved in. I knew it was important, but I was surprised (to find out how important). I learned there are only two Division I schools in Cincinnati and almost everybody involved in the city had someone involved, either a friend or a relative that went to UC graduate school or undergrad, or Xavier. So everybody had some connection, an aunt or an uncle. So you learned as you got there."

The game became even more hotly contested after UC fired Yates and replaced him with the fiery Huggins. At that time, the Musketeers had won six of the previous 10 games.

"I think when Tony was let go, one of the mandates that went with the (UC) program was hey, let's beat Xavier like we used to," Gillen said. "I think that was one of the reasons Huggins was hired. That wasn't the main reason, of course, but that was a big thing. They were more determined than ever. Cincinnati thought, hey, we were the top dog for 20 or 25 years and we don't want to be sharing the spotlight or be a little behind Xavier. So yeah, I think it got more intense. We won the first one when Bob was there and then I think they won three in a row and we won the last one. There was a little bit (of tension). He's a competitor. I'm a competitor. It got a little uncomfortable. But that's competition. That happens."

It didn't take long for sparks to fly after Huggins arrived in town. In Huggins' first Crosstown Shootout, Xavier won, 90-88, in overtime on Jan. 31, 1990, after a controversial call by the officials. With the Bearcats leading by one, UC's Lou Banks had the ball and was being guarded by Michael Davenport, who slapped the ball away from Banks out of bounds with 17 seconds left in overtime. The officials ruled the ball hit off Banks before it went out of bounds and awarded possession to the Musketeers, which set up the game-winning 3-point shot by Jamal Walker.

"Honestly, I couldn't see what happened," Gillen said. "It might have been a bad call. We got the ball. I remember Jamal Walker hitting the shot. Then Cincinnati took a half-court shot that almost went in. It hit the backboard, hit the rim, and fell off so we won by two. There were big bodies all over the place so it very easily could have been a bad call, but I did not see exactly what happened. I know they were upset about it."

Several years later, there was talk, mostly from Huggins, about discontinuing the rivalry.

"That was never going anywhere," Gillen said. "We wanted to play. It was never going to go that far. There was brief talk. It was after the hostility of the Handshake Game. You've got to play because it's good for the city, good for the fans. We were going to play. That was never under serious consideration."

Gillen still follows the Shootout and watches it every year unless he has a conflict with a game he's broadcasting.

"I text (Xavier coach) Chris Mack the day before that game every year," he said. "I don't talk to him. I just text him good luck or whoever the coach is. I did it when Skip (Prosser) was there. I don't always watch the whole thing. But yeah, I watch it every year. If I can, I will."

A few years ago, nearly 20 years after the Handshake Game, Gillen was in Morgantown preparing to broadcast an upcoming game between Huggins' West Virginia team and Duquesne.

"I had a week off before, so I went to see West Virginia," Gillen said. "I drove from my home in Charlotte, about four hours. I'm crazy, but I had time so I went to see them play. I got there early and was up getting some stats. The sports information guy said, 'Hey, Bob's doing his radio show down there.' He said, 'Why don't you go talk to him?' So I said, 'All right, I'll do it.' Bob was great. We talked for a while and he said, 'Why don't you come over to my house for a beer afterwards?' I was surprised he said that. You know, we were cordial, and I said, 'Sure I'll go.'

"He played the game and they won. I went back to the hotel. I had given him my number and he called me and said, 'Why don't you come over to the arena?' My hotel wasn't far from the arena so I went over and I was there for two and half, three hours, drinking beer with him and a couple of the high school coaches. It was great. Some people are surprised by that. I didn't put it on a plane and fly it around, you know, Huggins and Gillen are okay now, but it was good. The women's coach was there from West Virginia and a couple of assistants and a couple of high school coaches that he knew....there were about eight or 10 people. I had three or four beers and then went back to the hotel. I was glad that we did that. I think that's more of a story and it was by his invitation. He was the guy who precipitated it, so it's to his credit.

"I've said this before: Huggins is one of the top three or four guys I've ever coached against and I've coached against Larry Brown with Kansas. I coached against Eddie Sutton at Oklahoma State and (North Carolina coach) Roy Williams and (Duke coach Mike) Krzyzewksi. And I mean it. I'm not saying that because we're talking."

*UC coach Bob Huggins, right, had great respect
for Xavier coach Skip Prosser, left.*

BOB HUGGINS

UC head coach, 1989-2005

"I got ordained with a black hat."

S ome of the most memorable moments in the history of the Crosstown Shootout occurred while Bob Huggins was the head coach at UC.

But Huggins, who went 8-8 against Xavier during his 16 years as the Bearcats' head coach, said the game never meant that much to him because he had bigger goals, especially during his first few years at UC when he was trying to resuscitate a long-dormant program that was on NCAA probation.

"I didn't worry about Xavier until it was game time," said Huggins, who went from UC to Kansas State to West Virginia, his alma mater. "My whole thing coming into the Metro Conference was that I wanted to be Louisville. I wanted to be the team that everybody respected, everybody wanted to play, the team that was ranked nationally, the team that was on TV all the time. I honestly never thought about Xavier until game week or whatever. We didn't really recruit against each other much, maybe once in a great while, but not very often. I was more focused at that time on trying to climb the ladder in the Metro Conference."

When it was suggested that Xavier was just beginning to come into its own during that time, Huggins said, "They didn't play anybody. I didn't pay attention other than the fact that every time we burped it was a story and they could do whatever they wanted and nobody cared."

Huggins' first game against Xavier was a classic. The Bearcats squandered most of a seven-point lead with a minute and a half left in overtime, but still led by one and had the ball with 24 seconds left only to lose by two.

Huggins said he remembers very little about the game.

"I remember a lot of stuff about them but I don't remember which one came in what order," Huggins said. "Was (Jamal Walker's shot) on an in-bounds play? Honestly, I don't remember. I remember losing at the buzzer quite a few times but I don't remember that one. I've coached almost 1,200 games."

Huggins does remember the first time UC lost to Xavier, on Nov. 26, 1996, when the Bearcats were the nation's top-ranked team. In that game, UC point guard Charles Williams dribbled the ball off his foot out of bounds as he was trying to set up a potential game-winning shot for UC after Xavier's James Posey tied the score. Fortson, who had fouled out, watched from the bench as Lenny Brown scored over Darnell Burton to win the game for Xavier as time expired.

"Who was it, Lenny Brown or somebody made a jump shot?" Huggins said. "What was that, Danny's junior year? You want to know the truth? After the Kansas and Xavier games, that's when I knew it was time for Danny to go (to the NBA) because he wasn't going to get a fair shot. If you go back and look at the film, he didn't foul people. I mean, he was smart enough to stay away from them and they'd still call fouls. They'd fall down and it was always Danny. I told the guys in the conference office, you guys are chasing out the best player in the league, somebody who's a marquee guy for us."

As for the Williams turnover that set up Brown's game-winning shot, Huggins said, "That was my fault. I had him going left and he couldn't go left. I should have ran him the other way where he could get it into his right hand."

Huggins said he could not remember the second time No. 1-ranked UC lost to Xavier, even though it occurred just three years later.

"Who was playing for us?" he asked. "Was that Kenyon?"

The 1994 Handshake Game, as it has come to be known, occurred after an 82-76 Xavier win in overtime. Huggins said during his post-game press conference that he refused to be a phony by shaking hands with Pete Gillen after some of the things that were being shouted in his direction during the game from the Xavier bench.

"I would say we probably both did things we probably wouldn't do again," Huggins said. "Everybody knows what it was. The whole thing came out on WLW (radio) with Bill Cunningham. The whole story came out, but it was always the handshake, it was never the other deal."

It has long been assumed that Xavier assistant coach Bobby Gonzalez was the one yelling at Huggins from the Xavier bench, but Huggins said it wasn't only Gonzalez.

"It was Pete," Huggins said. "Sure it was Pete."

Asked if he now regrets not shaking Gillen's hand after the game, Huggins said,

"I'm not sure. I haven't thought about it. That's something I have to think about for awhile."

It was no secret that Huggins and Gillen didn't get along in those days, although they both say they buried the hatchet several years ago. Huggins said he always got along with Gillen's successors, Skip Prosser and Thad Matta.

"It was probably because of everything that happened," Huggins said. "I think just probably the way the games went, just the way things were. I shouldn't say we didn't get along. We didn't communicate, where Skip and I talked a lot. Thad and I talked.

"It's just that Pete and I didn't have very much conversation until that week. Like I said, we didn't recruit against each other. I saw Skip and (Xavier assistant coach) Dino (Gaudio) way more than I saw Pete. I didn't really dislike Pete. I kind of disliked the treatment that they got. The same things went on over there that were going on at our place, the same things that go on just about everywhere, but it was like they never did it.

"I never viewed Pete and (my) relationship as bad, it was just kind of non-existent. We just had no communication whatsoever. I saw Skip more, I guess. Skip and I would sit together in the airport. Skip and I would sit together during the summer at games. I never saw Pete really that much. It wasn't like I wouldn't have sat with him, I just never saw him."

> " **Honestly, I don't remember. I remember losing at the buzzer quite a few times but I don't remember that one. I've coached almost 1,200 games.** "

Huggins talks effusively, almost lovingly, about Prosser, who died in 2007 of a heart attack five years after Huggins survived a heart attack in the Pittsburgh airport.

"He was down to earth," Huggins said of Prosser, "unpretentious, a good guy. I thought he could really coach. When I had a heart attack, I wasn't allowed visitors other than my mom and dad and my kids and my wife and Skip got back there and (current Kentucky coach John) Calipari got back there. Skip and I have always been close."

The night before Huggins' heart attack, he was having dinner with a friend. "I can't remember who I was with," he said, "but Skip and Dino (Gaudio) were sitting right across from us."

Huggins said when he found out that Prosser had suffered a fatal heart attack, his first thought was, "That can't be."

"I was kind of teasing Skip because he was running and losing weight," he said. "I was kind of joking around with him about it. When I went into the viewing, the first guy I saw was Dino. We were hugging each other. It's kind of, what's the word, surreal?"

Huggins said he doesn't think much about why he survived and Prosser didn't because it's not part of his nature to ruminate about the past. He would rather talk about his friendship with Prosser and what made him a successful coach.

"He was really a good X and O guy," Huggins said. "We had great games when he was at Wake. He put guys in position where they could win. That's what we do. You can't make shots for them."

Huggins' last game against Xavier was a 65-54 UC win at Fifth Third Arena, although no one knew at the time that it was his last.

"It meant a lot more to them than it did to us because they were always the underdogs," Huggins said. "I just think they heard it a lot more than we heard it. We were more focused on the national schedule that we played. I mean, Skip tried to schedule after he became head coach, but their league obviously wasn't as good."

Eleven years have passed since Huggins was forced out at UC in August, 2005. He seems content coaching at his alma mater. His office is in an impressive new $24.1-million basketball complex of 64,000 square feet. A lounge, complete with flat-screened TV, bar and fireplace, is accessible from his office and overlooks the Mountaineers' practice gym.

The Crosstown Shootout has long receded into Huggins' past. But some of the scars from it remain.

"I got ordained with a black hat," Huggins said. "It's not near what it used to be. I think probably being here has a lot to do with it. Unfortunately it got started in Cincinnati and then it became a national thing. We had thugs and we had this and we had that. And most of that shit never happened, but it was like, well, we have to send it to the grand jury or people will think we're showing favoritism when they knew damn well it didn't even happen. Art Long didn't punch a police horse. It didn't happen.

"But all that stuff got so blown out of proportion that it tainted what those guys were and what they did and that's a terrible shame because that's not what they were. The only thing that really bothers me is how our guys were portrayed when that really wasn't the case. Did we have a few? Sure. Does everybody have a few? Sure. It's not like it hasn't happened at Carolina or Duke or wherever – Michigan, Ohio State, wherever – it has. But we became the national thugs and that wasn't fair.

It wasn't fair to Bobby Brannen and people like that who got characterized in that regard. And it all started in Cincinnati. The whole thing started in Cincinnati and that ain't right."

Huggins understands the importance of the Shootout to the city of Cincinnati, where he says he was blessed to have coached. But he said it was blown out of proportion by the media.

"It meant something to the city for four or five days or whatever and that was all because of (the media)," he said. "It didn't mean as much as a league game. We tried to win league championships. We were about hanging banners. I don't think you hang any banners when you beat Xavier.

"For such a long time, nobody nationally knew about it. Then it started getting a little bit more recognition. It's a great rivalry. But so is West Virginia-Pitt, so is Duke-Carolina.

"You guys (the media) make it like a holy war. That's the whole deal in Cincinnati. It ends up being a holy war. I've been a part of the Pitt-West Virginia game and it's a heck of a rivalry but it's not as personal – husbands and wives, best friends."

Huggins said he never downplayed the rivalry while he was in Cincinnati, but he was also careful never to make more of it than it was.

"What am I going to say, Xavier is so important but Louisville isn't?" Huggins said. "Xavier is so important but Memphis isn't? I guess Xavier was a constant probably, but when you're playing Penny Hardaway four times? That's what we did that they didn't do. That's the difference. It wasn't the game of the century for us. At least it wasn't for me. We were playing people, man."

Huggins said he didn't especially like coaching in the Crosstown Shootout and he doesn't go out of his way to watch it on television. He clearly doesn't miss it.

But he does miss Prosser.

"Skip and I were very, very good friends," Huggins said. "Dino and I were good friends. Thad and I were good friends and we're good friends today. I mean, Skip and I talked about going back to Cincinnati when we retired, spending a night or two together a week, and sitting around watching games and enjoying life."

Dino Gaudio, right, first met Skip Prosser, left, as his assistant coach at Wheeling (W. Va.) Central Catholic High School. He became one of Prosser's closest friends and worked under him as an assistant at Xavier and Wake Forest.

DINO GAUDIO

Xavier assistant coach, 1987-'93, 2000-'01

"Enjoy it, don't endure it."

*W*hen Skip Prosser took over at Xavier in 1994, the tension that had permeated the series-at least among the coaches-almost instantly disappeared. Huggins had nothing but good things to say about Prosser and Prosser had great respect for Huggins. The rapprochement was not the result of any diplomatic effort on the part of Prosser. He won over Huggins simply by being himself.

"I don't think Skip came back to Xavier and said, 'I've got to make friends with Bob Huggins,'" said Dino Gaudio, who worked at Xavier as an assistant coach with Prosser under Gillen, and later as an assistant coach under Prosser when he was the head coach at Wake Forest. "I don't think that happened at all. I just think it was a genuine relationship based on mutual respect and friendship. It just went from there."

Perhaps more than any Xavier coach, Prosser embodied the Crosstown Shootout. He embraced the rivalry and urged his players to do the same. He also had a lot of success against UC, twice knocking off the Bearcats when they were ranked No. 1 in the country. Overall, he was 4-3 against Huggins and the Bearcats.

"He talked about the importance of the game and the importance of the game in the city of Cincinnati," Gaudio said. "He would always say, 'Enjoy it, don't endure it.' In other words, there's so much pressure on it, but man, we're going to enjoy this experience."

Gaudio was much more than Prosser's fellow employee. He was one of his closest friends. He was the best man in Prosser's wedding and Prosser was the godfather for Gaudio's daughter, Alyssa. Their 27-year friendship began in Wheeling, W. Va., where Prosser was the head coach at Wheeling Central Catholic High School and Gaudio was an accountant at Wheeling-Pittsburgh Steel in 1981.

"I had my little cubicle and my little calculator and I was like, man, I can't do this for the rest of my life," Gaudio said. "I was wanting to coach and I went back in the evenings and got my education degree."

One day in August, 1980, he saw a newspaper ad for a basketball coach/business teacher at Wheeling Central Catholic and applied for the job. The next day he received a call from a secretary at the school asking him to come in for an interview. He drove the the hour and 20 minutes from his home in Yorktown, Ohio, to Wheeling, and interviewed with the principal, Dr. Joseph Villietta. His interview lasted an hour. Before the day was over, the job was his.

There was just one problem. Prosser knew nothing about it. When he found out, he wasn't pleased.

"At the time," Gaudio said, "Skip wanted this other guy. The other guy didn't have the business teaching degree and would have had to work outside the school and then come to practice afterwards. Skip goes, Doc, who'd you hire? He says, 'I hired this young kid, Dino Gaudio.' Skip says, 'Doc, how do you know he can coach?' And the principal goes, He told me he could. And Skip goes, Doc, do you hire every teacher that tells you they can teach? That's how it started. Three days later, they have an open gym. I go to the gym and I meet Skip for the first time.

> **We could have terrific arguments and two seconds later he would say, 'All right, where are we going for lunch?'**

"He was just a genuine good person. One of the things I said during his eulogy was that coaches in the ACC cried and the cafeteria workers at Xavier cried because he treated them all the same. He brought that common touch. That's just the way he was. I never heard anybody in this crazy business, with recruiting and guys doing something underhanded, I never heard anybody say a negative word about him. Nobody. He was genuine.

"He was the best teacher in the high school. Our rooms were right next to each other. I learned so much from him about teaching, education, your classroom, and how to handle young kids. And then he taught me just a wealth of knowledge about basketball and coaching values. In all the time that I was with him, he was really demanding on kids, but he never swore. That just taught me a lot about how you can be tough on kids without cursing at them.

"We had a unique relationship. Skip was really non-confrontational. We'd have meetings sometimes where we could have arguments and it was usually me arguing and trying to make my point and he would always say, 'Dino, sometimes right, sometimes wrong, but never in doubt.' We could have terrific arguments and two seconds later he would say, 'All right, where are we going for lunch?' "

It's no surprise to Gaudio that Prosser's Xavier teams were able to beat UC twice when the Bearcats were ranked No. 1.

"Of all the redeeming qualities Skip had as a coach, and I say this when I'm on the air (on ESPN), Skip coached confidence so very well," Gaudio said. "Kids played confidently when he was on the sidelines. They weren't looking over their shoulder. It wasn't pressure like, man, we have to win this game. And Skip enjoyed all the activities surrounding (the Shootout), the radio, the thing they did downtown. Skip played more to the idea that we were the little brother, we were the little train that could, if you will. Pete understood the magnitude of it, but It was a little more confrontational thing with Pete and Huggs and I think it became such because the game became so very big to both of them."

Gaudio's first game against UC as an XU assistant came complete with an impassioned pre-game speech from Gillen in the locker room, but it's not Gillen's speech that left an impression on him.

"Pete, God bless him, pours his heart out in the pre-game talk," Gaudio said. "He's literally trying to motivate the kids. He turns around and there's a door behind him and he hits his fist on the door. He says, 'This is your house! They are coming here to take what you own!'

"The players go and huddle up by the door. That team was Byron Larkin's team. And Byron huddles those guys up and I'm right by the door before they go out. They're in the hallway there, the coaches aren't there, but I've got my ear in the huddle, and Byron goes, boys, you know what this is all about. This if for all the women in Cincinnati. And those guys are like, yeah, yeah, yeah – one two three, let's go! I walked in and I told those guys, 'Can there be better motivation?' It just put everything into perspective."

As the years went by, both Prosser and Gaudio came to have great respect for Huggins as a coach. Not only did they enjoy the experience of trying to beat the Bearcats, who were one of the best teams in the country in those days, they learned about the game from competing against him.

When Xavier won, Gaudio said, "It was a tremendous sense of accomplishment because not only were you beating Cincinnati, you were beating Huggs. And I'll say this: when we went to Wake Forest in 2001, we led the nation in rebound differential.

Skip always would talk about how the Cincinnati teams were so tough and it showed up on the backboard. That's the page he borrowed from Huggs. I guess you could say that's one thing from facing those Cincinnati teams that he learned from.

"We were always, always a good rebounding team. And I think one of the reasons was it's what Skip emphasized. It's a page he took from facing Bob's teams because they were just maniacal on the backboard. He used to say the fight started when the ball was in the air when you played Cincinnati. Because when it was in the air up on the backboard, that's was where the game was won or lost."

After Prosser died, Gaudio said, "Huggs came to the funeral service and then one day I was calling a West Virginia game and Huggs goes, 'Come on over to the house after the game.' That was a 9 o'clock game, so it's over at 11. He gets done with media at about 11:30. We go down in his basement in Morgantown and he just said, and I have no idea why he said this, 'I'm here and Skip's not.'"

THAD MATTA

Xavier head coach, 2001-'04

"I lost 15 years of my life coaching in that game."

Seven games into his first season as the Xavier head coach, Thad Matta committed the cardinal sin. He lost to UC. And he lost big, 75-55.

"The first year I had no clue," Matta said. "I had no idea. I can remember some buddies of mine from college came over from Butler for the game and we lost and afterwards, they're saying, 'These people were trying to cut your head off, the Xavier fans, for losing the game.'"

If he didn't know before that incident how much beating UC meant to the Musketeer faithful – and to the Xavier players – he found out during his first Shootout in 2001. The Bearcats were looking for revenge, having lost the last two games to their crosstown rivals – each by two points.

By the time Matta arrived from Butler to take over for Skip Prosser, the Xavier players were hungry to extend their winning streak.

"I still remember this, going into the locker room (before the game) and the guys are going crazy," Matta said. "They're all jacked up. And I remember saying, 'Calm down, calm down, it's only a game.' When I walked out (onto the Cintas Center floor) and I felt that energy, it was like, 'Oh my gosh, what is this all about?' You could just feel it when I walked into the arena."

Matta stayed at Xavier for only three years before leaving to become the head coach at Ohio State, a position he still holds. He rallied to win his last two Shootouts, the last coming on a basket by Lionel Chalmers with 26 seconds left to lift the Musketeers to a 71-69 victory over the 10th-ranked Bearcats. At the time, Xavier was a pedestrian 10-9 seemingly headed nowhere after going 26-6 and advancing to the second round of the NCAA Tournament the year before behind national player of the year David West, who had moved on to the NBA.

"We were big-time underdogs and I thought for sure that was going to be the worst day of my life because I didn't think we could win the game," Matta said. "Lionel wanted the ball. I knew he was going to take the shot. He wasn't passing it. That was the type of player he was. He wanted to take those shots. I just remember it going through and me thinking, oh my God, I think we're going to win this game, which was a huge upset.

"That gave us a shot of confidence. We battled some injuries and we were a little bit disheveled. At times, we were playing great basketball, but we just weren't consistent enough. For whatever reason, that kind of sparked us a little bit and maybe refocused us. It gave us more belief in what we were doing."

That was the first of seven straight wins for the Musketeers. They lost only one more game-by six points to Duquesne at Cintas Center-then won nine more in a row before losing to No. 6 Duke by three points in the Elite Eight. They finished 26-11.

During West's junior year-Matta's second as Xavier's head coach-UC forward Jason Maxiell called West "soft" during an interview session with reporters the day before the Shootout. West responded by scoring 23 points in the Musketeers' 50-44 victory.

"I coached David in two of them," Matta said. "In the first one he sprained his ankle. The second one over there, he was on a tear. He got a cheap foul that was not a foul. It was a blown call and I had to sit him because we were up big. They made a little bit of a comeback. But that was David's game. He was a prideful person and a very competitive person."

Matta remembers Maxiell's comments about West supposedly being soft.

"I knew David wasn't soft," Matta said. "I don't even remember if I said anything to him (about it) or not. Honestly, nothing surprised me during that week leading up to the game. I still laugh every time Huggins and I are together. We were at that stupid dinner we used to have, the Crosstown Chili cookout-I don't know what it was-so Huggs tells us, 'Whatever you do-I think it was Robert Whaley-take him off your scouting report. I got into it with him today in practice. He is not playing tomorrow night.' So about eight minutes into the game Robert Whaley's at the scorer's table (getting ready to come into the game). I looked down at Huggs and he gives me like the palms up and a big smile on his face."

Matta and Huggins got along well, much like Huggins and Prosser did.

"He really helped me out when I got to Xavier," Matta said of Huggins. "We would talk, not a ton, but I always appreciated how he treated me in terms of him being a basketball coach in Cincinnati and knowing the city. When we ran into

Thad Matta found out how important the Crosstown Shootout was when he lost his first game against UC as Xavier's head coach.

each other, we would talk. He told me, 'Hey, these are the people you need to know, where to live, all that stuff.'"

Matta said he didn't have to prepare his players very much for the UC game, "because they knew what it was about," and he agrees with the theory that the rivalry is more of a players' game than a coaches' game because the crowd noise prevents the players from hearing the coaches.

"That is definitely the case," Matta said. "You have to make plays in that game because there are no secrets, that's for sure. You only coach in a couple of those a year. That one was just kind of a players' game, a fun night, if you will. I've always told people that I lost 15 years of my life coaching in that game because that game can take five years off your life and I did it three times. Once that thing was over, it was like, thank God, let's move on to the rest of the season."

Now that he's at Ohio State, Matta doesn't see the Shootout every year, but he did see the 2011 game that ended in a brawl. He said he wasn't surprised.

"If I'm around, I'll definitely watch it and I'll laugh knowing what the energy is in the building," Matta said. "I haven't seen it a whole lot lately, but I did see the fight. Honestly, it was very, very unfortunate. You felt something like that could happen, but my initial thought was hopefully that will reel the magnitude of that game back in a little bit in terms of the fans because the one year that they beat us I got home and there were UC signs in my front yard. Hopefully, people said, 'Okay, wait a minute, this is getting a little bit out of hand.'"

What used to be just a local event has grown in recent years into a rivalry the rest of the nation has become aware of, but Matta said fans in other parts of the country have no idea what the game is really like.

"Not many people know," he said, "but the people in Cincinnati, they know. When I was in Indiana, I didn't know anything about it. I always knew it was a great game and I remember when Bob and Pete got into it a little bit, but even being up here in Columbus, a couple of hours away, people have no idea of the energy in that game."

ANDY KENNEDY

Interim head coach, 2005-'06
Assistant coach, 2001-'05

"It's hard to prepare guys for that environment."

*H*aving inherited an seemingly impossible situation as UC's interim head coach in the wake of Huggins' forced departure, Andy Kennedy focused on only one thing, and it had nothing to do with trying to persuade athletic director Mike Thomas to make him the permanent head coach.

"I didn't ever openly come out and say this because I just didn't think it would serve a purpose," said Kennedy, now the head coach at Mississippi, "but I was never going to be the head coach at Cincinnati. I never had one day of thought that I was going to be the head coach at Cincinnati simply because of my relationship with Huggs. That was not going to change. Because of the manner in which Huggs was let go and how close I was to the situation, I was a stop-gap. I appreciate them giving me the opportunity because of the kids that were in that program then who deserved to have an opportunity to compete and have some semblance of continuity, and that was really my purpose there."

The Crosstown Shootout couldn't have come at a worse time for the Bearcats that season. Already struggling against the odds with a depleted roster trying to compete for the first time in the mighty Big East Conference, things took a turn for the worse at Connecticut on Jan. 9, 2006, when starting forward Armein Kirkland, who was having the game of his life, went down with a torn anterior cruciate ligament that ended his season and his college basketball career.

"I remember standing in the hall afterwards and thinking, okay, what's next?" Kennedy said.

Before that game, Kennedy and the Bearcats had found a way to win 10 straight games, including a 2-0 start in the Big East. As they took the floor to face the fourth-ranked Huskies, they had been ranked in the Top 25 for the first time that season, checking in at No. 25. Without Kirkland, they lost to UConn, 70-59.

Desperate for players at that point, Kennedy recruited tight end Connor Barwin from the UC football team. The Bearcats lost their next game at home to Syracuse, 77-58, and were scheduled to face Xavier five days later at Cintas Center.

"We were just trying to find our way," Kennedy said. "We had Devan (Downey), who had never been in the series. We had Cedric McGowan, who had never been in the series. We picked up a kid, Ron Allen, who was part of Hurricane Katrina. We didn't have a lot of depth. We traveled light. We probably saved some budget money."

But they also had a core of veterans in Eric Hicks, James White, Chadd Moore and Jihad Muhammad.

"Those guys that had been a part of it," Kennedy said, "they were certainly excited to play Xavier. Kids aren't going to make excuses. They're gonna go out and try to battle and conquer the world. So we really depended upon our veterans who at least had been through the experience before and tried to shepherd those young guys along.

"It's hard to prepare guys for that environment but we had already experienced it at Marquette, which is obviously a hostile environment, so (the newcomers) had at least experienced a tough environment, even though they had never been part of the Crosstown Shootout."

The Bearcats gave it all they had, erasing a six-point deficit in the final 30 seconds with a chance to win in regulation, but Downey-who scored 22 points-missed a 3-point shot from the wing with less than five seconds left and the game went into overtime.

They had another chance to win in overtime after Justin Doellman missed a free throw with 3.9 seconds left and Xavier leading by two. White accepted the in-bounds pass, dribbled down the middle of the court and launched a 3-point shot that hit off the backboard as time expired, preserving a 73-71 victory for the Musketeers.

"It was a real deflating moment for us," Kennedy said. "It was on a Thursday and then we turned around and played a Big East opponent on Sunday. I remember after the loss the emotional letdown from that, especially for our seniors, who were not going to get another opportunity. It was a challenge to make sure that mentally we got back right so that we could carry on our conference season.

"Anytime you play in that game, whether you win or you lose, there's going to be a lot of energy expended, not only on the court but off the court because of

Andy Kennedy lost to Xavier by two points in overtime during his one season as UC's interim head coach after Bob Huggins was fired.

all the other things. When you lose a really close game and an overtime game, it takes its toll."

Kennedy's first experience in the Crosstown Shootout turned out much better for the Bearcats. He had arrived at UC in 2001 with a basic awareness of the rivalry in the manner that a casual fan from another part of the country might know it.

"As Huggs had taken Cincinnati basketball to a national level, Xavier was becoming nationally relevant," Kennedy said. "I knew it was a game that had some reverberations across the country. I didn't really have any idea of the passion involved because I didn't realize the proximity of the schools until I was a part of that rivalry. If memory serves, my first year there I believe was the first time it was in the Cintas Center. It was (Steve) Logan's senior year and he was dominant (in a 75-55 UC win).

"It was my first experience in that building, in that environment, in that game, and it totally lived up to the hype. I remember Cintas Center being a smaller venue than Fifth Third Arena and the fans being right on top of you. I remember the student section being right on top of our bench. You could feel the energy in the building. I remember us winning the game in a comfortable fashion if there is such a thing. The game was not one of many of the Shootouts where it was a one- or two-possession game but that did not take away from the magnitude of the moment."

Kennedy's combined record against Xavier as a UC assistant and interim head coach was 2-3. The Bearcats also won in Huggins' final season at UC, 65-54, at Fifth Third.

"I got a much greater appreciation of it," Kennedy said. "Now that I've stepped away from it in the SEC, I don't even know if I've seen one simply because you kind of get engrossed in your own deal. I watch a lot of basketball and I watch UC as much as I can because I used to be a part of that program and I'm proud for Mick (Cronin) and them being able to get it back to the level it deserves to be. I'm friends with Chris Mack and I watch Xavier and I pull for them when I can. It's a great, unique rivalry where you've got two storied programs, within what, a five-mile radius of one another? It's kind of unheard of. It's a unique dynamic. It's good for college basketball."

SEAN MILLER

Assistant coach Xavier, 2001-'04
Head coach Xavier, 2004-'09

"That game brings out the best and the worst in you."

*B*efore he experienced the Crosstown Shootout as a participant, Sean Miller began to learn about it while he was an assistant coach at Miami (Ohio) from 1993 to 1995. Miami is located in Oxford, about 35 miles up the road from Cincinnati, and the Redskins – they've since changed their name to the RedHawks – played both UC and Xavier.

"I think that had a real good feel for what it was like," said Miller, now the head coach at Arizona. "The game was always very personal is how I would describe it, much more so than a lot of other rivalries of its kind. I think it has more of a college football dynamic because it's a one-shot deal. It's either home or away and the win or the loss really lingers. It affects things moving forward depending on the outcome of the game. It had that kind of Ohio State-Michigan feeling on a smaller scale but in terms of college basketball I don't know if there's more of a personal feeling to a game than that one."

Miller coached at his alma mater of Pittsburgh and at North Carolina State before he became an assistant at Xavier in 2001. After three years as an assistant, he became the head coach when Matta left for Ohio State. During his eight total years at Xavier, Miller came to appreciate the Shootout and learned to embrace it for many different reasons.

"Everybody has a great deal of pressure and responsibility on their shoulders to

Sean Miller learned as the head coach at Xavier that the best way to approach the Crosstown Shootout was to embrace it.

win the game," he said. "It didn't matter where the game was played. It didn't matter what the other team was ranked. Many times you would see UC ranked very, very high and Xavier being the underdog. That's changed over the years, but all that was out the door. The expectation was to win the game and if you didn't you had to recover from it and use that as a learning experience to become better. If you won the game, you had to be careful that the euphoria of winning it and feeling a sense of accomplishment didn't affect you negatively moving forward.

"Once I coached in the game, (I learned) that the aftermath of the game was very important, how you handled it, because you found that your team was physically and mentally beat up. I thought I had a very good grasp of how big the game was to the city of Cincinnati and both respective universities and programs, how it was a defining game to a season, especially a non-conference season. But once you get involved in it there's a buildup, a luncheon and all of that makes it, in a way, almost bigger than it needed to be because unlike college football you have 30 to 35 games that you're juggling and it's such a long season.

"When so much is put in a five-to-seven day period of time you started to worry about who you were going to play prior to that game and then certainly who you were going to play after that game. That's a seven-to-10 day window of time that was really important and how you managed all that defined a lot of things. The intensity of it, the importance of it to the fan bases, and the reaction to a loss is something that's very striking to me even to this day."

During his time as Xavier's head coach, Miller coached against three different UC head coaches – Bob Huggins, who was forced to resign after the 2004-'05 season; Andy Kennedy, who spent one year as the interim head coach in 2005-'06; and Mick Cronin, who has been the UC head coach since 2006-'07. Miller was 3-2 against UC as Xavier's head coach.

"The rivalry was really going through a lot of change as I became the head coach at Xavier," Miller said. "It was Huggs and then it became Andy Kennedy and then Mick. Their program was also going through a lot as well. There was more pressure on everybody to play bigger non-conference games, there was pressure to play in exempt tournaments, so there was more on that non-conference slate. As that game continued to be so big and so personal I could almost sense that it was just a matter of time before something would happen."

Three years after Miller left Xavier, something did happen. Players from both teams squared off in a brawl that ended the game with 9.4 seconds left and Xavier leading, 76-53, at Cintas Center.

"I couldn't have predicted that that fight would break out," Miller said, "although it always seemed to be close to that happening. You just sensed that it needed to be tempered and it seems like they've done that. I didn't see it, but I saw the highlights of it. They asked me about it in a press conference and I came across as saying that I was proud of the guys at Xavier. I really said that in a different context than it came out. The context that it came out in was that I had just finished watching the fight and I was just so proud of what I saw. That was just the furthest from the truth.

"My context was that in that game there's a toughness level that you have to be at in order to win that people don't understand unless you've been in that game. I use the word personal because it's personal with the players, it's personal with the coaches and it's certainly personal with the fans. That permeates in that building for that three-hour period of time.

"At Xavier, I think Coach Prosser did a great job of embracing the rivalry and making sure that he utilized the rivalry to better the program and looked at that, as hey, look, UC is known for their toughness and we have to have toughness within our own right now, because we're playing UC but (also because) that's what we need to get where we want to get to as well...I think in some cases people began to look at Xavier as being even more physically tough, mentally tough, willing to compete at the highest level. That's really what's required in that rivalry.

"It wasn't really about the fight. I didn't understand how serious that fight was as much as in order to compete and be successful in that game you cannot back down. I think that's the mantra that probably both sides have and that's what makes it such a competitive game."

Every head coach has to come up with an approach to the Shootout that he's comfortable with and that his players respond to. Miller was no different, even though he had been part of the rivalry for five years as an assistant coach before he took over for Matta in 2004.

"I thought so highly of Thad," Miller said, "I believed in what we did and I tried to keep a lot of those same concepts in place and I still do to this day, but you have to be yourself. In the first Crosstown Shootout when I was the head coach we played at Cincinnati. Bob Huggins was the coach and we were clearly the underdog. We had a very, very young group. We weren't able to reach that pinnacle of competition and toughness in our own right. We didn't really have that at that time."

UC won that game, 65-54.

"Until you're in it, going from an assistant to a head coach, you don't realize how important of a game it is, how personal the battle is and how intense that it is. I feel like I've been in a lot of games now, even as a player in the Big East Conference a long, long time ago, and I can't think of a game that reminds me of the Xavier-Cincinnati game just in terms of how it feels to be a part of it.

"Looking back on it, once you go through it the first time I think you're more prepared but after that first game I no longer would talk the talk of this isn't a big game, it's just another game, and try to undersell it to our players. I went opposite. I said this is the biggest game because in my opinion it was such a beast that you might as well embrace it and have your team as ready as you could because I don't know if the other way is going to work in that situation. That's how I felt. I don't know if it worked or not but from that first game on, whether we won or lost we really competed for 40 minutes.

"You do (feel more pressure as a head coach) and I think that's part of handling that game. Your players feel it, your team feels it. Everybody feels it, especially if you're on the away court, especially if the team you're playing is better, if they're more veteran or a higher ranked group. You know it's not going to be an easy fight. The other thing at Xavier that you inherited was that there were so many great games where Xavier was clearly the underdog but won the game that it's almost like when you play UC it didn't matter if you were the underdogs. It was almost like, who cares, because we win whether we're the underdog or not. So there was an inherent extra pressure, I would say, on everybody involved. How you learn how to handle that pressure will define how you perform in that game and my way came to be to try to embrace the fact that it is a big game, and you had to have a fight to win. And I don't mean a fist-fight but an amazing ability to not back down.

> **Until you're in it, going from an assistant to a head coach, you don't realize how important of a game it is, how personal the battle is and how intense that it is.**

"You learn from coaches and I learned so much from Bob Huggins as a young coach. There's no coach that I admire more than him. The level of toughness and physicality that his teams at UC played with was unlike anything that I saw and even to this day, to me, I always use that in my mind as the gold standard. When you want to be a big, physical, strong team, a tough-minded team, you think of UC's teams under Huggs. That's obviously a great compliment to him, but that's really how I felt when I was at Xavier."

Miller's second Shootout as Xavier's head coach – and his first win in the rivalry – was on Jan. 19, 2006, with Kennedy as UC's interim coach. The Musketeers won, 73-71, in overtime at Fifth Third Arena, holding on when UC's White missed a 3-point shot at the buzzer.

"One of the things I remember was that Huggs was there at the Cintas Center in a (private) box," Miller said. "I got such a kick out of that. I think that said a lot about him, how much he loves basketball, how much he loves UC and Andy Kennedy. If that was me, the last place on earth I would probably want to be would be in that arena. That game could have gone either way. I think you leave that game grateful that you won."

The following season, UC posted a victory as an underdog. Cronin was the new UC head coach. In the aftermath of the messy breakup with Huggins and the decision by UC athletic director Mike Thomas not to retain Kennedy, Cronin had started over with almost an entirely new roster of players, most of whom had no Division I experience and certainly no experience in the Shootout. Somehow the Bearcats managed to win, 67-57, at Fifth Third Arena. The Musketeers responded from the loss to go 25-9 and advance to the second round of the NCAA Tournament.

"We learned a lot from that game," Miller said. "That would have been my third year at Xavier. If you followed that path of my third season, November and December were still a growth (period). Like the old standards of college basketball, we had a lot of younger players and they grew up a little bit in our second year. Now we're in our third year. We still were very much growing so that game being on the away court, I'll never forget that Stanley Burrell had a really difficult game especially. It was after that game that he made his mind up that he was going to be much more than a scorer and a shooter. It was one of the many things that helped our program hit new heights in really the next year and a half, two years.

"Again, when you're faced with a tough situation, a loss, a failure, that game brings out the best and the worst in you. But if you're smart enough to learn from it, you'll leave that game better, even if it doesn't happen right away. I really looked at that loss as something that we learned a lot from because we got into February and March of that year we really became a Top 25 team and really a Top 25 program moving forward."

As Miller looks back on his experience in the Shootout, he has mixed feelings. He doesn't miss it, he says, but if anything his respect for the rivalry seems to have grown.

"I didn't dread it," he said, "but I didn't look forward to it. I would say I'd probably be in the middle because I think some of the things that as a coach you would dread are the dinner or the banquet because (as a coach, you don't like) anything that gets in the way of normal weekly preparation, especially because you recognize that you're in November or December and we're judged on a 35-game season, not in a five-day span. But really, in that city and during those five days, there's really only one thing that matters and that is the winner of that game.

"So I think for you as a coach you have to embrace it. You don't enjoy everything about it, but I came to say my job is to have this team the most ready we can to compete. That became kind of the mission. I think in year four and year five, not only because we were more talented and better, I thought that we moved to a different category of competitiveness and toughness, physical and mental. We were a big, strong, nasty type of team. Those two teams were almost built for that game.

"I really admire college basketball in Southwest Ohio," Miller said. "When you come to a place like Arizona, we have our fair share of marquee games for sure, but the emotion, the personal nature of everything that's involved in that game, what's at stake, how it feels, the physicality, the competitiveness, I have not seen that, not just at Xavier, but I've never really felt that (anywhere else). When I was at NC State as an assistant we played Duke and Carolina. There was an underdog hatred for Carolina at that time but it wasn't a great rivalry because it was lopsided. You had a personal nature to that game, the same thing with Arizona-Arizona State. Arizona and UCLA is really big, but I can't really compare it to the Crosstown Shootout. I love the city of Cincinnati and Xavier is a special place for me. There's no question, that game, unless you covered it, been at it, seen it, kind of lived it, you don't truly understand what it feels like."

*Mick Cronin was praised nationally for the way he handled
the aftermath of the fight at the end of the 2011 game, won by Xavier.*

MICK CRONIN

UC assistant coach, 1997-2001
Head coach, 2006-present

"You've got to play that game with reckless abandon."

*D*uring 10 years as the head coach at his alma mater, Mick Cronin has re-built the program virtually from scratch and led UC to six straight NCAA Tournaments, including a Sweet 16 appearance in 2012.

But to many fans in Cincinnati, his finest moment at UC occurred moments af-ter the brawl that ended the Crosstown Shootout on Dec. 10, 2011 at Cintas Center. During his post-game press conference, a visibly upset Cronin declared that the players from both teams needed to understand they were representing respected institutions of higher learning and that it was a privilege to play college basketball.

Nothing in those remarks was prepared, said Cronin, who said he has never watched the video from that press conference.

"I think it may have affected people's opinion of me from what I've been told," Cronin said. "That fight obviously was ridiculous. I don't even like talking about it. Everybody ought to be thankful they're playing college sports and people actually care. I tell my guys all the time, 'What if you ran out of the tunnel and there was a band, cheerleaders and nobody in the stands? You've got to understand that this is a privilege, it's an honor and you've got to handle yourself with a measure of class and some humility that you do represent universities.'"

The fight, Cronin said, was the culmination of animosity that had been building between the players from both schools for several years.

"There was a punch (actually an elbow) thrown in the game the year before by Tu Holloway on Ibrahima Thomas late in the game," Cronin said, "but it didn't connect. It was addressed behind the scenes with the league offices. There was too much talk going on and I was concerned about where it was heading. At halftime, the ref called Chris (Mack) and I together. The lead guy, he said, 'There's too much talking. We're gonna give guys technical fouls' and I said, 'You should have already given about three or four technical fouls' and he looked at me. I said, 'You need to start giving T's before this gets out of hand.' I told him right there and he looked at me and I said, 'I'm talking about my guys too. You need to get control of the game.'

"We had always had a real strong crew on that game of Big East officials. But that year the A-10 commissioner said, no, we're going to assign our own officials and they were all A-10 officials on a Saturday. Since it's the A-10 and not the Big East or the ACC, it wasn't co-assigned and then you don't get the top guys. The Big East takes them, the Big Ten takes them, the ACC takes them and you end up with three guys (Michael Roberts, Jeff Anderson and Tony Crisp), they haven't been in a game like that, and it was a recipe for disaster.

"These guys were completely in over their head and I knew it when I talked to them and the guy looked at me like this guy's telling me to 'T' his own team, and I'm trying to explain it to him. The two- or three-year buildup to it was bad. (Kenny) Frease and Yancy (Gates) had had a bad history, things had gone on and it was just bad. There was just too much bad blood. Obviously what (Andy) Furman did with (Sean Kilpatrick) was infuriating. That shouldn't surprise you that he would do that. It needed to be handled and they just weren't capable of handling it."

Cronin was referring to a radio interview that Kilpatrick did with Furman the day before the game in which Furman pressed Kilpatrick to answer a question about whether Holloway would start for UC. Kilpatrick said that with the players the Bearcats had, he didn't think Holloway would start. That interview apparently angered Holloway, who referred to it in the post-game press conference.

The UC coach said he knew nothing about the Kilpatrick interview until someone told him about it.

"I was upset with some people here in our athletic department because I would never have let SK go on that interview," Cronin said. "That was done without my approval. He just baited him, which is a real classy thing to do to a college kid, but that stuff happens."

Cronin said he never advocated discontinuing the game permanently after the fight because he knew what it meant to the city. But he thought it would be a good idea to suspend it for two seasons because he believed the rivalry had become too heated – among players and fans.

"I'm smart enough to know that (some fans) want to hate another team," he said. "That's their enjoyment of it. I could cure poverty and all sickness in Cincinnati and there would still be Xavier fans that dislike me and vice versa for Chris. It had gotten to be embarrassing and it got to a point where it wasn't even about basketball."

The compromise to keep the rivalry going was to move the game to U.S. Bank Arena for two years and rename it the Crosstown Classic instead of the Crosstown Shootout. Cronin was in favor of the move downtown; Mack was not. After two years, it was moved back to the schools' campuses beginning in the 2014-'15 season.

"I still think it should be played downtown," Cronin said, "but that's just my opinion. I think it eliminates a lot of the hatred of the game. This game brings out a lot of the worst in people instead of the best."

Having grown up in Cincinnati, Cronin has always been aware of the rivalry, its history and the arguments it engenders among family members and friends. He has vivid memories of his dad, Hep, getting into arguments while he was attending La Salle High School and his dad was coaching there.

"At La Salle, there was Gene Jessee, who was my JV coach, and my dad, who were the only UC people in the whole building," Cronin said. "Everybody else rooted for Xavier. I used to talk to Bob Freemal about that all the time. He was my homeroom teacher (and phys ed teacher) and he was an ex-coach. You used to do a lot of useless sports in gym class and I didn't have to do them because we would sit and talk basketball and everybody else would play kickball. He had Xavier season tickets and he was a huge Xavier guy.

"Because I was always playing and my dad was always coaching, I don't have any memories of going to the game until '92 at the Gardens when Terry (Nelson) predicted the victory. Somehow we came upon two tickets and my dad and I went to that game. I remembered the Gardens. I had probably been there as a kid. My dad had taken me to see stuff, but I remember thinking how bad the Gardens was. UC just dominated the game. I thought, oh my God, Coach Huggins is going to kill Terry if they don't win this game because by then I knew Terry and Coach Huggins.

"I always had friends at Xavier. Even to this day, Steve Gentry and I are very good friends. He played at Withrow, I played at La Salle, and we still are (friends) to this day. When you grow up as a kid and you're really close friends with someone, even though I wanted UC to win, I always wanted Steve to do well. While he played (for Xavier) that was a really unusual time during the game for me."

Cronin's next memory of the Shootout is from 1999-'00 when he was an assistant coach. That was the first of two times the Musketeers upset the Bearcats when they were ranked No. 1 in the country. This game was played at the Gardens.

"They played great," Cronin said. "Darnell Williams made every shot. It was my scout and I blame myself for that. That environment was crazy because we were so good. We had multiple NBA players. I remember Kevin Frey having the game of his life. You shake your head at some of that stuff. I remember talking to Coach Prosser before the game. I had great admiration for him as a person. You could not dislike him and he was similar to my dad as a high school teacher and coach. I looked at a guy like him and I thought if he can make it, I can make it."

Cronin's first Shootout as UC's head coach occurred on Dec. 13, 2006. The UC program was a mess, having been decimated by Huggins' forced departure, and Cronin was in the early stages of piecing it back together. UC was not expected to win, but this time the Bearcats pulled the upset, 67-57, at Fifth Third Arena, behind 24 points from freshman guard Deonta Vaughn.

"I'm sure Sean Miller is shaking his head over how we won that year," Cronin said. "I still don't know how we won that game. My recollection was that it was early in the year and they were trying to play their best guys and they were playing a kid named Justin Cage at the three and he couldn't shoot, so we didn't guard him. It made me look smart. We just basically had an extra defender standing in the lane the whole game so anything they tried didn't work."

Cage made five of eight shots and scored 14 points, but perhaps because of the extra defensive player at the Bearcats' disposal as a result of not guarding him very closely, they were able to do a better job on Stanley Burrell, who was 0-for-10 from the field.

"On the other end," Cronin said, "we had some guys make some shots. That year early we were 9-3 in the pre-conference schedule. We beat some other teams – we beat Temple, we beat NC State. We were able to upset some teams because we weren't beat down yet. I think some people hadn't figured out yet that we only had one guy that could shoot – Vaughn. We didn't have an identity. You couldn't scout us because we had a new coach and all new players.

"But I knew what was coming in the Big East. We're playing Marcus Sikes at center. It's not gonna work when we get in the Big East. But it's memories that the kids can always have. When you're the underdog and your guys are captivated that 'Okay, this game means a lot and we've got to give everything we've got for this game, (it helps).' But it's impossible to play a team sport with that type of emotion every night, so I think a team like that, if it has some pride, has a little bit of an advantage, the emotional edge, if you can get your team to believe that hey, we've got to play unbelievably hard in our best game of the year to have a chance. That's something that over time you lose and your guys tend to think that we're really good and we've just got to go play.

"I will tell you, too, that since the fight it's a concern of mine. I'm so concerned with that never happening again that I think it's been a disadvantage for me in the way I approach it because I don't want anything to happen again like that. As a coach, I've got to forget about it. Our guys have got to get back to you've got to play that game almost with reckless abandon physically and mentally. It's the only chance you've got to win that game. You can't approach it like other games, but it's a fine line because guys get too on edge and obviously we all know what can happen when it gets to that point.

"It's been tough because of what happened in '11. That was my concern with the game going forward: how do you prepare your team for a game like that? But at the same time you just want to get out of there without a fight. I need to let it go. I don't talk to the team like that, but I'm telling you the truth. I still think we've got to get back to playing with the proper intensity in that game. You've got to get your guys at a different level for that game. You just have to or you're not going to win. That's a different type of game. It's more physical than every other game you're gonna play. It's more intense than every other game you're gonna play. You still do that with your team but in the aftermath of the fight, in the back of your mind as a coach, you're saying, okay, I've got to get these guys fired up but at the same time I don't need to get them to a point where somebody undercuts a guy or somebody takes it too far and the then the next thing you know we've got another problem."

Cronin, who's 3-7 in the Shootout, said he doesn't hate Xavier, and certainly doesn't dislike Mack.

"We've known each other since we were kids," he said, "but we never played on the same team as kids. He played on my brother's (Dan) team a little bit. He's in-between us. But we've always known each other. We have similar friends that we all played hoops with. What Chris and I understand is that we're both fortunate to have the jobs that we have and we both are old enough to understand the good and the bad that goes with our job. When he struggles, his popularity goes down when his team loses a few and the same with me. We get it.

"We don't socialize, but we have a mutual respect for each other and we both know what the other guy is going through.

"I think playing the game has definitely helped escalate the (Xavier) program. If you're having a mature conversation with somebody with integrity and class like Gary Massa and Joe Sunderman, Xavier people that are great people that would speak with maturity on the situation, there's no doubt that playing the game and having some success in the game helped them elevate their program. That's what you face every time you go to play them. With all due respect, it's never been that way here. It's never been the thought process here that you need to beat Xavier to elevate your program. It doesn't mean you don't try to win the game. That's far from what I'm saying.

"If you talked to Bob Huggins about some benchmarks to elevate your program, him and Tony Yates would tell you you have to beat Louisville. They've won national championships. They're demographically a similar school. In my opinion, we'll always be at a disadvantage mentally in (the Xavier) game because the name of the city is on our chest and the other school's fighting to say it's their city. Whether we win or not, the name of the city is still on our chest."

Because most of his players are not from Ohio, let alone Cincinnati, Cronin said it takes a while to get them to understand the importance of the rivalry. Of course, it's true that most of the Xavier players also are not from Ohio.

"The (UC) guys didn't come here to play in that game," he said. "It's not being condescending or dismissive of the game, but it's not the recruiting sell. It's not in the pitch at all. It's something that they learn once they're here. The dynamic for me is to get them to a point of the importance of the game and how hard you're gonna have to play. If you don't want to win that game really, really bad, you're at a distinct disadvantage. That's the challenge you face as the Cincinnati coach. In a smaller school, it is an immediate thing in their program, that, hey, we beat Cincinnati. That's important. We've got to beat Cincinnati. It'll be interesting to see if that continues now that they're in a bigger league.

"The good thing is both teams are really good so basketball-wise you learn about your team (in the rivalry). It's a good game RPI-wise, for your strength of schedule and all that. But just from a basketball standpoint you learn some stuff about your team when you put yourself up against a good team. So that part of it is good, that part of it I like, but the hatred part in this day and age with Twitter, with all that stuff…the game should be about basketball, but it's tough to keep it that way. It drives fans nuts. I have fans and I have boosters that would rather win that game than our league. And they'll tell you. What happens, you learn in life, is that people care about their own plight, what affects them. And they'll laughingly tell me that because they play golf with another Xavier fan and they don't want to have to hear it…I'm like, okay, that's why we'll win. It all goes with the territory."

CHRIS MACK

Xavier player, 1991-'93
Director of Basketball Operations, 1999-2001
Assistant coach, 2004-'09
Head coach, 2009-present

"If we could play them 32 times a year,
I'm ready to tee it up 32 times a year."

The toughest day of Chris Mack's career as a head coach was the day of the fight between the UC and Xavier players at the end of the Musketeers' 76-53 victory in 2011, over UC. It was a victory that Mack was unable to fully enjoy because of the brawl.

"We pleaded with the A-10 to make sure we had a crew on the game that could handle the emotions of it," Mack said. "For years, there had always been a very strong officiating crew that wasn't going to take any nonsense."

These officials lost control of the game, even though coaches and players from both schools said afterward that they could see the fight developing because of the talk among the players on the court.

"We had just come off the heels of getting our asses kicked over at UC when Yancy (Gates) was hitting 17-, 19-foot fade-aways at the end of the game," Mack said. "We had some competitive dudes in that locker room. It just went the wrong way. There was a little bit of talk before the game and it just really intensified to the point where it shouldn't have. And then afterwards we didn't make it any better by our guys going up there and talking at the press conference. I still to this day feel like they were misrepresented a little bit. I didn't know what they had

Xavier head coach Chris Mack was against moving the Shootout to U.S. Bank Arena because, "I felt like it was a little bit odd."

said. I wish I had."

Mack was talking about his starting guards, Tu Holloway and Mark Lyons.

"We got disrespected a little bit before the game, guys calling us out," Holloway said at the post-game press conference. "We're a tougher team. We've got grown men over here. We've got a whole bunch of gangsters in this locker room, not thugs, but tough guys on the court. We went out there and zipped them up at the end of game."

"At the end of the day, if someone puts their hands in your face and tries to do something to you, where we're from, we're going to do something back," Lyons said. "We're not going to sit there and get our face beat in by somebody like Yancy Gates or somebody like that. We're not going to let that happen."

"I look back on what they said, knowing those two guys," Mack said. "I know what they meant to say. It didn't come off very well, but I didn't have that at the time. You learn a lot. You have to address that stuff going in and make sure guys know that, hey, no matter how intense it gets…it's got to be officiated the right way and our players have to handle themselves the right way on both sides.

"It was certainly a bad moment, a tough moment, one that we certainly hope will not happen again. We had never really talked about that before the game because it never was really a part of the game. It's just how you grow up playing. You go at the opponent as hard as you can and at the end of the game, you shake hands and you go your opposite ways. That obviously didn't happen.

"I've been maligned at times, like why doesn't Mack take out his starters, like why are those guys in there when they're up 17 or 18 points? The reason I didn't take them out was ironically because I didn't want to rub it in. It's one of those things where when you take them out, they're going to walk off the floor. They're not going to run or sprint right to the side and sit down. They're going to put their hands up and then you're going to have the opposing coach and staff looking down there like, you're rubbing it in. We just wanted the time to evaporate.

"When faced with that situation now, I don't hesitate. We'll take a timeout if necessary and we'll (put in) the subs. But again, you're still going to have that same problem that I was trying to avoid and that is guys celebrating in the moment and it really becomes from an opponent's standpoint, looking like you're rubbing it in as they walk off the floor.

"I thought it would be more subdued if the time just ran out and the guys that were on the floor were on the floor. If there's two minutes on the clock and you're up 17 and 18 points, everybody's saying why aren't you putting walk-ons in? From a coaching standpoint, if I put those walk-ons in and UC continues to press or any team continues to press, an 18-point lead can go to about nine in about 40 seconds.

That's why it sort of happened down the stretch the way it did in terms of an Xs an Os standpoint."

The Xavier players believed that UC's Sean Kilpatrick had "called them out," to use Holloway's words, when he said during a radio interview the day before the game that he was a better player than Holloway and that Holloway would not start for UC.

"I know it really impacted Holloway," Mack said. "It really set him off. That's why he was sort of barking at the bench at the end of the game. I'm not saying Sean was wrong. Two wrongs don't make a right. Again it's what happens when you're in the Cincinnati-Xavier rivalry and you're a part of this and you're sitting in the city where all the media attention is being driven and again rightly so because the game itself has a great story, a great tradition. The schools are three miles apart. There have been some classic games but that's what really bothered Tu because UC had whupped us the year before and they were telling him about it leading up to the game."

> I think the game has to be treated differently. We talk to our guys all the time about it being a players' game because it's going to be so loud.

Players from both teams were suspended after the fight and there was talk about ending the series or at least postponing it for a few years. Instead, the athletic directors and presidents from both schools decided to move the game to a neutral court at U.S. Bank Arena in downtown Cincinnati for at least two years and to change the name of the rivalry from the Crosstown Shootout to the Crosstown Classic.

"We wanted the game to be played," Mack said. "We just felt like on our watch we didn't want that game to crumble because there are so many people that the game means a whole heck of a lot to on both sides of the equation. For us to be the ones that dropped the torch would have been really upsetting, so regardless of where the game was played we wanted to play it.

"I felt like it was a little bit odd (on a neutral court). I think the dynamic of what happened the year before sort of affected the mood. The crowd was just a little bit different, the fact that both sides were there. I know people tried to point to the Missouri-Illinois game but that game doesn't have the same intensity and the same feel as this one. It was probably a good break but not necessarily one that I felt could be sustainable over time."

Mack, who has been the head coach at Xavier since 2009, was born in Cleveland but grew up in Cincinnati. He was neither a UC fan nor a Xavier fan as a kid. He played basketball at St. Xavier High School, then went to the University of Evansville to play for Jim Crews, a former assistant coach at Indiana under the hard-driving Bob Knight. After two years, Mack decided he wanted to transfer.

"I had two good years of playing but (Crews) comes from the Bobby Knight cloth and I wasn't ready for that," Mack said. "It wasn't what I expected. I should have been smarter in knowing that he played for Knight for four years and coached under him for six. But when you're a high school kid and you don't have the internet, you don't know any of that stuff.

"Toward the end of my sophomore year I just dreaded going to practice and basketball wasn't fun. This was something that you put so much time into-I remember spending seven, eight hours a day playing basketball-so I just wanted a fresh start, to go somewhere where I really enjoyed going to practice. I sort of masked it by saying I wanted to get closer to home. I didn't want to hurt anyone's feelings so I said that."

Mack said he was offered a scholarship by UC and Xavier but chose Xavier because the Musketeers played in the same Midwestern Collegiate Conference as Evansville so he was more familiar with their program. He also knew some of the Xavier players from playing in open gym with them while he was home during the summer. He ended up being a two-year captain for the Musketeers in 1991-'92 and 1992-'93.

He was 0-2 against UC as a Xavier player. His first experience against the Bearcats was a 69-56 UC win during the year Mack had to sit out under the NCAA's rules for transfers. The following year UC manhandled the Musketeers, 93-75, making good on a prediction by UC forward Terry Nelson that the Bearcats would blow out Xavier.

"He was right," Mack said. "We got blown out. It's funny because a lot of times when guys have those types of quotes they generally backfire and I remember our guys were excited to play, but my gosh, they were good. They got off to a really good start and they never looked back. I remember that Coach Gillen came in and in front of the team, he basically said, we're not responding (to Nelson's prediction). We're not saying anything. We're not retaliating. We're not playing this out in the media. We're going to do this the right way.

"There were a couple of guys that were fuming and wanted to go at (Nelson). Obviously we ended up getting drilled so we couldn't have wanted that much revenge. There were some guys upset (about the prediction). A couple of guys thought he was a complete clown, but you know, Muhammad Ali talked a lot and he backed it up."

Mack has fared much better against the Bearcats as the Xavier head coach, going 5-2. His approach is to emphasize the importance of the game with his players and encourage them to enjoy the experience. It would be a mistake, he said, to treat it like a normal game because it's not.

"Even if you want to, the media, the fans, people around the city (won't let you.) When you walk into Xavier for the first time as a scholarship player, when you go play over at the Deveroes Summer League or you walk into Kenwood Mall and somebody identifies you and says where do you play, and you say Xavier, the first thing they ask you about is the Crosstown Shootout, and it's one of two things: 'I root for you guys every game but one,' so now you know what side of the fence they're on.'

"I think the game has to be treated differently. We talk to our guys all the time about it being a players' game because it's going to be so loud. You have to be aggressive. You can't worry about trying to run your offense. Both teams are going to know each other inside and out. You have to give those guys the freedom to attack and not look over their shoulder and just make it a players' game and let those guys know, 'I want you to have the time of your life. I want you to play loose, play free, have fun.' But it's tense leading up. There's no coverage like that for any other game you play during the regular season.

"And when you're in the NCAA tournament, you're off at some remote site so all of that stuff being reported is in a different place than you're at. Here you're sitting in the city of Cincinnati while all of these stories are coming out, while all of this coverage is going on. You have the VIP reception and the players are sitting in the middle of that."

Asked if believes the game means more to Xavier than it does to UC, Mack said he couldn't speak for what it means to UC, "but I can tell you that it does mean a whole lot to us. I know this is how I feel. Anywhere I go in the city of Cincinnati at some point, if I'm in a restaurant for a couple of hours, I'll get heckled. It may not be what that fan perceives as heckling, but there's, 'Coach, I love what you do, I love ya, but I've got to tell you I'm a Bearcat.' There always has to be a precursor to our conversation. I get it. We can't go to Oktoberfest anymore with our family. That's a bad mix. You've got 20-somethings with alcohol, so I don't know if it means more to Xavier, but I do know that you're reminded of it every day."

Unlike Gillen, his former coach at Xavier who said he didn't enjoy coaching in the Crosstown Shootout, Mack said he loves it.

"If your personality as a coach is to not enjoy a heightened game, a heightened coverage game, a rivalry game," he said, "I think your players are going to feel that. I love playing UC, I love playing Dayton, I love playing Butler. To me, those are the games where the fans are really into it. If you're a player and you're running through that tunnel, as excited as all get out, and if your coach is sort of on edge and nervous and doing things outside of what he normally does, I think your players are going to feel that. I tell those guys all the time if we could play them 32 times a year, I'm ready to tee it up 32 times a year and I want our players to feel that way."

Mack, who was an assistant coach at Wake Forest under Skip Prosser for three years, says the Crosstown Shootout can match any rivalry in the country, including Duke-North Carolina.

"I can't say that I've sat on the sideline for Duke-Carolina or Louisville-Kentucky," Mack said, "but I have been part of the ACC and I certainly know those staffs and players that have played in it and it doesn't take a back seat to any of those rivalries. It just doesn't. A couple of them have a lot more Final Fours and national championships than both of us but just the familiarity between players and the programs and the fans and divided families…you have families that have UC graduates that have Xavier kids and vice versa. I see it in my own family."

The rivalry has been back on campus for the past two years and there have been no incidents to detract from the games. Still, Mack would like to see the fans dial down the vitriol they feel for the other school.

"You're not going to be able to control that," Mack said. "That's part of Mick's job and my job, to make sure that there's a respect level among the teams, among the coaches, that it's not a venomous thing. I don't know how you control it outside of the locker rooms and the venue. Fans are going to be fans. The loyalties run deep. I think (fighting among the players) is in the past because at least at our end we've certainly addressed it and I know that Mick's always been a class act when it comes to that. His kids, they respond the right way. I don't foresee it being a problem, at least during my time."

UC associate head coach Larry Davis filled in for ailing Mick Cronin during most of the 2014-'15 season.

LARRY DAVIS

UC acting head coach, 2014-'15
Associate head coach, 2006-present

"I should have gone with my first instinct."

*W*hen Mick Cronin was forced to sit out most of the 2014-'15 season after he was diagnosed with an arterial dissection, associate head coach Larry Davis ran the team and seemed to push all the right buttons. With Davis in charge, the Bearcats went 23-11, made it to their fifth straight NCAA Tournament and knocked off Purdue in overtime in the first round before falling to No. 1-ranked Kentucky in the second.

But there is one decision that Davis regrets as he looks back on that season, a decision that received little attention at the time and that Davis has carried with him ever since.

It happened during the Crosstown Shootout. The Bearcats had rallied from a 12-point halftime deficit to take a one-point lead on two free throws by Troy Caupain with 19 seconds to play at Fifth Third Arena. At that point, Davis thought about replacing freshman forward Gary Clark with senior forward Jermaine Sanders, one of UC's best defensive players.

But he didn't listen to his own instincts and left Clark in the game. On the Musketeers' next possession, Clark tried to steal the ball from Xavier freshman Trevon Bluiett only to foul him. Bluiett made two free throws with 11 seconds left to give the Musketeers a one-point lead.

UC still had a chance to win but Farad Cobb's 3-point shot was off the mark with four seconds left. A free throw by Myles Davis gave Xavier a 59-57 victory.

"We had ourselves in a position to win," Davis said.

Davis decided to leave Clark in the game because, he said, "Gary had played pretty well and he had just scored (with 1:10 to play). It was hard to do. You always look back and say that's the one thing I wish I would have done. Gary almost stole the ball but he shouldn't have gambled. Jermaine Sanders wouldn't have gambled. He might have fouled the kid or the kid might have made the shot but he would have had to make the shot over the top of Jermaine. He would have been solid and done the right thing as a senior and he would have made (Bluiett) earn it. I thought about it and we didn't do it. It was happening so quick, but I should have just gone with my first instinct. Usually in coaching, your first instinct is right. A lot of it was the faith I had in Gary. Even for a freshman I had a lot of faith in him. The second half of that game he kicked their ass. He went right at every one of them and scored on them.

"The truth of the matter is Farad Cobb got a look. We still could have won the game. If I had to do it over again, I'd sub (Clark). That one stands out, but like you tell players, normally one play doesn't win or lose the game. If Farad comes down and hits the shot nobody thinks about it. Despite what he says, he thought we were down three because he had an opportunity to shoot a pull-up and he didn't. He actually could have gotten fouled. He side-stepped and shot the three. He should have taken one dribble and shot the pull-up two. I don't know why he thought we were down three."

Cobb took the crucial shot only because Caupain did not drive the ball to the basket where he might have gotten fouled.

"We put it in Troy's hands to make the play and he made the pass," Davis said. "Sometimes the play is to shoot it and sometimes the play is to pass it. I think in his sophomore year his mindset was to make the pass at the end of the game and not go make the bucket. And now his mindset has changed to I've either got to go make the bucket or I've got to draw everybody and then find the guy."

Davis' first exposure to the Shootout was during the 2006-'07 season, his and Cronin's first year at UC. The Bearcats were basically starting the program from scratch and were underdogs against the Musketeers but found a way to win, 67-57, in what was probably the highlight of the season for an outmanned UC team that finished 11-19 and at one point lost 16 of 18 games.

"We probably caught them by surprise a little bit," Davis said. "That early group was so bought in, it was such a sense of pride with them. It was an accomplishment that they could actually pull off. Winning the Big East, we weren't going to do that, but winning that game, that was possible, and I think they saw that in their minds. They were a tough group and they toughed it out.

"I think it gave everybody a glimpse of hey, good things are going to come. It may take a while but we can get this thing back to where it's a Top 20 program, winning, being as good as anybody in the country. That gave everybody hope. It was a good spark early on because it was going to be a tough road because of the league we were in."

Davis was on the UC bench at Cintas Center in 2011 when the brawl broke out near the end of the Shootout and like other UC staff members and assistant coaches he did his best to pull the Bearcat players away from the fracas, but it was too late. The fight had already gotten out of hand.

Cronin was praised for the way he handled the fight's aftermath, speaking philosophically about the value of college athletics and the shame the fight had brought to both programs and their players. He spoke from the heart and fans across the country listened and approved. It wasn't long afterward that Davis began to notice the effect it had on UC's recruiting.

"Mick handled it unbelievably well," Davis said. "Sometimes in recruiting I'll make a call and I'll talk to somebody for the first time. I talked to a guy in Florida about his son and he brought that up. He said, 'I've always liked your program. I've always liked your coach, ever since the Xavier fight, how your coach handled that. Because of that, I would send my son there to play.' As a recruiter, that is an interesting byproduct of the game. His actions and how he handled it after the game … I can't tell you how many times I've run into that lately where people have said that. I don't bring it up. Other people bring it up."

Senior forward Yancy Gates was among four UC players suspended after the game.

"I think it humbled him," Davis said, "because basketball has always been there for Yancy. I think all kids take basketball for granted, particularly the more talented players. It's like, I'm good, it's always going to be here. And for the first time in his life he was in real danger of getting basketball taken away from him. He could have been done here. There was an outcry of people who wanted all of those guys to be permanently kicked off the team and never play at Cincinnati again."

Instead, Gates was suspended for six games. Without him and the other players who were suspended, the Bearcats had to reinvent themselves in a hurry.

"We got together as a group," Davis said, "and Mick, as he was dealing with everything, said, 'You guys get together and figure out a way that we can play small. How can we play offensively small and how can we play defensively small? Write every idea you have on the board.'

"We had a meeting. He had ideas in his mind but we went kind of down that list and we started to fashion a game plan. Mick was great with them. He told them we're not going to feel sorry for ourselves. This is where we're at. We're going to find a way to win. And that group of guys – I have to say that was one of the most fun times in my whole coaching career (because of) the intensity that they played with and that they prepared with.

"I always say this because I've been a mid-major coach and a low-major coach, in games where I was going to play Florida State, Minnesota, whoever it was, Ohio State, those games, those are the easiest prep games you ever have as a mid-major and the reason, despite what everybody says, is that kids are scared to death that they're going to get embarrassed, so they tune in more. They play harder. They listen. They just do. The low- to mid-major team knows if you don't play that way, you can get beat by 30 and be embarrassed. I think our guys had that mentality. They didn't want to be embarrassed. We came up with a style of switching everything, trapping everything, and spread people out and made them guard us. Wright State was the first game and they didn't want to go lose to a mid-major team, so they went out and won. Then we went to Pittsburgh and we found a way to win that game and that served us well."

The Bearcats won 10 of their next 11 games. When Gates and the others returned, they blended in with the new system and UC ended up in the Sweet 16. The Musketeers lost five of their next six games, but they, too, advanced to the Sweet 16.

Even though he lost the one Shootout he directed as the acting head coach, Davis says he's glad he had the opportunity to run the show in at least one Crosstown Shootout. Davis has been around college basketball for 31 years. Before he took the job at UC under Cronin, he was the head coach at Furman for nine years. He has also coached at Minnesota, Ball State and Wake Forest. He says he has never seen anything like the Crosstown Shootout.

"I've been in the ACC, I've been in the Big Ten, I've been to Duke, I've been to Indiana," Davis said. "I've been to some places, man, and I have to say that's one of the most intense atmospheres, whether it's downtown, at Xavier, or here, that's one of the most intense atmospheres I've ever seen."

TAY BAKER

UC head coach, 1965-'72
Assistant coach, 1959-'65
Xavier head coach, 1973-'79

"I still had coaching in my blood."

*I*magine the reaction in Cincinnati if Xavier had hired Bob Huggins to coach its men's basketball team after he had been forced out of UC in 2005.

Okay, that never could have happened, given the way Xavier fans felt about Huggins and the way he felt about Xavier. But there was a time when a UC coach did become the head coach at Xavier shortly after he left UC.

Tay Baker was the head coach at UC from 1965 through 1972. He was out of coaching for one year after he was replaced by Gale Catlett. He then resurfaced at Xavier to replace Dick Campbell after the Musketeers had gone 3-23 in 1972-'73, their fifth straight losing season. Baker remains the only person to be the head basketball coach at both schools.

"I was sort of semi-retired and it was just about the lowest point in the history of Xavier University basketball," Baker said. "I had a personal connection there. I got a call and I talked to them about it and I thought about it and I still wanted to coach, so why not take a shot at it? It was very difficult, but it was an opportunity and I didn't have to move. Of course, I was sort of concerned about being a Protestant who played at UC. I thought what it amounts to is, can you get into a situation like that and do a job and be accepted for what you do, not for where you played ball or where you went to school or what religion you had, but what the results of your tenure there would be? I was still young enough and I had enough coaching in my blood."

Tay Baker is the only coach to be the head coach at both UC and Xavier.

Baker was 5-2 against Xavier while he was the head coach at UC. He was 0-6 against the Bearcats while he was the Musketeers' head coach. His final Xavier team narrowly missed knocking off the Bearcats the year before Xavier made its big breakthrough in the rivalry under Bob Staak. His overall record at UC was 125-60. He was 70-89 at Xavier.

College athletics in that era bore only a passing resemblance to what they are today, with million-dollar salaries for coaches and the influence of national television – and more recently, social media.

"When I was at UC, we were always faculty people," Baker said, "we were never on contract as coaches. We were always given professorial status. The paycheck came from the School of Education, not from the athletic department. It was a totally different scene at that time than it is now. We were obligated for 12 hours a semester. At that time, though, there was a regular physical education requirement for the liberal arts college so we taught all of those phys ed classes plus the speciality classes in your sport. When I first went to UC I took a $500 cut from Wyoming High School because I was a UC guy and I had the opportunity to go back there. I jumped all over it. The first two years I coached over there I was also the track coach and cross country coach."

When he started at Xavier as an assistant coach, Baker was also a member of the faculty, which is the way he wanted it.

"The only condition I had when I went over there was that I could transfer my status on the educational staff and have guaranteed tenure," he said. "That was the main point in the whole discussion. We'll put you on faculty and award you with tenure because you've been a college teacher for 13 years or something like that. With tenure, you have some degree of security. It's not going to be a situation where you have to go in every year and tell them how many games you won or lost or why you won or lost.

"I'll be very truthful with you. I really liked it at Xavier. I really felt like I was accepted over there, but not by everybody. Because when you have a situation where you're at two universities, both great universities, Xavier and Cincinnati, and you come from one to the other, some people are going to have some negative feelings about that. But the president of the university and the athletic director, they were just wonderful people and I got along with them very well. There was one other person in the phys ed department and he and I hit **it** off real good so it was a good working situation."

The program he had been hired to turn around was much different from the traditionally successful one he was accustomed to at UC.

"They had like five coaches in six years (actually three in 10 years) or something like that and the facility (Schmidt Fieldhouse) was a horrible facility," Baker said. "It was an old, old fieldhouse and people just didn't have interest in going to watch games there. It served a purpose at one time but when these other state universities started building their big arenas and getting into the TV aspect and the financial aspect and income of what collegiate basketball offered, that changed the picture pretty readily."

At the time, both schools operated without a league affiliation, the Bearcats having left the Missouri Valley Conference in 1970. UC's independent status lasted only until it helped form the Metro Conference in 1975. Xavier was still trying to figure what to do about a conference when Baker arrived in 1973.

"When I met with (athletic director Jim McCafferty), he said, 'Coach, listen, we're forming a new league' and he named the teams off that were all set to go into this thing, and it would have been a great league," Baker said. "It was Xavier, Dayton, Marquette, DePaul, Loyola, Detroit, like 10 teams of that nature. And I said, 'Well, look, you actually cannot exist as an independent. You can't do it. Marquette can do it. Notre Dame can do it, but aside from those two schools, there's not a university in the United States athletically that can exist unless they're affiliated with a conference.' He said, 'We're getting that.'

"They had a final meeting and it was supposed to be maybe a year from when I went over there. Here's what I was told: All of the ADs were there and they were discussing schedules and all that kind of stuff. DePaul said if Loyola is gonna be in that conference, we're not gonna be in it. DePaul, at that time, they were the king in Chicago, not Loyola.

"So then Marquette said, 'If DePaul is not gonna be in this thing, we're not gonna be in.' It fell apart is what happened. It was like another five years before they ever got that thing organized…but it was a conference and that, as far as I'm concerned, was the factor that changed the whole complexion. With that conference, once you get in there, it's motivation for you that if you win this conference, you're gonna be in the NCAA. That to me is the factor that changed the whole complexion of basketball at Xavier University."

Xavier became a charter member of the Midwestern City Conference in 1979. By then, Staak had replaced Baker as the head coach. But Baker said he felt no bitterness, even though he had pushed so hard for a conference.

"I felt good for them," he said. "I had no animosity toward the university. Mac couldn't help it that DePaul said we're not gonna be in that conference if Loyola's in there. It turned the thing around for them. Really, I'm very, very happy that it happened the way it did."

Staak and others at Xavier have credited that victory over UC as the catalyst that put the Musketeers on the path to where they are today as a nationally-ranked program. But Baker believes the conference affiliation was as important, if not more important, than the upset of the Musketeers' crosstown rival.

"I don't think the individual games like that had anything to do with it," he said. "They had the right group of people together at the right time to go ahead and agree to form a conference. It's just like what UC's going through now with that Big 12. They either get in there and get some money or they're gonna have to bite the bullet."

The modern version of college basketball has also greatly changed the rivalry that Baker knew at UC and at Xavier.

"Then it was a local game," Baker said. "That game and Miami and Dayton were probably the big teams on the schedule. It didn't have the national attention or respect that it has now. UC won a couple of national championships. They've always been traditionally a Top 20 or 25 team. Xavier has reached that point, too, that they're nationally known."

Baker's first game coaching against his old school was a 68-56 loss to UC on Feb. 29, 1994 at Cincinnati Gardens. And yes, it did seem strange coaching against the school where he played from 1948 to 1950, worked an assistant coach from 1959 to 1965 and head coach from 1965 to 1971. He's also a member of the school's James P. Kelly Athletics Hall of Fame.

> **When you coach, you can't be emotional. You've got to think, what do I have to do with my players to get them best prepared for the team that we're playing against?**

"When you coach, you can't be emotional," Baker said. "You've got to think, what do I have to do with my players to get them best prepared for the team that we're playing against? You can't eliminate that from that basketball game, but you try your best not to let it become an emotional issue and forget what you're there for and that's to coach the basketball game. I tried as much as I could."

Having coached at both schools, Baker was appalled when the fight broke out between the UC and Xavier players in 2011.

"I was really kind of ticked off at both schools," he said, "because I think the thing originated, kind of festered a little bit more with that radio thing with (Sean) Kilpatrick. Then it just boiled up from that. I wasn't too proud of anybody at all in that situation. You've got to blame both schools, both administrations and players from both schools."

Baker still follows the rivalry and although he loved his time at Xavier and wants only good things for the Musketeers, when they play against his alma mater, he roots for the Bearcats.

"I've got UC blood in me," he said. "If it's a well-played game and there's no problem, I kind of hope UC wins. But I love (Chris) Mack and the way he coaches and the university and the progress they've made over there and I got to know Skip Prosser real well and had great respect for him. But it's still a basketball game. Somebody's got to win so I'm probably hoping that it's not decided by an official's call or something like that, that it's a well-played game and there's no interruptions. And I think for the most part it's been that way. But that fight was a bad deal for everybody concerned. Nobody gained anything from that. It's a special game and it always will be, but I think now the coaches, even though they're close to each other, they've got to be thinking more about their conference and conference championships and things like that."

XAVIER PLAYERS

*Gary Massa, a Cincinnati native, scored 12 points
in Xavier's historic 1980 upset of UC.*

GARY MASSA
1977-'81

"It gave me chills."

A 1977 graduate of Cincinnati's St. Xavier High School, Gary Massa traded one Jesuit school for another, one X for another, and stayed home to play for the Musketeers. The sharp-shooting forward played his first two years under Tay Baker before Bob Staak arrived on the scene.

"The program wasn't anywhere near what is today," Massa said. "It didn't have the resources, didn't have the fan base."

Massa attended Staak's introductory press conference and liked what he heard. Perhaps it would be more accurate to say that he was shocked by what he heard.

"He talked about getting to the NCAA Tournament," Massa said. "The few media that showed up that day snickered. It was like, you've got to be kidding me… Bob Staak came in and demanded things. We didn't have money to paint the locker rooms back then in Schmidt Fieldhouse. He came in a young buck, 31 years old. He knew how to make it work. He had kind of a vision."

The transformation didn't occur right away. There was a lot that needed to be fixed at Xavier. But three years later, in 1983, the Musketeers made only the second NCAA Tournament appearance in school history and the first since 1961. XU was chosen as a No. 12 seed to face Alcorn State on March 14 at UD Arena, where it lost, 81-75. The following year the Musketeers beat Ohio State, 60-57, in overtime in the National Invitation Tournament at Cincinnati Gardens.

Both of those accomplishments would have been difficult to imagine during Staak's first year.

"He cobbled together a few junior college guys and myself and a few others and that first year we were 8-18, not pretty, but then we got in a league and beat UC," Massa said. "That was a big deal for us to lift our presence in the city. From that point on, I think we lost one and then we won a couple and then it was like, man, this is now a rivalry. People paid attention to it. It was really good for the city, like it is now."

Massa, who scored 12 points in Xavier's upset of the Bearcats in 1980, said he will never forget Staak's bold proclamation near the end of the game.

"We were on the bench and the microphone was in the huddle," he said. "There were like 17 seconds left, the place was going crazy for Xavier and he said, 'In 17 seconds, we own this city.' It gave me chills because it was such a cool thing. Xavier had never experienced that in a long time. Back maybe to the '58 NIT team is my guess. There was just not much pride around the place."

Now Vice-President for University Relations at Xavier, Massa has no doubt that Staak, even at that early stage of his tenure at Xavier, knew exactly what a win over UC would mean for the Musketeers' program.

"There was an extra hop in his step during that week in practice," Massa said. "He really made it clear that we can do this. We got a little momentum going and hit some shots. That's what happens. That's one of the cool things about sports. You've seen it happen a million times. You give a team a little confidence, a spark, and you've seen what happens. On the other hand, if you punch them in the mouth right away, a lot of teams just pack it in and fold up.

"I remember that every possession was intense. And certainly being from Cincinnati, it meant that much more. There were a lot of times when you'd play back in that day, at Detroit or Cleveland State or Hanover, and there wouldn't be that many people there. As a player, you want to play in the big games in front of the big crowds and this is one where people came out. The games had an intensity factor like no other and that's truly the way it is today. That's what makes it so much fun.

"In that game, the thing I do remember is that we knew damn well it wasn't over until it was over. It wasn't like we were used to being in that position. Going back to that timeout, there was still a level of intensity. Coach Staak was sweating. He was still very much into the game even though we had a lead. I think we were up five or six or something like that at the end. So I remember just making sure that we hung on and didn't blow this thing.

"We played kind of a matchup zone. Bob really knew what he was doing. We all felt confident because of his game plan. And we all knew each other from playing in the summer. That really was the case back then and I'm sure Eddie Lee was the guy we needed to stop. UC even today is always big and athletic. Once in a while when they're good they have somebody who can put it in the basket in a consistent way and he was the guy back then and if we stopped him we thought we'd be in good shape."

It wasn't until Keith Walker provided the exclamation point with his dunk late in the game that Massa allowed himself to believe that the Musketeers had won.

"Keith was really not a very big guy," Massa said. "I'm not sure that we had ever seen him dunk before. He was our point guard and I don't think he was more than 5-10. When he did that, it was like, you know what? That's done. That stuck a fork in 'em. At that point, our fans went crazy.

"Xavier was not used to this. Our students were delirious. I can remember going to Dana Gardens (near the Xavier campus) afterwards and it was crazy. So many times back then we were the little guy. It was part of what built that rivalry. We were the little Catholic school down the road compared to the big, bad state school. That was just always the way it was. It was like David and Goliath for sure and honestly at the time I don't think anybody thought that this would be a common occurrence."

After playing two years with Tay Baker running the Xavier program, playing under the demanding Staak was a culture shock for Massa. Practices were much tougher, the intensity was higher and so were the expectations. There were no guarantees that Staak's way would be any more successful than Baker's, but Massa welcomed the change in approach.

"It was pretty much roll the ball out (under Baker)," he said. "It was not very demanding. It was pretty loose. We had guys like Steve Spivery and Nick Daniels. It kind of had to be that way. Bob came in and it was tie your shoes on tight and get ready to battle every day, screamin' and yellin'. I'm convinced that it was like playing for Bobby Knight. You bust your butt every day. It's a war. You hated the guy, but as the dust cleared, if you made it through, you'd go through the wall for the guy. And it was the right time for that kind of guy at Xavier."

There was more to Staak's plan for Xavier than solid game strategies and demanding practices. Staak was active in the community and sold the program, doing whatever it took to let people know that he was serious about waking up sleepy little Xavier.

After his playing days, while he pursued his master's degree in business, Massa witnessed the hard-driving Staak at work off the court.

"He was trying to build a program," Massa said, "like Brian Kelly with the football program at UC. He would be out and about. He was very popular with our alums. He was a very social guy, believe me, sometimes too social. He helped me get a scholarship from the NCAA to get my master's degree in business. So I was in the athletic office a lot after I graduated. He would take me to play golf with an alum or whatever and that wasn't just what you were doing. At 2 o'clock in the morning you found yourself somewhere. It was like, 'Oh my God, this guy's incredible.' He was funny and he was fun to be around, so he was building the program and he loved it and had fun doing it."

In 1991, Fr. James Hoff took over as Xavier's president and began to pursue an aggressive strategy of using the basketball program to promote the university as a whole. The school moved its home games out of Cincinnati Gardens in 2000, and into 10,250-seat Cintas Center, its new state-of-the-art on-campus arena.

"I don't think anybody, even after beating (UC) could have thought that our program would have progressed to the point where unbelievably we've got a nicer arena (than UC) and a better league (the Big East vs. the American Athletic Conference) and more NBA players and higher rankings and more wins," Massa said. "It's just amazing.

"I've been here for 17 years raising money for the university. Ninety percent of what's been raised in the history of the university has been raised in the last two decades and clearly, whether it's right or wrong, the academic progress, the building on campus, the progress, has all been parallel with an intentional strategy focused on basketball. You can't buy that kind of visibility and exposure. There's a lot of people that don't really think that athletics should be at the level that it is – people in academics in particular – but the reality is you don't get the kind of notoriety and national publicity that you get from basketball through your physics program."

Massa believes it all started with that win over UC on Feb. 4, 1980.

"There's no doubt that we thought we could do it," he said. "It wasn't like it was some kind of ridiculous thing, but to actually see it happen, feel it happen, it was a big deal back then. Today, you beat UC and you move on, you've got to play Villanova on Saturday."

Massa remembers the Crosstown Shootout not just for the 1980 game and what it meant to the Xavier program, but for the fun of competing against the UC players he knew from playing against them during the summer and whom he genuinely liked. He was especially fond of Badger.

"People talk about this hatred and stuff," Massa said, "but I always got along with their players fine and Ed Badger in particular. He was always very nice when we walked off the court. I can remember sitting with a bunch of buddies at the High Rise Inn over in Clifton and he sent a pitcher of beer over. So think about that today, if that happened today. It would never happen."

STEVE WOLF
1980-'83

"That was our NCAA."

*P*erhaps no Xavier basketball player has ever been a bigger UC fan than Steve Wolf, who played for the Musketeers from 1980 through 1983 and was a co-captain during the 1982-'83 season.

Wolf, who now does color commentary on CBS Sports TV, is the son of Charley Wolf, who coached the NBA Cincinnati Royals from 1960 to 1963. He grew up following the Royals but also the Bearcats. At the time, the NBA used a territorial draft, which meant the Royals had first crack at UC's players, some of whom played for Wolf's dad.

"Let's face it," Wolf said, "everybody followed Cincinnati basketball, including me. I didn't follow Xavier basketball."

Over the years, Wolf personally knew a lot of UC players-Oscar Robertson, Ron Bonham, Pat Cummings, Connie Dierking, Bob Miller, Steve Yoder, Steve Collier and Puffy Kennedy-to name a few.

"I got to be good friends with them," Wolf said. "Pat Cummings took me under his wing my senior in high school. I was on his summer league team. When I was at Xavier and we'd go to Milwaukee to play Marquette, he was with the Bucks and we'd go out. He was always really good to me. Doug Schloemer lived down the street from me in Kentucky. Bobby Austin and I played against each other in high school and in All-Star games together. I knew all those guys. I knew all about Cincinnati basketball. That's what I was raised on."

Wolf will go so far as to claim that he was "anti-Xavier," even though his older brother, Marty, played there for two years.

"I didn't like anything that was going on there," he said.

After he graduated from St. Xavier High School, Wolf signed with North Carolina State where he played for coach Norm Sloan. He spent one year in Raleigh before he decided to transfer back home. He talked to the head coaches at UC, Miami and Dayton. And despite his misgivings about Xavier, he talked to Bob Staak.

"The program was not a program (before Staak's arrival)," Wolf said. "I went to basketball camp there in the 70s when Dick Campbell was coaching and it was just an abysmal program. The only reason I went to Xavier was because my dad told me if you go back to NC State, let Norm Sloan be your dad, because you're not going to come back home. That's not the program for you.

"(Bob) Staak was great. He told me everything I wanted to hear. He said we're going to change things here. He talked about playing games at the Coliseum and at the Gardens. He really had it on line of what to say and he meant it. He was probably too young and too dumb at the time to understand what it was really going to take. I don't think he would have taken the job if he realized how much work had to be done."

So just like that, Wolf switched his allegiance. He was on the bench, sitting out his transfer year under NCAA rules, during the 1980 game when Xavier turned the tide in the rivalry that had long been dominated by UC.

"The hardest game to play for me ever was the UC-XU game because it put a lot of pressure on me," Wolf said. "You always want to play a great game."

Xavier went 1-2 vs. UC during Wolf's three years as an active player with the Musketeers. His only win was a 53-51 victory on Jan. 27, 1982 at Riverfront Coliseum. Wolf had broken his right foot in the season opener vs. St. John's but by the time the UC game rolled around, he had recovered to the extent that he believed he might be able to play against the Bearcats.

"(Staak) took me up in the gym," Wolf said. "I remember taking five Advil and he said, 'We're going to see if you can play tomorrow.' He said, 'Let me watch you run.' I couldn't limp. If I limp, I'm done. So the next game I played and we just walked the ball up the floor.

"My dad said, 'If you can't play hard, don't play.' I was out of shape. (UC's) David Duarte goes up for a shot and (Xavier's) Dexter Bailey blocks it. I drove down the court and (UC's) Junior Johnson trailed me down there. I dunked it right in his face.

"After the game was over, we're excited about winning and my dad looks at me and says, 'You need to have your head examined. You sit out for 11 games. You're hurt. Just go down and lay it in.' He was really upset with me. But it was a pretty neat moment down at the Coliseum."

As he looks back on those games, Wolf realizes that he probably tried to do too

*Steve Wolf, whose father Charley coached the NBA
Cincinnati Royals, grew up a rabid UC fan, but ended up playing
for Xavier after he transferred from North Carolina State.*

much against the Bearcats.

"My dad told me before the game," Wolf said, "'just remember, in big games, the little things make the difference – not turning the ball over, boxing out, keeping your man in front of you. I remember thinking every time the ball came to me that I had to do something positive and that was hard to do. That puts a lot of pressure on you. I put too much pressure on myself to make every play instead of doing the little things.'"

During Wolf's time at Xavier, the NCAA Tournament was not a realistic goal for either team. "It was a pipe dream," he said.

The Musketeers were in the early stages of their rebuilding project. UC had just come off NCAA probation and was in a long down period in its impressive basketball history. That added to the pressure of the Crosstown Shootout because it was the biggest game of the year. Today both teams make regular appearances in the NCAA Tournament.

> **I've always felt the game meant more to Xavier. UC's a big school. Xavier's a small school. We're a private school. We've got a chip on our shoulder.**

"Back then, that was our NCAA," Wolf said.

Wolf never found it uncomfortable playing against the team he rooted for as a kid. He was so into the rivalry when he was growing up that he still has T-shirts that were printed up for the two programs-Badger Brigade shirts for UC fans, Staak Attack shirts for XU fans.

"UC wasn't the program at that point in time that I loved," Wolf said. "There weren't any Robert Millers or Pat Cummings where I looked at them as always being a Top 20 team. So if we won, it wasn't a national thing, it was totally a local thing. I go back to when Xavier beat UC when they were No. 1 in the country (in 1996-'97). I was like, man, this is a double dip. That was a big thing for us. For somebody who was there from the beginning that was a big deal when Lenny Brown hit that jumper. And then when Kevin Frey did it again (in 1999-'00), to think that we had come that far."

In 2015-'16, Xavier fielded one of the top teams in the country, a team so talented that it knocked off eventual national champion Villanova, 90-83, at Cintas Center when the Musketeers were ranked fifth nationally. But Wolf still believes

UC will always be a measuring stick for the Musketeers, who beat the Bearcats the same year, 65-55.

"If you want to see how good your offense is, play against UC," Wolf said. "That's my feeling. I think UC has always got one of the best defenses in the country."

Wolf remains a UC fan and roots for the Bearcats when they're not playing Xavier.

"I've always felt the game meant more to Xavier," Wolf said. "UC's a big school. Xavier's a small school. We're a private school. We've got a chip on our shoulder. That's just the way it always was. When you've got a chip on your shoulder, you play a lot better. Right now Xavier should win. Now the tables have turned.

"It makes no sense to me for anybody from Xavier or UC to say they don't root for Xavier or UC when they're not playing each other. If Xavier beats UC and they lose all their games, that doesn't help us at all. It never made sense to me because they're the ones with the city written on their chest. If you're a UC fan and you look at Xavier now, I think it's all the things that I wanted back in the day – respect."

No matter how successful Xavier becomes, Wolf said, the Crosstown Shootout will always be important to him. He pointed to his heart as he tried to explain it.

"You don't forget," he said. "It's implanted here."

Byron Larkin, the leading scorer in Xavier history
with 2,696 points, won three of his four games against UC.

BYRON LARKIN

1984-'88

"Fighting against the evil empire."

*B*yron Larkin thrived on pressure during his basketball career at Xavier. He wanted the ball in his hands when the game was on the line. He was a capable outside shooter, but his strength was slashing to the basket, getting fouled, and making the defense pay at the free throw line.

During his four years at Xavier, the graduate of Cincinnati's Moeller High School scored 2,696 points, which made him the leading scorer in school history, a distinction he still holds. He was at his best in the Crosstown Shootout, where he averaged 21.5 points in four games against UC. The Musketeers won three of those games.

"My team needed me to play a role and that was to score points and I said, 'Okay, I can do that.' I don't know how, I just did it," Larkin said. "I didn't want the moment to be too big for me. Sometimes it's late in the shot clock or a situation where guys back away, you know, they don't come to the ball or necessarily want the ball in those situations. I always wanted to be that guy that my team relied on.

"(UC) had tough players. I was fighting for our program against the evil empire. That's how I felt. It was definitely more fun playing on their court just because of all the hatred that you would feel and the venom (coming) out of their mouths. It started when you walked out to shoot. The fans would get there early and I'd hear them yelling my name, 'By-ron,' 'By-ron,' trying to intimidate me. I just wanted to shut them up with my play. It energized me to play even harder."

Larkin, the younger brother of former Cincinnati Reds Hall of Fame shortstop Barry Larkin, has done color commentary on XU radio broadcasts for the past 17 years, which means he has either played in or broadcast 21 of the 36 shootouts since the Musketeers' breakthrough in 1980.

But before he arrived at Xavier, he hadn't paid much attention to the rivalry, even though he grew up around it.

"I was too much into my games," Larkin said. "I never even watched it on TV. I was usually out playing in the back yard. I had never gone to one before I played in it. After I signed at Xavier, I noticed that a lot of people were talking about the game way before it even started, so I was like, maybe this is kind of important. But as soon as I got to Xavier, they were like, 'Hey, we want to go to the NCAA and beat UC.' That's how they determined the success of the season.

"UC recruited me a little. I was kind of on their radar. But they didn't come after me full bore. They had Roger McClendon. They had their scoring guard. I think I played against him every year. They made a big deal out of both of us because we were both the leading scorers on our team and we played the same position. They built that up around the game."

The only game that Xavier lost to UC while Larkin played for the Musketeers occurred during Larkin's junior year in 1987 when UC's Joe Stiffend made a game-winning 17-foot jump shot for the Bearcats. Larkin scored 24 points in that game, McClendon 29.

"I recall trying to guard McClendon down at the Coliseum," Larkin said. "Man, he was rockin' and rollin'. He was really hard to stop. He was like spidery, with long legs, and he could really shoot and elevate and had quickness. He was a tough matchup.

"That was the only jump shot that Joe Stiffend ever hit in his entire career. He was 6-2 (actually 6-3) and had a 40-inch vertical. He was a linebacker, man. He was really strong and he did all his damage inside. He hit that jump shot running away from the basket. That one stung."

The Shootout wasn't a game between strangers, especially during Larkin's era.

"We knew all those guys because every weekend we'd be on their campus for parties," Larkin said. "UC had all the girls, so every weekend all the guys would pile in the car and we'd go over to UC's (Tangeman Center). In the summertime, we would play with those guys. They would come to our gym at Schmidt (Fieldhouse) and we would play pickup and we would go to (UC's) Armory Fieldhouse.

"We had a pretty good relationship with them and honest respect. When we would see those guys at a party, you'd look at 'em and pull your head back, like, yeah, we got ya all. It was unspoken. When we would be in the huddle before the game we would say, 'Hey, man, we're gonna beat their team and take their women.' That's what we would say in the group right before we took the court."

Larkin remembers how important the rivalry was to Bob Staak.

"He was really into it," Larkin said. "He really wanted it bad. My freshman year we played down at the Coliseum. We got on the bus and he had the radio on and they were talking about the game. Whoever was on the radio said, 'Yeah, it's clear that Xavier is the better team.' He turned down the radio, turned around and looked at us and said, 'Did you hear that?' He was really, really into it.

"We prepared for UC just like any other game but the difference was that everybody else around talked about it, all the students, all the professors, all of our friends. That's when you know there's got to be something to this. You'd run into 20 people in the daytime and 19 asked about the game. You never had that with any other game on the schedule.

"You could tell when you walked into the arena two hours before tip-off and there was an intensity in the air that just wasn't there for any other game – an anticipation. It would just build to the tip-off and started when you walked in. Then you go in and change and get taped up and come out to shoot. The fans were there then. And then that's when you feel it. You could feel it in the air.

"When the game started, all that hype and stuff goes out the door and you just concentrate on playing basketball. The opponent is irrelevant. You just play basketball, but with the intensity of that game, you fight for every square inch on the floor the entire time. It's a special level of competition that is just very rare. It's like an NCAA (tournament) game. NCAA games are that intense because of what's at stake. You either win or you go home. That makes for a very intense situation, but that's what the Crosstown Shootout was like. I think (the Shootout) was a little more intense. Both teams are trying so hard because you want to beat your neighbor worse than anybody because you're gonna see 'em a lot. When you play a team in the NCAA Tournament from the other side of the country, you're not gonna see those guys. You're not familiar with them. You don't see them on TV or see them at the movies walking around.

> " **When the game started, all that hype and stuff goes out the door and you just concentrate on playing basketball. The opponent is irrelevant.** "

"During that time, my perspective was that UC was the big university and Xavier was fighting for their space in the city. That was the general perception, not to us in the program, but that's how I felt the general public looked at the two programs and it gave us a little chip on our shoulder. These guys are at a bigger school than we are but they're no better than we are. That was kind of our edge that we played with."

In Larkin's senior year, the Musketeers beat UC, 98-80, at Cincinnati Gardens, going on a 16-2 run after UC's Keith Starks took a swing at XU's Dexter Campbell with 3:56 to play. Both players were slapped with a technical foul. Another technical was assessed against UC because the players on the UC bench went onto the floor. That led to Larkin's favorite Crosstown moment.

With Xavier leading, 79-74, Larkin was awarded four free throws; McClendon was awarded two. McClendon missed both of his free throws. Larkin made three of four.

"The other players were off the lane," said Larkin, who scored 26 points. "It was almost like a contest. You bring your best and we're gonna bring our best."

Larkin's memory is a little bit off. He remembers making all four of his foul shots. But he clearly recalls the emotion he felt after he made his first one.

"I just looked at those guys, like, 'Yeah, this is our house,'" he said.

Larkin was behind the microphone at Cintas Center on Dec. 10, 2011 when the fight erupted.

"We were always told even back when I was playing that you don't want to give any bulletin board material to the other team," Larkin said. "I never did against UC or anybody. You've got to act like you've been there. Now you've got Twitter, social media, it's just magnified tenfold. That led to the fight with Yancy and Kenny Frease. That was all pre-game hype. That was fueled 100 percent by that. It's just a lesson learned. You better believe that will never happen again. Both programs were kind of embarrassed by what happened. It's a learning lesson, just like raising kids, man. Some of the best lessons I learned were when I screwed up the worst. It was like, I'll never do that again. It was a teaching moment for the Xavier program that this is what this can lead to.

"We've always had something go on every year. Before the Gates and Kenny Frease deal, (UC's) Myron Hughes punched Eddie Johnson in the face. They called a technical and we just went on about our business. Had that happened today, it would be all over. It would be national news. It was just different. It was more about basketball as opposed to the hype. It's all about hype now. The downside of all this is how quickly information is disseminated now. The other side is you get a lot of popularity. People know about what you're doing. Unfortunately, they know about the bad stuff too."

Larkin didn't like it when, as a result of the fight in 2011, the Crosstown Shootout became the Crosstown Classic for two years and was moved from alternating campus sites to a neutral site downtown at U.S. Bank Arena.

"I thought it was terrible (playing downtown), Larkin said. "I thought it punished the fans and the fans didn't have anything to do with the reason why they changed it. There weren't fights in the stands. There was none of that. It was on the court. But now when you get it off campus, it lost the energy. The one thing about college basketball is that it's a great college experience. That's one reason why you go to college, to be with your buddies, guys drinking in the stands, acting crazy, they can scream as loud as they want. You do it on campus. That's part of campus life, you know? Taking it away, taking it off campus, just hurt the Xavier fans and the UC fans.

"I just thought it was an overreaction. The powers that be decided we've got to do something but maybe in retrospect it gave everybody a minute to breathe and kind of soak in what happened and kind of focus on the mistakes that were made and what led up to it to make sure nothing like that ever happened again."

Both programs have experienced success in recent years. Xavier has advanced to the Sweet 16 in five of the last nine years and in 2015-'16 was ranked in the Associated Press Top 10 for most of the season. UC suffered a down period in the aftermath of Huggins' departure in 2005, but played in six straight NCAA Tournaments from 2010 through 2016, with one Sweet 16 appearance.

"I think the game doesn't mean as much to either team as it did before," Larkin said. "When I was playing and Xavier was in the (Midwestern Collegiate Conference) UC was a huge game for us. But now Xavier's in the Big East and UC, they play such a great schedule. The schedule is so much better from Xavier's standpoint, non-conference and conference. Xavier's just had their number. I can't explain why. I'm just really happy that they have."

Michael Davenport admits that when he deflected the ball while guarding UC's Lou Banks, the ball went out of bounds without touching Banks, but the official ruled otherwise, setting up the game-winning shot for the Musketeers in 1990.

MICHAEL DAVENPORT

1987-'91

"I knocked that thing out."

In Bob Huggins' first Crosstown Shootout in 1990, UC led by four points with 24 seconds left in overtime, when UC's Lou Banks was called for traveling. Xavier's Michael Davenport then made his second 3-pointer in less than a minute to cut the UC lead to one with 20 seconds left.

That's when Huggins learned that in this rivalry it's always dangerous to assume anything.

The Bearcats' seven-point lead in overtime had nearly disappeared, but UC still had the ball and a scant lead. After Steve Sanders passed inbounds to Banks, Davenport slapped the ball away and it went out of bounds. Official Ken Falkner ruled that it hit off Banks before going out and awarded possession to Xavier with 17 seconds to play. Davenport knew better, but who was he to argue?

Xavier set up a shot for Derek Strong, who missed it with 10 seconds left. After a struggle for the rebound, the ball went out of bounds off a UC player and again was awarded to Xavier. Jamie Gladden accepted the inbounds pass from Jamal Walker, who then slipped back onto the court uncovered. Gladden passed back to him and Walker released a 3-point shot that dropped through the net to give the Musketeers a 90-88 lead.

There were still seven seconds to play, enough for UC's Levertis Robinson to get off a 35-foot shot, but he was unable to connect and the Musketeers celebrated a win at Cincinnati Gardens.

Whenever he's asked about the call that awarded the ball to Xavier, Davenport, who scored 16 points in that game, is quick to point out that the call was made by an official from UC's Metro Conference. Twenty-six years later, he refers to it as "that bad call."

"I knocked that thing out," Davenport admitted. "Banks looked at me, like, 'You've got to be kidding.' We were down seven points (with a minute and a half to go in overtime). I remember seeing people start to leave. Jamal hit a three to put us up two and if you go back and watch the film, Levertis Robinson gets the ball. There's probably about seven or eight seconds left. We're up two now. He dribbles down the court. In-between half-court and the 3-point line, he shoots the ball. It hits the back of the backboard and it does everything but go through the net. It kind of rimmed in and rimmed out."

> **The city was electric and I just remember the week of the buildup to it. It was a great environment.**

Bob Huggins was so upset by the out-of-bounds call and the outcome that after he talked briefly with his players in the locker room, he stormed out and walked across the court, his suit jacket slung over his shoulder. He stood for a few seconds at the rail looking up at the emptying seats muttering angrily before heading back to the locker room.

When reporters asked Davenport after the game about the call that went against Banks and UC, he was coy.

"I'm sure I said it was a good call," he said. "It's only speeding if you get caught. Most of the refs don't miss much. It think it was just kind of a bad angle. I tried to clap and just walk out of bounds just to maybe encourage him a little bit. Some of those games were just great games. You play a lot of games over the years, there's a few that stick out. For me, that game against UC my junior year when we came back in overtime and then won, that was fun. It's a very memorable game."

Playing against UC, Davenport said, was a treat. He went 2-2 against the Bearcats.

"The cool thing about that is that it was just right here," said Davenport, who ranks 30th on Xavier's career scoring list with 1,172 points. "It was in-town. The city was electric and I just remember the week of the buildup to it. It was a great environment...I really liked them and rooted for them to win all their games except one. It's kind of like a family relative. You want to do better than them. You want them to have success, but you still want to do better."

After he graduated from Xavier, Davenport, from Grand Rapids, Mich., enrolled at UC's law school, earned his law degree and became an attorney. He said going to

UC after having competed against the Bearcats for four years in the Shootout wasn't as awkward as one might think.

"Once you finish undergrad, nobody cares about the fact that you played college basketball," Davenport said. "For me, it was nothing. I would visit the (UC) basketball offices and see coach (Larry) Harrison and Huggins. Huggins was as nice to guys like us as anybody. Just the fact that you were playing college basketball, he was in your corner. You'd see him out and about. A lot of people think things about Bob Huggins, but to me he is a great coach, obviously, and he was great for UC at that time."

*Jamal Walker's 3-point shot with seconds remaining
gave Xavier a 90-88 win over UC in 1990.*

JAMAL WALKER
1987-'91

"I knew automatically it was going in."

*J*amal Walker had played so much basketball on the playgrounds of New York City that he knew exactly what to do after he passed the ball inbounds to Jamie Gladden.

"I ran to the corner and I was wide open," Walker said. "The instinct of a basketball player is always to go where the ball's at, so once I threw the ball to Jamie everybody ran to him. What I always explained was regardless of the controversial play, you still have to make the shot."

That was no problem for Walker.

"I knew automatically it was going in," Walker said. "I've been in that situation plenty of times in my career. It felt real good. Honestly for me, it was more that we won the game and then for the fans. It was really good because of the rivalry situation and the history of the rivalry. It became as big as day. You would think I was Steph Curry."

Curry, the NBA's current long-range shooting sensation, wasn't even born yet when Walker made his famous shot, but don't blame Walker for making the flattering comparison, especially since he was not considered a great perimeter shooter. As the Musketeers' point guard, it was his job to penetrate defenses and set up shots for his teammates.

"My game was to pass first and make the team better," Walker said.

But he found ways to score, too, and ranks 22nd on the Musketeers' career scoring list with 1,333 points.

Xavier went 2-2 against UC during Walker's four years with the Musketeers.

He was a flamboyant, entertaining player who was nicknamed "Jumpin' Jamal" by Xavier play-by-play voice Andy MacWilliams. "Jumpin" Jamal, give me the ball!" MacWilliams would say when Walker scored.

Walker's game-winning 3-point shot remains one of the most memorable in XU history, but he doesn't rank it as the biggest shot he's ever made.

"I've been playing basketball since I was five or six years old," Walker said. "I've hit plenty of shots in bigger games. I'm from New York where games in the streets were big. That's just how it was for me. We had to make plenty of shots to stay on the court."

Nonetheless Walker, who scored 21 points in the 1990 Shootout with five rebounds and eight assists, savored the moment. He had fun doing all the post-game interviews, a skill he had gradually acquired at Xavier.

When the interviews were finished, he knew better than to dwell too long on his heroic moment. There were a lot more games to be played and a lot more at stake for the Musketeers, who were ranked 23rd nationally. The win over UC was the fourth in what became a 12-game winning streak. Xavier went on to finish 28-5, winning the Midwestern Collegiate Conference regular-season championship and advancing to the NCAA Tournament's Sweet 16 for the first time in school history.

"You have to humble yourself real quick," Walker said, "because you have to get ready for your next game. We were ranked at that time so you didn't want to have a letdown in that situation. I was very focused. I didn't party too much. I didn't do too much hanging out. I don't know if I went out (after the game) but I do remember I got interviewed and it was very exciting and people talked about it. But the next day I was back at practice.

"It's more for history," he said. "It's more for the alumni from both schools to discuss. I'm just happy I was part of the whole history of playing in that game and I'm humbled about it. To this day, my boy Andre Tate (UC's point guard) says he was the MVP of the game and I say, 'Well, you can't be the MVP if you take an 'L.' The media thought UC had won the game so they named him MVP and then they had to give it to me."

Playing in the Shootout, Walker said, is "exciting and overbearing and all those adjectives that you talk about as far as being a basketball player. You want to do well. Sometimes you're going too fast, sometimes you're going too slow. Sometimes you miss little layups and sometimes you miss shots that you usually make. It just comes to the point at the end of the day, like an All-Star game, where you play the first three quarters and when that fourth quarter comes it's time to get ready and get busy and pull your jock strap up and tighten it up. Now you realize you're in a gang fight."

Walker, now the basketball coach at Cincinnati's Princeton High School, said he doesn't talk much about his game-winning shot unless his players bring it up.

But he does plenty of talking with the former UC players.

"Me and Andre Tate have been playing one-on-one since that day," Walker said. "We ain't never been on the court but we talk it. We've been playing with our mouths. During the last UC-Xavier game (which was won by Xavier), I hung out with him and Corie Blount and Terry Nelson. It was at some UCATS function that Terry Nelson put together. He invited me over. I thought we were just going to BW3's and I ended up going to a UCATS function with a whole bunch of Xavier stuff on, so that was good. I didn't have to talk. We were winning. When you're winning, you don't have to say anything."

Brian Grant, who played 12 years in the NBA, felt slighted during a recruiting visit to UC and signed with Xavier.

BRIAN GRANT

1990-'94

"I wanted to prove them wrong."

*I*f Brian Grant's recruiting visit to UC had gone a little differently, he could have spent his college career playing against the Xavier Musketeers instead of for them.

Okay, Grant's visit would have had to go totally differently because it didn't go well at all. In fact, it was so bad that it left Grant angry and insulted.

"I wouldn't necessarily say that UC recruited me," Grant said. "I went there for a visit and when I got there for the visit I was asked to go with the assistant coach and the other recruit was asked to go with Bob Huggins. When I went there, they basically made me feel like they didn't want me and later I heard from them that they didn't think I was going to make the grades. I was like, really? You think that I wasn't going to make the grades at UC? And then when we were in the locker room they put me and my coach in the back of the locker room and they put the other kid on the bench with the starters. After that, my coach said, 'We're not staying.'"

Grant, a 6-foot-9, 254-pound power forward, is from Brown County, Ohio, about 40 miles southeast of Cincinnati. He played at Georgetown High School and was not considered an elite recruit. So when Gillen offered him a scholarship he quickly accepted it.

"At the end of my senior year, Pete Gillen came out and told me there was one scholarship left," Grant said. "It was between me and a kid from somewhere in Cincinnati and I could get it right there. When I went down there as a freshman, I wasn't supposed to be playing until my junior year. I wasn't an All-American or anything. I was just happy that I was going to college."

Gillen's decision to offer Grant his last scholarship turned out to be one of the best moves he ever made at Xavier. Grant far exceeded expectations. He finished his college career with 1,719 points, which ranks 10th on the Musketeers' career scoring list. He was a ferocious rebounder with a soft shooting touch whose 59.4 percent career field goal accuracy is a school record. He was a two-time Midwestern Collegiate Conference Player of the Year, an Associated Press Honorable Mention All-American in 1994, and in 2011 became the fourth player in Xavier history to have his jersey (33) retired.

Grant was an NBA lottery pick, drafted by the Sacramento Kings with the eighth selection overall in 1994, and played 12 years in the league for five different teams, making the NBA all-rookie team in 1994-'95.

When he arrived at Xavier, he knew very little about the Crosstown Shootout. Even though he grew up in what is considered part of Greater Cincinnati, he considered himself a country boy.

"I knew about it but it wasn't that big to me because I lived in Brown County," Grant said. "We were close to the city but it was almost like we were a million miles away too. The week of the Crosstown Shootout was always on TV but it wasn't that big living out in the country."

Getting a chance to play against UC, the school that he believed had snubbed him, was not on Grant's mind when he reported for duty at Xavier.

"When I got there and met the other guys, I didn't know if I could make it as an athlete," Grant said, "and I definitely didn't think I could make it as a student because I got into college with a C-minus in pre-algebra and that was the last year you could do that before they raised the curriculum. I wasn't thinking about UC. I was just trying to figure out how I was going to stay eligible."

In that sense, then, UC's concerns about his grades seem reasonable.

Grant's first experience in the Shootout was on Jan. 30, 1991, at Shoemaker Center against a UC team that featured Lou Banks, Levertis Robinson and Keith Starks. It was the first Shootout played in The Shoe, which had opened the season before. UC won, 69-56.

"They had a decent team," Grant said. "We were just a young team. We should have and could have beat them but they had the new arena at the time and we played over there. It was a good game but we lost. The second year is when Nick (Van Exel) and all those boys came in."

That was the year UC's Terry Nelson predicted the Bearcats would blow out the Musketeers.

"I don't think they blew us out, though, did they?" Grant asked.

In fact, they did, with a 93-75 victory at Cincinnati Gardens. Grant doesn't remember the blowout but he does remember Nelson's prediction

"I was upset," Grant said. "I wanted to prove them wrong. Terry Nelson, that whole group of dudes that came in, they were different than the guys who were there the previous year. It seemed like they came in with some swagger and some mouth but they backed it up. We would never say anything like that in the media and if we did we'd be in trouble. Pete didn't teach us that. He taught us to be humble and say the right things."

Grant didn't dislike the Bearcats, though.

"People thought that we all fought," he said, "like when we would see each other during the summer there was a big brawl between the players. But it wasn't like that at all. We'd hang out. We'd see each other out and give each other props. They beat us so they had bragging rights. As far as hating one another, we didn't hate each other at all unless we had a personal issue outside of basketball."

It was Grant's misfortune to have to play against the Bearcats when they had some of their best teams. In 1993, the Musketeers lost to fourth-ranked UC again, 78-67, leaving Grant winless in his first three games against the Bearcats, who went to the Final Four the year of Nelson's prediction and to the Elite Eight the following year.

"For us, by the second and third year, (beating UC) became something that we wanted and had to do because we weren't doing as well as they were doing during the regular season," Grant said. "They were tough. They had a whole lot of fire. The only way we could try to get back at them was to beat them in the Crosstown Shootout. My freshman year didn't mean that much to me but that second and third year, because of Terry Nelson's prediction, they were just so verbal, but they could back it up. It was irritating but it wasn't like that was the end of my world."

The breakthrough for Grant and the Musketeers came on Jan. 19, 1994 when they beat the Bearcats, 82-76, in overtime in what became known as the Handshake Game after Huggins refused to shake Gillen's hand.

"It wasn't like we blew them out," Grant said. "They had some young guys. It was a whole new batch of guys that came in. We ended up taking it into overtime and winning finally. That meant a lot. If I had went the whole four years without winning the Crosstown Shootout that would have been crazy."

As for Huggins' refusal to shake Gillen's hand, Grant chalked it up to Huggins being Huggins.

"He got mad," he said. "That was Huggins, though. He said a couple of words and Pete said a couple words back. I didn't expect that to happen at that moment because Huggins was kicking our butts for the three previous years and then all of a sudden he's upset because of taking the 'L?' It was kind of like, whatever. I don't know what he was upset about."

When he was told that Huggins claimed both Gillen and assistant coach Bobby Gonzalez were shouting things at him during the game, Grant was dismissive.

"If he was upset about that, you're going to do what you're going to do and I guess I wouldn't expect him to do anything other than that," he said.

During his NBA playing days, Grant established the Brian Grant Foundation to assist seriously ill children and underprivileged youth. He retired from the NBA in 2006 and was diagnosed with Parkinson's Disease in 2008. After his diagnosis, he re-created his foundation, which is based in Portland, to raise money for research and to promote awareness of Parkinson's.

Despite winning only one of four games against UC, he remembers the rivalry fondly.

"I think it's one of the best rivalries in college basketball," he said. "I know there are some other schools that have big rivalries but for us, and I'm sure the other guys will tell you the same thing, the week of that game, everything else kind of went out the window, whether you were ranked or not ranked or whether you were having a bad year. The hope was that if we beat UC that's okay. Even though we didn't make the (NCAA Tournament) we at least beat UC.

"Unfortunately the first three years that didn't happen. We made it to the NIT my senior year. We didn't make the (NCAA), but because we beat UC it was okay."

Grant takes great pride in Xavier's recent success against UC. The Musketeers have won eight of the last 11 Shootouts.

"UC dominated three years of my college career and I don't think they were feeling too bad for me," Grant said. "The (Xavier) program has come a long way, not just the program but the school. It's a totally different school than it was when I was there. Now you've got Cintas (Center), you have all these new buildings going up. Xavier has bought most of Dana Avenue. It's a real college.

"When kids would come to Cincinnati and they would do two visits, one to Xavier, one to UC, they would have this huge campus and Xavier had this, well, where's the campus? Where's everything at? That was great for me. I was from a small town. I didn't want to come to a big campus anyway. The program has really grown thanks to the success of the coaches there like Chris Mack now. Chris and I played together. He was always injuring his knees so he never really got a chance to play, but he's a hell of a coach. They have something really good there. I hope he stays until we get our first national championship."

STEVE GENTRY

1990-'94

"You can never stop being loyal to a friend."

W hen the Crosstown Shootout rolls around every year, Steve Gentry is faced with mixed emotions. Even though he played for the Musketeers and graduated from Xavier, he has a hard time rooting for his alma mater because he wants his friend, UC coach Mick Cronin, to do well.

"I've been playing against Mick Cronin ever since I was a little kid," Gentry said. "We played community ball against each other. We had to be maybe nine or 10 years old.

"I played against him in high school. They beat us when I was a junior at Withrow and he was a junior at La Salle. And then the following year we beat them in the Martin Luther King Classic down at what was Riverfront Coliseum. It was always competitive. He was one of the top guys in the (Greater Cincinnati League) and I was one of the top guys in (Cincinnati Public Schools) so it was always a battle. It's been a battle since we were 10 years old. Nothing has changed. He was always short but he played hard. I always want UC to do well because of Mick and I want Xavier to do well because that's where I went to school. I try to stay neutral in that game but it's very hard. I always wind up rooting for Xavier, even though Mick and I are good friends."

Getting the chance to play in the rivalry he had followed since he was a kid remains one of the highlights of Gentry's college career.

"Growing up in the city, you're watching those guys go to battle for that one game and you're watching them during the regular season, seeing how this team is playing and how that team is playing," Gentry said. "I had the jitters, man. I was

Steve Gentry, basketball coach at Cincinnati's Deer Park High School, became friends with UC's Mick Cronin when they played against each other in high school. They have maintained that close relationship.

anxious to get on the court. It was a long time coming and being the first person on either side of my family to play Division I basketball, there was a huge amount of stress on my shoulders."

A point guard known for his defense and running the offense, Gentry played in two of the best-known games in the Crosstown Shootout-the 1992 game in which UC blew out Xavier as predicted by UC's Terry Nelson and the Handshake Game.

First the Nelson prediction.

"I was a little feisty and rowdy," Gentry said. "I took it personal. That made me play harder. I'll never forget that. Terry Nelson was on the news and he said, 'You know, they're a good team but we should beat them by at least 20.' And they did it. Back then they had Nick Van Exel and Anthony Buford, Corie Blount, Terry Nelson, Erik Martin, Herb Jones. They had a good team, man.

"I just wish we could have made better adjustments during the game. I was guarding Van Exel. Buford ended the game with like 32 points (actually 29) or something like that. I was telling my coaches at halftime, 'Hey, switch me off on this guy. This guy's killing us. Let me get him. Nick is not doing nothing.' (He scored 15 points). They said, 'No, you stay on Nick.' And Anthony Buford killed us. But they thought if I guarded Buford then Van Exel would start killing us. They call him Nick the Quick, but I was quick, too, back in those days so it really didn't bother me. Defense is my forte so anybody that I guarded it didn't bother me because I knew either I was faster than them or I was stronger than them."

Gentry didn't know about the Huggins-Gillen tiff until he got home and saw it on the TV news.

"I was too busy celebrating," he said.

You can't blame Gentry for missing the biggest story to come out of that game because the biggest story to him was that he had finally beaten UC for the first time in his fourth and final try. To make it even sweeter, he made a 3-point shot in overtime, prompting Huggins to single him out in his post-game remarks.

"I remember Bob Huggins coming on the news and saying, 'Man, you've got Steve Gentry shooting the three. Who would have thought that he would have knocked a jump shot down?'" Gentry said. "That's my fondest memory of the Crosstown Shootout. They just left me. I wasn't known for a guy who was going to shoot a lot of threes, even though I could do it. I was the point guard. I was the setup man. I would drive to the basket and drop it off. I led the team in assists and I led them in defense. I guess he was surprised that I even took the shot."

Gentry made two 3-pointers in that game, with six assists and no turnovers in 32 minutes.

After he finished his playing career, Gentry, like Cronin, got into coaching. He started as an assistant coach at his alma mater at Withrow under George Jackson, who years later became an assistant coach at UC under Cronin. His first coaching job, he said, was mostly done as a favor to Jackson.

"It kind of fell in my lap after I got done playing," Gentry said. "One year turned into seven years of helping out. When he retired, I said I was done, but he was like, you can't be done. I left this for you. You're the next man up, so you've got to take this job. He made me take the job, so I did what I was told. I always talk to him and tell him I don't know how you did that all those years coaching basketball, especially in CPS. Now I'm on my 15th or 16th year. I'm doing the same thing he did."

As Gentry moved from Withrow to Aiken High School to Shroder, he watched with pride as his friend, Cronin, climbed through the college coaching ranks to become the head coach at UC.

"I thought it was amazing to see him go from a JV coach in high school to video coordinator at a college to assistant coach to associate head coach to head coach to the man at the University of Cincinnati," Gentry said, "and he's from Cincinnati. I always tell everybody that Mick and (Xavier coach) Chris (Mack) are good friends of mine. We all grew up together."

That's how it was when Gentry played at Xavier, too. The XU players and the UC players played together and hung out during the summer, even going out to eat together after playing in the Deveroes Summer League. So it was painful for Gentry to see the fight that occurred at the end of the 2011 game, with Withrow graduate Yancy Gates in the center of it for UC.

"That was super tough to watch," Gentry said. "That was distasteful for a lot of reasons. One, it was Xavier and UC. Two, it was Yancy Gates, and where did Yancy Gates come from? Withrow High School, my high school. That brawl would have never happened back when we played. We might go hard at you, we might hit you with an elbow, but I don't think it would have come to a fist fight because we were good friends. We respected them and they respected us. It was just that game where all deals are broke. We're going at each other for 40 minutes. That's just the way it was."

Gentry's friendship with Cronin still means a lot to him, but so does Xavier.

"He would come and pick me up and we'd hang out together in high school and college," Gentry said. "You see a lot of UC people that don't have a relationship with Xavier people. And a lot of Xavier people don't have a relationship with UC people. It just happens that I've got a good relationship with a UC guy and he just happens to be the head coach. You can never stop being loyal to a friend."

GARY LUMPKIN
1995-'99

"We never took into account what the odds were."

Gary Lumpkin is not the type to shoot off his mouth after games, probably because the one time he did he heard about it from the Xavier coaching staff.

It happened during his first Crosstown Shootout on Jan. 17, 1996. The Musketeers lost to No. 3 UC, 99-90, at Cintas Center when UC's Danny Fortson scored 40 points and pulled down 17 rebounds, dropping Xavier's record to 6-7.

"We were within two baskets toward the end of the game and were keeping it close," Lumpkin said. "That was the one time in my career that I actually got chewed out by my coaches because in the press conference after the game I made one of the stupidest comments ever in my life. I made the comment that I felt like if UC was ranked No. 3 in the country, then we should be in the Top 10 and we weren't ranked anywhere near that at the time.

"We were so young and our record was so bad, but we were losing some pretty competitive games. We weren't getting blown out. We knew that in years to come we would be reckoned with. We just didn't have the experience to really get over the hump during that year. Danny was a man among boys. Coming in as a freshman, I remember that was the year that Huggins had his weightlifting team out there. They were muscle-bound from top to bottom. Quite honestly, that was a measuring stick for us, but Danny was on another level. The weight room was a big, big emphasis for us going into the next year."

Ten months later, Xavier upset then-No. 1 UC, 71-69, at Shoemaker Center on a last-second basket by Lenny Brown.

"Our team had a conversation about (the next UC game) not long after (my freshman year) was over," Lumpkin said. "We had discussed our goals and everything and it was a big emphasis so that Coach (Skip) Prosser wouldn't have to prepare us for that game to motivate us. X's and O's yes, but motivation to go play and be competitive, he wouldn't have to do that.

"We never took into account what the odds were. That year might have been the most confident team we had at Xavier during my years there. There was nothing we felt like we couldn't conquer. Going in there, our big thing was that we were going to shock the world. Even getting down a few times, even going back to the huddles, they were always positive. They were always, 'Hey, just keep playing, we're gonna pull it out. Just keep playing. We're gonna get a chance at the end.'

"We had a great offseason that year. We trained really hard. We became closer as a unit. I remember playing a lot more open gym together and pushing each other. Individual workouts were a lot better. We were more focused on improving on what we did that prior year."

The Crosstown Shootout seemed to bring out the best in Lumpkin. He can't explain why, but the guard from New Castle, Del., played some of the best games of his career against the Bearcats. He scored in double figures in all four games, averaging 18.7 points, and the Musketeers won two of four games against the Bearcats during his time at Xavier.

"The UC game was the one game I knew I was going to play well in every year," Lumpkin said. "I think I had 23 in junior year and senior year I had 25. It was just a matter, I guess, of your competitive nature kicking in playing against your crosstown rivals. I had never been involved in a game of that magnitude before. It kind of had me shaking a little bit at first. But once the jump ball went up I remember being okay and confident."

Brown's game-winning shot against UC is one of the most famous in Xavier history, but if the play had been executed the way it was drawn up it would have been Lumpkin who had the chance to play the hero instead of Brown.

"People don't know this but I was supposed to get that shot," Lumpkin said. "If you look at the play, I was doing a flare screen to the wing for a jump shot, but Lenny didn't remember what to do, so they said, 'Get the ball to Lenny and get out of the way,' and I was okay with that.

I could have been (the hero). But I don't think I would have made that shot. I think it was meant for Lenny to make that shot.

"Lenny might be the most misunderstood guy I've ever known. What people saw and who he really was weren't the same person. If you got to know Lenny, Lenny had a huge heart. Lenny was a great, great guy. I think sometimes the way he came off may have been cold or kind of distant, but that wasn't Lenny. He had his

*Gary Lumpkin, who had some of the best games of his career against
UC, scored 25 points against the Bearcats in his senior year.*

moments as would anybody, but at that time, to come from a school in Delaware and hit a major shot on a national stage and the fact of what he went through to get that – his mother passing away at a young age and him having to step into adult shoes – I was so, so proud of him. Coach Prosser put it best: He had the courage of a cat burglar. There is no situation that he's not confident in."

Playing for Prosser was one of the joys of Lumpkin's career, if not his life.

"He was the best, the best, the most amazing coach I ever played for in my life," Lumpkin said. "Skip was the kind of coach that once he believed in you there was nothing anybody could do or say to make him think otherwise. I remember I had a horrible senior year and I thought I was going to get benched. We played Purdue. I had 11 turnovers and five assists and was sure I would get benched and he brought me in and said, 'Listen, I'm riding with you. I trust you, I believe in you. I need you to have confidence in yourself because I have confidence in you.' And that did a lot for me. He was definitely a loyal guy. I don't think I would have gotten that anywhere else.

> **That year might have been the most confident team we had at Xavier during my years there. There was nothing we felt like we couldn't conquer.**

"I really don't know who didn't like Skip. A month ago, I talked to a custodian up at Xavier who had been there and he mentioned, did you play for Skip? I said, yeah, and he said, 'Man, you wouldn't know this, but Coach Prosser came and got me one day from the job, took me to the store and bought me a brand new suit and a brand new trench coat.' Skip told him, 'Hey, this is from me to you. I don't want anything in return. I appreciate what you do.'

"He said he even came out on the floor one time, mopping the floor on the basketball court and Skip came to him and said, 'Hey, show me how to do that.' And he said he showed him and Skip said, 'I'll take it from here.' Some of the things I've been hearing since he's been gone, I really believe I played for an angel, I really do believe that in my heart of hearts."

Lumpkin, who lives in Cincinnati, ranks 17th on Xavier's career scoring list with 1,507 points. Since graduating from Xavier, he has earned his master's degree in education with an emphasis on special education, and works with special education children.

Being part of the Shootout, he said, "was definitely an experience like no other. I really loved the competitive nature of it. To this day, I'm good friends with quite a few guys on their team-Mel Levett, Damon Flint-there were good friendships formed from that. For the most part, the only time we didn't like them was when we played them."

Lumpkin enjoyed the Shootout more when the game was played on UC's home court because he believes it defined the character of the Xavier players, but he always appreciated the motivational boost Musketeers fans gave him and his teammates at Cintas Center.

"They were kind of like a lion getting ready to eat meat," Lumpkin said. "They were like, you guys have got to win. Their motivation to push us to be great and beat them definitely rubbed off on us."

Now that Xavier has turned the tables in the series, Lumpkin said, "It's like redemption in a way because UC always had that 'bad boy, we rule the street' kind of mentality. From the time we came in, it seemed like the tide started to turn and even after we graduated, they beat 'em again when they were No. 1. I was really happy that the tide had turned like that and Xavier was finally getting noticed for being a really, good, tough team, that we had toughness on our side too."

Pat Kelsey, who grew up in Cincinnati as the ultimate Xavier fan,
felt a "palpable energy" when he played in his first Crosstown Shootout.

PAT KELSEY
1996-'98
Associate head coach, 2009-'11

"The world stood still for me."

The first time Pat Kelsey checked in at the scorer's table to play in the Crosstown Shootout the feeling was almost overwhelming.

"I remember thinking I'm actually on the freaking floor for this game," Kelsey said. "There was just so much anticipation, knowing I was playing in my first Shootout, such an excitement when your name's called."

Kelsey was the ultimate Xavier fan growing up in the Cincinnati suburb of Finneytown. His dad, Mike, played at Xavier in the late 1960s and early 70s. The family had season tickets and for Pat, the Crosstown Shootout was one of the highlights of every sports year. He listened faithfully to Andy MacWilliams and Joe Sunderman broadcast Xavier games on radio.

"I lived and died with Xavier basketball," Kelsey said. "I was at Bob Staak's last basketball camp at Xavier when I was eight or nine and then I went to Pete Gillen's camp. We had season tickets and watched every single game. I thought Andy Mac was a god and that he and Joe Sunderman were the voices of God like (Reds Hall of Fame play-by-play man) Marty Brennaman.

"I remember begging my teachers at St. Vivian during my sixth, seventh and eighth grade year to allow us to watch the Xavier tournament games during the school day. I talked them into putting TVs out in the hallway. I lived and breathed it. Every Crosstown Shootout was when the world stood still for me."

Kelsey developed into a pretty good player in his own right, first at Cincinnati's Roger Bacon High School and then at Elder High School where he played point guard on the Panthers' 1993 state championship team. He was not recruited by Xavier, though, and chose to play at Wyoming, a Division I school coached by former Miami (Ohio) coach Joby Wright.

Kelsey started 22 games during his freshman year at Wyoming but wasn't happy and decided to transfer to another school after the first semester of his sophomore year. While he was home during Christmas break, his dad, part of the management team at McCluskey Chevrolet, ran into Xavier assistant coach Mark Schmidt at the dealership. He told Schmidt that Kelsey had received his release from Wyoming, was looking to transfer to another school, and asked Schmidt if Xavier would be interested.

"My dad called me and said, 'I think they'd have in interest in you, but I don't know if it would be a scholarship right away,'" Kelsey said. "I was washing cars for my dad at McCluskey and they called my name over the intercom and said I had a phone call. I'm the lot guy. Nobody ever calls my name over the loudspeaker. I walk in, press the button, and I hear, 'Pat this is Skip Prosser.' My heart skipped. I was like, are you kidding me? He just said, 'Why don't you come over to practice on Monday at Schmidt Fieldhouse?'"

When Monday arrived, Kelsey went to the fieldhouse at the appointed time, still not believing that this was happening. He walked in at street level, which is at the top of the seating area. The floor is at the bottom of a long row of steps.

"I don't want to be a disruption or bother anybody," Kelsey said. "I sit way up there in the corner. Practice is going on and it was different from what I knew at Wyoming. There was an energy. Guys were flying around and they're going up and down. It was fast-paced. I was sitting up there going, this is awesome.

"There's a break in practice. They're shooting free throws and Coach looks up and he sends a manager up and he says, 'Coach wants you to come down and sit by the court during practice.' I go down and sit right there on a chair in the middle of the court on the side. Coach came over in the middle of practice with a whistle around his neck. He shook my hand. Practice keeps going on and I'm just so juiced up.

"At the end of practice, every single one of them were drenched with sweat. It was like carnage. Bodies are lying all over the place. They finish stretching and Coach brings them into the middle for the huddle in the jump circle. He goes, 'All right, bring it in.' Everybody puts their hands in and he goes, 'Hold on fellows.' He moves some bodies out of the way and he goes 'Kelse!' I run in there and he goes, 'Put your hand in here.' And he says, 'Fellas, Kelse is on our team now.' From that moment on, I would have run through a hundred walls for that guy."

Playing at Xavier, Kelsey said, "was one of the greatest experiences of my life."

The first day of class in the second semester is when I could start practicing," he said. "I walk in and he's already got my name plate up on the locker and a practice jersey with my name on the back. Wearing that jersey that first day in practice was a moment in time that I will never ever forget."

Under NCAA transfer rules, Kelsey had to sit out the first semester of his first season at Xavier, although he was allowed to practice. He didn't get to play in the Shootout until Jan. 17, 1996 when he played two minutes and did not take a shot. The Musketeers lost that game to third-ranked UC, 99-90, but that didn't detract from the experience.

"There is a palpable energy and feel and it's heavy," Kelsey said. "There's something about the atmosphere of that game that is different almost than any other game, venue, competition that I've ever been a part of."

After the 2000-'01 season, Prosser left Xavier for Wake Forest, where he remained until he died of a heart attack in July 2007. Kelsey worked for Prosser at Wake, first as the director of basketball operations and then as a full-time assistant coach. He stayed at Wake for two more years after Prosser's death working under Dino Gaudio and then became the associate head coach at Xavier under Mack. He's currently the head coach at Winthrop College in Rock Hill, S.C.

"We were really good for those eight years we were at Wake," Kelsey said. "We were No. 1 in the country on several occasions. We had Chris Paul. We played at (Duke's) Cameron Indoor Stadium in big games or at North Carolina where No. 3 was playing No. 4 on national television. So much was on the line. And yes, those games were packed to capacity. Every seat was filled.

"I'm not saying that it trumps it head and shoulders and maybe it's because of my background and how I was raised and how much the Xavier and UC rivalry means to me because I'm a Cincinnati kid, but I always felt like that feel of the Shootout was different. Even if every seat was taken in other games that you played against other people, it felt like there were more. It felt like people were sitting closer together. I don't know how to describe it. You just felt like even though maybe every eye within the I-275 loop was on that game, it felt like the whole world's eyes were on that game.

"During those years, it wasn't nationally televised. It was televised on WXIX, Channel 19. There wasn't regional cable. There wasn't Fox Sports Ohio back then. But it was such a big deal, I always felt like the city was standing still. The world stood still on its axis, at least in my world."

Kelsey loved the way Prosser sold the Shootout to his players.

"Coach Huggins', or UC's thing always was, at least publicly, we're not making more out of this than it is," Kelsey said. "It's just another game. It seems like that was always their message: We play this game, it's on our schedule, we have to, but the more important one is when we're playing a Conference USA foe in a couple of weeks.

"A least with Coach Prosser-and I know Coach (Chris) Mack is this way-we made it a big deal. It goes against Coaching 101. It goes against what most coaches do to circle a game on the schedule and put more emphasis on that game than any other one, but Coach Prosser made us understand that this is the biggest game on our schedule."

The year after UC dominated Xavier in the 1995-'96 game, Prosser made a point of telling his players they needed to be more competitive against the Bearcats.

"He said, 'Fellas, rivalries cease to be rivalries if you don't win a game every once in a while,'" Kelsey said. "He was challenging us a little bit, like, hey, people are going to stop calling this a rivalry if UC is the top dog program in the country and just kicks our butt every year."

That was the year Lenny Brown made a last-second jump shot to upset top-ranked UC.

Kelsey played for three years at Xavier, but played in only two Shootouts. The Musketeers lost the first, but won the second. He was mostly a role player whose job was to distribute the ball to his teammates. He did his job so well that he was named a team co-captain for his senior year in 1997-'98. That was also the year he earned a scholarship after playing for two years as a walk-on who had to pay his own way. He was voted Xavier's Most Inspirational Player in 1996 and 1998.

His second appearance in the Shootout was on Dec. 13, 1997. He played six minutes in that game without scoring. Overall he played a total of eight minutes against UC and cherishes every one, even though he never took a shot.

"I do remember stepping on that floor (against UC) and I'm like, I'm one of the 10 dudes out here in this game," he said. "I'm in here and it matters. The clock's ticking and it's close."

DARNELL WILLIAMS
1995-2000

"It's a little better the second time."

arnell Williams is proud to be the answer to a trivia question.

Williams is the only Xavier player to play in both of the Musketeers' upsets of UC when the Bearcats were ranked No. 1 in the country. The first occurred on Nov. 16, 1996 at Shoemaker Center, the second on Dec. 18, 1999 at the Gardens. The first was played at Shoemaker Center; the second at the Gardens.

In the first upset, Williams, a forward from Brooklyn, N.Y., was a sophomore. He played 24 minutes but scored only four points before fouling out. He was on the bench when Lenny Brown made the game-winning shot as time expired, giving the unranked Musketeers a 71-69 victory.

"We had the confidence," Williams said. "We knew deep down inside from playing pickup (with the UC players) in the summertime that we could play with them. Then as the game started going on and the minutes started ticking we just felt like, we can win this. During the timeout (before Xavier's final possession), when they were drawing up the play, I said, 'Lenny, you just got to get the ball. There's not enough time for a play.' Me and (assistant coach Jeff Battle) were yelling, 'Lenny, go to the ball!'"

When Brown's shot went in, Williams said, "It was just a feeling you can't even really explain. It was a feeling of great joy because you did something that you figured no one ever thought could be done. We just shocked the nation. The whole nation is watching and they see that score come across the board. We just did something that will go down in history."

But once was not enough for Williams. Three years later, the Musketeers did it again. And again they were unranked.

Williams was in his fifth year at Xavier by then. He sat out the season following his junior year after having surgery to repair a torn anterior cruciate ligament. This time he played a much bigger role for the Musketeers, scoring 16 points, all in the first half, to lead Xavier to a 39-31 halftime lead. UC battled back to tie the game with 1:43 left, but Kevin Frey made two free throws with 29 seconds remaining to break a 62-62 tie, then scored on a breakaway layup with 8.9 seconds left to give the Musketeers a 66-62 lead. The final score was 66-64.

Again, Williams experienced the unbridled joy of knocking off the nation's No. 1 team, made even sweeter by the fact that it was the Musketeers' crosstown rival.

"The first time was great," Williams said, "but being a senior, being considered a leader on your team doing that again, and doing it twice, it's a little bit better the second time. We really thought we could win again the second time around."

Williams and Reggie Butler were the only players on the Musketeers' roster who could relate the details of the first big upset to the other players. Butler was on the 1996-'97 team, but was redshirted that year, so he didn't play against the Bearcats.

"Coach Prosser found different quotes from different authors, from history, and just told us to believe," Williams said. "If you believe, anything will be possible. I told (my teammates) about the first one because a lot of them were asking about it. They wanted to know how tough the game would be. I said, 'Well, we have nothing to lose. If this game is close and we keep it where we need it to be, if we make the plays down the stretch, we ain't gonna have no pressure on us. Nobody don't expect us to win.' With all the intensity and energy that we had for that game, we didn't have to play perfect. All the pressure was on them."

Up to that point in the season, Williams was still trying to regain his rhythm after sitting out the previous year.

"It takes a you a while to get the rust off," he said. "You can have all the practice that you want, but the timing is the hardest thing to get back. I was struggling. I was just waiting for a breakout game. I just needed that one and it came at the right time. I had a big four-point play on the first play of the game. I hit a three-point shot and got fouled."

Before Williams' 4-point play, UC had jumped out to a 5-0 lead. Lloyd Price then made a 3-pointer, giving the Musketeers a 7-4 lead. By the end of the game, UC had shot 50.1 percent to 39.1 percent for Xavier, but the Musketeers made 7 of 17 3-pointers to 4 of 11 for UC. And they had a huge advantage at the free throw line, where they made 23 of 30 compared with UC's 10 of 13.

"I broke out in the first half and I was a decoy in the second half," Williams said. "We just had to find a way to win. They started cutting off the lanes for the shooting

Darnell Williams is the only Xavier player to play in both of the Musketeers'
upsets of UC when the Bearcats were ranked No. 1 in the country.

gap and played no help. It didn't matter because by them having to switch out on screens sometimes they would get mixed up and it ended up getting open shots for open people. Sometimes you've got to use yourself as a decoy. Anything to win a big game. I was fine with it because by the end of the game they weren't going to say, Darnell won, they were going to say we won."

It was a stinging loss for UC, which was 8-0 at the time, but not one that did lasting damage to its national championship hopes. Four days later, the Bearcats bounced back with a win at Oklahoma and went on a 16-game winning streak. They reclaimed their No. 1 ranking three weeks after the loss to Xavier.

By the end of the season, their upset loss to the Musketeers wasn't even their worst memory from that season. It was far overshadowed by the injury to Kenyon Martin, the National Player of the Year who broke his leg in UC's first game in the Conference USA tournament. At the time, UC again was ranked No. 1 and was expected to receive the overall No. 1 seed in the NCAA Tournament. Its season ended with a loss to Tulsa in the second round of the tournament.

Williams, who resigned as the head coach at Kentucky State at the end of the 2015-'16 season, still relishes his distinction as the only Xavier player to play in both memorable games, not just as a personal achievement, but because he believes it was another milestone on the Musketeers' road to national recognition.

"It makes you feel good about winning those games," he said. "It helped put Xavier on a national level. We were changing to the Atlantic 10 Conference and people didn't think we could really win in that conference. But when you upset the No. 1 team in the nation twice, that's a quick national spotlight for any school. The school was just going up.

"I tell Reggie Butler all the time that I'm the only one that got two wins against the number one team," Williams said. "It's a big thing. My career record against teams that are ranked No. 1 is 2-1. When UMass was No. 1 (in 1996), we lost to them in overtime."

Williams, who ranks 15th on Xavier's career scoring list with 1,572 points, agrees there was a time when the Shootout meant more to Xavier than it did to UC, but he says that's not the case anymore.

"Cincinnati had more of a national spotlight with Coach (Bob) Huggins, going to the Final Four, always being ranked in the Top 5," he said. "I think back then it meant more because we wanted the national attention. But now I think it's reversed. Cincinnati is still having success but not the national attention that Xavier has been getting. UC has to get tired of it, especially if you look back and remember that you used to win it all the time and now the roles are reversed."

LIONEL CHALMERS

2000-'04

"We knew each other's every move."

*A*s the ball fell through the net with 27 seconds remaining, time slowed down for Xavier point guard Lionel Chalmers. That basket would give the Musketeers a 71-69 upset over 10th-ranked UC at Cintas Cinter on Feb. 3, 2004 in a game that practically no one gave them a chance to win.

"It was like a movie," Chalmers said. "It was really an unbelievable atmosphere at that time, with all of the stakes on the line, being at home, beating UC in the midst of creating our identity as a team, just so much happened from that situation. That's how big it was. It was bigger than just making a shot to win the game."

Chalmers, who ranks 16th on Xavier's career scoring list with 1,556 points, wasn't supposed to take the shot-UC led by one at the time-but he relished the opportunity when it arose.

"I just like to win," said Chalmers, who scored 20 points in that game. "I love to put the weight on my shoulders and take that shot. We ran a play and there were a couple of options. It kind of broke down and I ended up with a big (man) on me, so I just went to one of my moves to create space and got the shot up and knocked it down.

"I was about two steps inside the 3-point line, about 17 or 18 feet. I think it was (Eric) Hicks who was guarding me. There was a breakdown in the defense. We were running a play and they ended up switching and I just took advantage of the switch and I had a nice step-back option and I knocked it down."

UC called timeout with 18.5 seconds left and tried to get the ball inside to Jason Maxiell, but when the Musketeers had Maxiell covered, UC guard Nick Williams tried to pass to Armein Kirkland only to throw the ball over his head and out of bounds. A free throw by Romain Sato with 2.2 seconds left accounted for the final score.

It was the year after David West had been named National Player of the Year and the Musketeers were struggling. They were 10-9 and had lost three in a row, five of their previous six. They were such overwhelming underdogs that even Xavier coach Thad Matta said he was expecting the worst.

"We felt like every game we played we could win but when you looked at the previous games that we played up until that point we were struggling to find our identity," Chalmers said. "Our consistency level wasn't there, so for you to think that we wouldn't win that game, it's what most people probably thought."

But as is often the case, when the Crosstown Shootout rolled around, the Musketeers hit their stride. UC overcame an 8-point deficit to take a 66-61 lead with 4:15 left, but Xavier rallied to tie the score a 66-66 with 2:37 to play. Maxiell gave the Bearcats a 69-68 lead with 56 seconds left.

The victory changed the Musketeers' season. They won six in a row after that and 15 of 17 to close the season, which ended in the Elite Eight with a 3-point loss to No. 6 Duke.

"It was a stepping stone for where we needed to go that year," Chalmers said.

Chalmers entered Xavier the same year Leonard Stokes enrolled at UC. They were close friends from their days playing together on the same AAU team in upstate New York, but Stokes had graduated the previous year. Stokes beat Xavier only once during his four years at UC. Chalmers won three of his four games against the Bearcats, two of three while Stokes was at UC, but they rarely guarded each other because they played different positions. Stokes was a shooting guard and small forward, while Chalmers played mostly point guard.

"It was fun (playing against him)," Chalmers said. "We knew each other's every move. We knew how to get under each other's skin, so it was great competition. We had a great relationship coming up in high school. He lived in Buffalo. I lived in Albany. But when we got together for the summer AAU tournaments we had a good time and we remained friends to the point where we were going to go to the same school."

Both players were planning to attend Providence, but that plan fell through.

"Something happened with the coaches and he ended up choosing Cincinnati and I chose Xavier," Chalmers said. "Providence was not the only school that was on the list. It was a school that we talked about going to together, but we had other schools on our list. It came down to the best choice for us individually. Coach Prosser recruited me since my freshman year of high school. They were one of the

Xavier's Lionel Chalmers, right, and UC's Lenny Stokes, left, were friends and AAU teammates in New York state, but became rivals in the Crosstown Shootout.

first that recruited me."

Chalmers' first exposure to the Crosstown Shootout came during the year he redshirted in 1999-'00, the year the Musketeers knocked off top-ranked UC at Cincinnati Gardens.

"That atmosphere was probably the best atmosphere I had ever been around up until that point," Chalmers said. "If you go back and look at that game, I had a shirt and tie on and you could see me jumping up and down during the whole game because of the energy and the excitement of the game."

> **Maybe because we're a smaller school, they like to say that it means more to us, but when you play in a game and it's for the city, it doesn't matter who you are, you want to win.**

The following season, when Chalmers first played in the Shootout, he had a good idea what to expect.

"It was an honor," he said. "I felt like we were carrying on the tradition and it was like pride to go out there and not only compete but win. It was for the city. It was for Xavier and the tradition that carries on. There was a big weight on our shoulders to perform and continue the legacy. That's the one game you want to win. It was tough (to deal with the nerves) because so much was on the line. But once you start playing you kind of get through that and you do what's necessary to win."

Chalmers doesn't buy the theory that the game means more to Xavier than it does UC.

"I think they come with the same fire and energy that we do," he said. "Maybe because we're a smaller school, they like to say that it means more to us, but when you play in a game and it's for the city, it doesn't matter who you are, you want to win. So for them to say that it means more to us than them, it's just ridiculous."

Chalmers said he didn't think about the Shootout until it was the next game on the schedule. The media coverage is a little less extensive now than it was when he played. One reason is that the schools now restrict access to their players and coaches to one or two days before the game, instead of providing virtually unlimited access back in Chalmers' time.

"You don't worry about it or think about it until they start to put it in the paper and talk about it," Chalmers said. "They compare player to player, coach to coach. They compare record to record and (talk about) the history of the game. For me personally, I didn't pay it any attention. It was more fun to look at it than anything else. Some guys took it personally and that was something that drove them to try to be more successful in the game, I guess, but for me, it was all in fun. At the end of the day, you have to go out there and play the game, so everything else didn't matter.

"Looking back, I would say it was a great experience. It was something that you remember because you don't really have too many experiences of an in-city rivalry like that on that level. I think you appreciate it. You look back on it and it's fun, especially when you won more than you lost. Being on the winning side of that gives it a little extra incentive. It was a great honor to be a part of that. I enjoyed it."

After he graduated from Xavier, Chalmers spent 10 years playing overseas in France, Italy, Spain, Bulgaria and Russia. He lives in Orlando and hopes to get into college coaching. That game-winning shot against UC in 2004, Chalmers said, was the biggest of his college career.

"Every once in a while when someone talks about it, it brings a smile to my face," he said. "I take pride in being able to say that I played for Xavier and graduated from Xavier and that's one of the biggest things that goes with Xavier is that rivalry. That makes me proud for sure."

It also helps that when he and Stokes decided to take different paths in college, it was Chalmers whose team got the best of his friend in their head-to-head match-ups.

"We don't really talk about basketball too much," Chalmers said, "but if we get to going at each other, I might bring it up."

Stanley Burrell scored 20 points in Xavier's 73-71
overtime victory against UC in 2006.

STANLEY BURRELL

2004-'08

"I never got the bill."

A deadly 3-point shooter, Stanley Burrell scored 1,612 points during his four years at Xavier to rank 13th on the Musketeers' career scoring list. He was 2-2 against the Bearcats and scored 20 points in the Musketeers' 73-71 overtime win in January 2006 at Cintas Center during his sophomore year.

That game is easily his best Shootout memory. It takes very little prodding to get him to talk about his worst, a 67-57 loss during his junior year at Fifth Third Arena in 2006 during Mick Cronin's first Shootout as UC's head coach. Burrell was held scoreless, going 0-for-10 from the field and missing all four of his 3-point shots in 31 minutes. He now calls it "a disaster."

"It was horrendous for me personally and for the team it was really bad," Burrell said. "It was a rough night. I kept trying to find it, trying to find, trying to find it and never could. They were set up to really take me out of the game the way they were defending me. I struggled like crazy. You remember those games because it motivates you to work even harder and not let that stuff happen again. Once your jumper's not falling, you try to get to the basket and guys would just crowd the paint. As a young fellow, you've got to be able to handle it correctly or it will take you out of your game. I really learned from that.

"It was really frustrating. I remember trying to find my rhythm the whole night, trying to find the opportunity to make a shot and get going. I might have forced a couple of them trying to get myself going, but it continued to just go downhill and I remember after the game going into the locker room and just destroying some stuff. I remember knocking some kind of paper towel dispenser off the wall or something. It was ridiculous. You've got to get that frustration out of you because you work so hard for those type of moments and then to get there and you have such a bad performance, it was hard to deal with."

Asked if he owed UC for the paper towel dispenser he busted up, Burrell laughed. "That's a good question," he said. "I never got the bill."

Burrell, a guard from Indianapolis, remembers being clued in during his freshman year about the significance of the rivalry by his older teammates, Will Caudle, Keith Jackson, Justin Doellman and Justin Cage.

"Everyone explained to me that the Shootout was coming up," Burrell said. "I saw videos from past games to understand the history of it and how important it is and then the media coverage and all that stuff showed me just how important the game was. I was just excited for the chance to play in such a big game.

> **"**
>
> ## During my time, we would play with those guys and we'd see them around. There was no problem until the game came around and then you look at each other differently.
>
> **"**

"You can have all the coverage and hear everybody talking about it but to actually be on the court and feel the energy after every single bucket from the beginning of the game all the way through, especially if it's a close game, it's incredible. I was nervous at first, that's for sure. We always had great fan support at Xavier, regardless of who we were playing, but that was just a different level. It put a little more pressure on you. In the beginning, you feel that burst of energy and then you settle in and do what you're supposed to do. But at the beginning, it's really nerve-wracking."

When Burrell watched the fight at the end of the December 2011 game, it brought back memories of how physical the Shootout was every year when he played.

"Even during my years there was a little extra stuff going on," he said. "But for us to let the media hype it up going into that game like we were really enemies, it's crazy. I would get like, I want to kill this dude, but now when I'm older and I look back, I'm like, should we really have been acting like that?"

Since leaving Xavier, Burrell has played professionally in Serbia, Belgium, Poland, Germany, Turkey, Russia, Japan, Cyprus and Hungary. Occasionally he runs into former UC players who are also playing overseas.

"During my time, we would play with those guys and we'd see them around," Burrell said. "There was no problem until the game came around and then you look at each other differently."

A few years ago, while playing in Israel, he ran into former UC forward Yancy Gates, who played a major role in the fight.

"I was like, man, that was crazy," Burrell said, "and he said it went too far. You bring it up because it's like the elephant in the room. I'm from Xavier and he's a UC guy. How can you not talk about that? But we're not hating everybody for life."

"I've been playing overseas for the last eight seasons. You're going to cross paths with other Americans that maybe did not play in that game, but they knew about that game, they saw it on TV. So when when it comes up , there's a level of pride behind it that you won these certain games. I played against (UC's) Deonta Vaughn last year in Cyprus. I knew him because we're both from Indianapolis. There's no issue when we run into each other, no issue at all. It's mutual respect."

Aside from actually playing in the Shootout, one of the things that stands out for Burrell is the sight of Xavier students camping out for tickets outside Cintas Center in the days leading up to the game.

"Seeing them camped outside and sometimes the weather conditions were really bad," Burrell said, "to see them out there being dedicated to stand in line and try to get a good ticket for that game, that was incredible. We really respected them so much. One time we came home and we brought all of them pizzas. We were delivering pizzas to their tents outside the Cintas Center. I don't know for myself if I would really live out in a tent just to get tickets to a game, but I do appreciate and respect everybody who did that. We really appreciated that love and support from them."

Josh Duncan, who grew up in Cincinnati, loved playing against UC in Fifth Third Arena, where he thrived on the animosity from UC's fans.

JOSH DUNCAN
2004-'08

"You wish you could go back and play again."

*P*laying the Crosstown Shootout on a neutral court, as UC and Xavier did in 2012-'13 and 2013-'14 wouldn't have appealed to Xavier forward Josh Duncan. The feeling just wouldn't have been the same.

For Duncan, the atmosphere – especially the atmosphere at UC's Fifth Third Arena – was the best part of the Shootout. He first experienced it as a freshman when the Musketeers lost to the Bearcats, 65-54, at Fifth Third in Bob Huggins' final year as UC's head coach.

"I do remember the feeling of that game," Duncan said. "There's a different energy, just the buildup beforehand, everybody talking about it, getting excited for it, the students, you just kind of feel the buzz around town about the significance of the game. I liked playing at home in that game too, but there was something about playing away, knowing how big the game was to Cincinnati, it was like us vs. everybody who hated us.

"There's certain arenas that just kind of really make you remember playing there and that's definitely one of them. I don't know what necessarily there is about it, maybe just the significance of playing in that game against UC and being on that stage. You just kind of soak in everything a little more. It was just a memorable place to play in. I always saw it on TV, but it's a different world when you're actually in there rather than just watching it on TV."

Duncan, who played at Cincinnati's Moeller High School, said he watched more of the Bearcats' games on television growing up than he did Xavier's. But when he was recruited by both UC and Xavier, he decided he'd rather go to Xavier, where he scored 1,210 points, which ranks 27th in school history.

"It's just one of those things," Duncan said. "Sometimes you just know in your heart. When I visited the campus everything about it, the people there, really made me feel comfortable with the place. I just had good a vibe about it. It felt like it was a good place for me. I really enjoyed all four of my years there. I often talk about how much I miss being there."

His first few weeks, though, were a little confusing. Duncan was recruited by (Thad) Matta but before he could get settled into a routine at Xavier, Matta left to become the head coach at Ohio State. Matta's assistant, Sean Miller, was named to replace him and coached Duncan during his entire Xavier career.

"Within a week or so after I got there, I happened to go down into one of the seniors' rooms and we were in there watching on TV that Thad Matta was about to leave," Duncan said. "That's how I found out. I was confused. I'm new to this whole college thing. It was very confusing to me, but I didn't think about leaving."

Duncan said Miller encouraged his players to approach the UC game like any other and Duncan did his best to follow those instructions, but he knew this was not just another game.

"To actually be a part of it," he said, "was just a crazy feeling you can't really explain – excitement, nervousness. Even to this day I always get nervous before games, not nervous like I'm scared, but nervous like I'm ready to play. In those games it was even at a higher level.

"There's so much hype with everything, especially with the media, that they just wanted us to really be focused in, like we would focus on any other game and try not to get caught up in all the outside noise that's going on, but to just enjoy it and have fun too. Of course you know how big of a game it is. It wasn't too hard but at the same time you want to soak it in too because you don't play those type of games all the time.

"You notice (the increased media presence)," he said. "You just try not to get caught up in that stuff. But for sure, you notice it and you start feeling the energy because you know everybody's covering the game, everybody's going to be watching it. You start getting that feeling that it's right around the corner, it's coming up. You try to be as professional as possible, at least that was my my mindset."

Duncan was 2-2 against UC. He got his first win as a sophomore, 73-71, in overtime on Jan. 19, 2006 at Cintas Center. The Bearcats had a five-point lead with 1:22 left in overtime but the Musketeers came back to prevail when UC's James White missed a last-second 3-pointer that would have won the game for the Bearcats. Duncan played 25 minutes in that game and scored six points.

He had his best Shootout as a junior when he scored 14 points in 27 minutes in a 67-57 Xavier loss at Fifth Third Arena, then capped off his college career with a 64-59 win for the 17th-ranked Musketeers at Cintas Center. UC led by five with just under seven minutes left, but Xavier rallied to outscore the Bearcats, 21-12, the rest of the way. Duncan scored 11 points before he was forced from the game with a knee injury with 10:46 left and did not return. It was a disheartening and premature end to his Crosstown Shootout experience.

"I got hurt on a freak incident," Duncan said. "We were going for the ball and somebody landed on my knee and twisted it up. I remember being frustrated that I got hurt, especially in that game. I remember being in the training room watching it on TV."

Next season will be Duncan's ninth playing professionally overseas He has played in France, Belgium, Israel, and Germany and will play in Turkey the 2016-'17. Last year, he played on the same team for a few months with Gates.

"I didn't know him on a deep level, but I knew of him just from growing up in Cincinnati," Duncan said. "He never was bragging about (the fight). He's a good guy. I think it was one of those things where, I'm not justifying it or saying that it was right, but I think emotions started flaring up. It's almost like a playoff game. I feel like any level, NBA or college, in a playoff game or the NCAA Tournament, emotions flare a little bit. The Crosstown Shootout is similar to that type of game."

Eight years after he left the Cintas Center court with a knee injury in his final Crosstown Shootout, Duncan says he misses it and appreciates the opportunity he had to play in the rivalry now more than he did then.

"Those type of games you wish you could go back and play in again," he said, "to be part of a team that got to play in that game…we fought hard every game. You're kind of making me want to go back in the files and find some of these games and watch them again. I think you realize it now more than back then. You kind of take it for granted. Just being younger, you don't realize that things don't last forever, but definitely looking back on it now, you appreciate those type of things. You try to appreciate all the moments that you have."

Xavier's Kenny Frease and UC's Yancy Gates had a long personal history that boiled over in the fight that ended the 2011 Crosstown Shootout.

KENNY FREASE
2008-'12

"It felt like somebody threw a brick at my head."

The first thing Kenny Frease remembered after getting punched by Yancy Gates was his father helping him off the court. At that point, he wasn't sure what happened. He didn't know who hit him and he had no memory of getting kicked in the head by UC's Cheikh Mbodj as he lay on the floor.

"I was pretty out of it honestly until I got to half-court," Frease said. "I felt like somebody threw a brick at my head. I had no idea where it came from. I didn't know until after the game when we went to the locker room that he was the one that hit me. I walked into the locker room and I was asking who hit me and they told me. Honestly, I had no idea."

It was Frease's senior year at Xavier. He had gone 2-1 against the Bearcats, the only loss coming the year before when Gates scored 22 points and pulled down 14 rebounds. Frease says he doesn't remember much about that game.

"If he scored 22 points and had a bunch of rebounds, I probably tried to get that out of my memory," Frease said. "Those games are just blurs because there's so much buildup to it and then it's over so fast. Normally I remember a lot about games that I played in, but those games were like pure instinct. You go out and let the cards fall where they may."

But Frease, a 6-foot-11, 280-pound center, remembers plenty about the fight that prematurely ended Xavier's 76-53 victory on Dec. 10, 2011 at Cintas Center.

"It wasn't me, but there was some sort of Twitter battle going on between some of the guys on the teams during the lead-up to the game," Frease said. "That was sort of what fueled a lot of the fire."

Conventional thinking is that the fight grew out of remarks that UC guard Sean Kilpatrick made in a radio interview the day before the game in which he said that Tu Holloway probably wouldn't start for UC. But if that were the case, Frease didn't know about it.

"Tu is the type of dude that he would always go out and play with such intensity that I don't think it was much different than if (Kilpatrick) hadn't have said it," Frease said. "We never really talked about it too much honestly because he was the type of person who just did what he had to do and he let his game do the talking for him. Maybe he had some more motivation for that game, but that's not something he would have talked to us about.

"I think just because of how bad we were beating them there was a point in the game where you could feel that it was turning from just a blowout game to…it was weird. You could feel it a little bit that it was building up, but I think it was more between the players. I don't think it was something the coaches or even the fans may have even seen. I could definitely feel it happening but I didn't think it would ever turn into something like that."

As the pushing and shoving began in front of UC's bench, Frease said, he walked into the middle of it with the intention of breaking it up. Instead he got punched just below his left eye. Blood ran down his face and the area around the eye was swollen as he later walked off the court with his arms raised in triumph.

Asked if he was surprised that Gates had hit him, he said, "I think I was more surprised by the fact that anybody would have done it because I went into that group with the feeling that we're just going to break this up and it's all going to be done. I didn't think it was going to turn into what it turned into. We had guys on our side that were involved, too, that were in the middle of the fight. A lot of people lost their cool on both sides. It was an unfortunate thing. You like to have this rivalry and it sort of takes away from the whole thing. I walked in and had my hands out to my side and I was trying to move people out of the way. It just escalated a lot quicker than I thought it would and you saw the outcome."

It wasn't the first time that Frease and Gates had a confrontation. During Frease's freshman year, in his first Shootout, he head-butted Gates at UC's Fifth Third Arena, but Gates did not respond.

Why the head-butt?

"Who knows, man?" Frease said. "He probably got in my face and my teammates were all around me. I don't know. I just remember it being played on ESPN like 15 times. I probably had a hundred people sending me a video on their phones talking about me on ESPN."

Frease and the 6-foot-9, 260-pound Gates were not strangers to each other.

Frease grew up in Cleveland, Gates in Cincinnati, and they played against each other on the AAU circuit. So when Frease chose to attend Xavier and Gates picked UC it was inevitable that there would be a personal rivalry between the two big men.

"Yancy and I, we've known each other for awhile because he's from Ohio too," Frease said. "I wouldn't say we're friends or enemies. He's one of those people that you see and you play against them and you don't really know them that well. I wouldn't say that I have any feelings either way towards him.

"It was a big rivalry not only for the team, it was a big rivalry for us, too. Not only between us, it was something the fans really built up, that matchup between me and Yancy. It's hard to say if it was personal. I always remember going to those games thinking, 'I can't play bad in this game,' but I don't think it was ever personal between me and him. It was more of the fact that I didn't want to let my teammates down.

"He's always been a little bit quicker than me, maybe a little bit more than a little bit, so I was always trying to keep him in front of me, and for him it was trying to keep me from being able to get close to the basket to the point where I was able to get in scoring position. We had a little bit different style of play where he had more agility and was quicker than me but I think that I had a little bit of the strength advantage on him."

After the fight, Frease said, Mack "told us to stay off social media, we're going to handle this in-house. I don't want to hear anything on social media. Don't talk to reporters about it. He wanted to keep everything under control. He didn't want it to escalate anymore than it already had. I got (seven) stitches in the training room. After it happened, honestly, it was a semi-normal night. I went out to dinner with my family and hung out with some of my friends and that was it. Everybody was talking about it, but I was hanging out with some of my buddies and we stayed at their house. We didn't really go out in public. I really didn't feel like talking about it."

During the post-game press conference, Holloway and Xavier guard Mark Lyons made comments that attracted a lot of negative attention.

"We're grown men over here," Holloway said. "We've got a whole bunch of gangsters in this locker room, not thugs, but tough guys on the court. We went out there and zipped them up at the end of the game."

Frease's reaction was that his teammates were misunderstood.

"I think what they said was construed into something a lot bigger and a lot worse than what it was," he said. "I think they were trying to say in their own words that we're going to protect each other. They used the wrong words, I guess, but their meaning was good. They just were all heated up and the words that they used probably weren't the best words to use on national TV."

Gates was suspended for six games for throwing the punch.

"It was unfortunate what happened and I don't think there's any room for that in college sports," Frease said, "but I think that (the suspension) was just a knee-jerk reaction. I think that a suspension was needed, but I'm glad that it wasn't like a whole season or something like that. I wouldn't want somebody's season to be ruined because of a split-second reaction that they made in a really heated environment. I'm glad that it wasn't a big suspension honestly."

Frease, who has played professionally in Germany and Turkey since he graduated from Xavier, said the only contact he has had with Gates came in the form of a phone call he made in the days immediately after the fight.

"There were a bunch of rumors going around that I was going to press charges," Frease said. "That was never even a little bit true. I just sort of wanted to get it out to him to know that I wasn't planning on doing anything like that. That's the only time I've talked to him. It was a two-minute phone call, maybe not even two minutes, just to let him know what was going on. He said he was sorry and that was it."

Frease had no inkling just how intense the rivalry was when he first arrived at Xavier in 2008.

"It's a big part of the Xavier basketball community, so yeah, you hear about it right away," he said. "When you think about going to Xavier and being a part of that game, it's a big deal for both sides. That was something that when you first get there, your first day on campus, it's something that they're all talking about, so right away you get this feeling how big of a deal it is, not just for the players, but also for the school and the city.

"After they go through all the facilities and talk about the different things about Xavier basketball and how big of a family it is, then they really start getting into that stuff. There's pictures all over the Cintas Center from it, different memories that people have. My first Shootout was at UC. When you go into a hostile environment like that, you step back for a second, like holy crap, this is a big deal really.

"The fans are screaming things. Everybody's trying to get under your skin. It was an unbelievable experience. You walk out onto the floor for warmups and you have all the nerves and then as soon as the game starts, it all goes away and you just focus on getting the win and how big of a win it is. Some of the things that the students would say, you can't repeat them now. But I wouldn't say that I was scared or anything. It was just mostly nerves for the first 10 minutes of warmups and you see all these people that absolutely hate you, so that part of it takes you back a little bit, but as soon as the game starts it all sort of just melts into the background."

In four Crosstown Shootouts, Frease averaged 8.5 points and 6.5 rebounds. His best game was the last one, in which he scored 13 points with 13 rebounds and four blocked shots. That game will always be remembered not for his statistics, but for the punch he took from Gates.

"I think it's unfortunate, a blemish on the Crosstown Shootout, because it's always been such a huge rivalry," Frease said. "Basketball is a really physical game, people get hurt, people get elbowed, people do stuff like that. I think it just took it to a different level. I just think it's to a point now where it's going to be so over-officiated that people are going to go into the game hoping nothing happens and I feel like that's going to take away from how great a rivalry it was.

"(The Shootout) games were always super-high intensity games and they were a lot of fun to play in," he said, "but the thing I remember the most about them was that at the end of the day, win or lose, the outcome didn't really have a huge effect on the season. There was a big buildup to the game and then once the game was over it was like, okay, now we have a whole season to play. All of the buildup just sort of goes away when you go to March and you're playing in the Sweet 16. Those are the games that you remember more than a big rivalry game."

Matt Stainbrook, who transferred to Xavier from Western Michigan, described the feeling of playing in the Crosstown Shootout as one of "complete and utter joy."

MATT STAINBROOK
2013-'15

"One of those once-in-a-lifetime experiences."

Matt Stainbrook considers himself one lucky fellow.

Not only did he get to continue his college basketball career in the Big East Conference after spending his first two years in the Mid-American Conference at Western Michigan, he got to play in the Crosstown Shootout, one of the great rivalries in college basketball. And to make his experience even sweeter, the Musketeers won both of the Shootouts he played in.

But he did miss out on one key part of the Shootout. He never got to play UC at home at Cintas Center.

"I truly was (disappointed)," Stainbrook said. "Once I transferred (to Xavier) I made a lot of friends and they used to talk about how they used to camp out in line for tickets. The atmosphere was just extremely insane for a home game and I wasn't going to get that opportunity. It was disappointing. It took away from the game but it didn't totally devalue it. I wanted to play a home game."

Stainbrook, a 6-foot-10 center, took a circuitous route to the Shootout. He grew up in Cleveland and accepted a scholarship out of St. Edward High School to play at Western Michigan. It was the only offer he had from a Division I school.

"I was planning on going to Case Western," Stainbrook said. "(Western Michigan) offered me in April. I go to Western and I play two years. I had a good two years but a little bit of rockiness. I didn't get along with my coach. I didn't really fit in with the team necessarily. We had our issues. After my sophomore year, my coach brings me in and tells me, 'We're not renewing your scholarship,' basically kicking me off the team.

"At that point, I had no idea what my value was. I was freaking out, calling my parents, saying, 'Hey I'm gonna have to come back and probably just go to school and be a normal student.' Little did I know I was gonna wake up the next morning, turn on my phone, and I've got 25 voice mails from tons of colleges. Xavier ended up being the highest profile one and being in Ohio, it was something I wanted to get back to. So I go on the visit, I was there on a Sunday until Monday. And I got an offer. I waited until I got back home but then I called (Chris Mack) and told him I wanted to come. It was such a whirlwind. At that time it was the A-10, but then it became the Big East. To go from the Mid-American Conference to the Big East, it was a jump that I was not expecting."

Stainbrook had seen the Crosstown Shootout on TV the night of the fight so when he decided to go to Xavier his thoughts turned to the prospect of playing in it.

"I knew that it was going to be something that was very intense," Stainbrook said. "I was excited for the opportunity. With the hostility and the emotions that sort of ran wild there, it showed that the city, and the teams and the universities and the players all really cared about winning this game. It was something that I was excited to be a part of. It's just kind of one of those once-in-a-lifetime experiences."

Before he arrived in Cincinnati, Stainbrook's only experience in a college rivalry was the one between Western Michigan and Central Michigan.

"They made a whole week out of it, like Western and Central week," he said. "There's lots of name calling, lots of buildup, tailgating, so that was something similar, but on a much smaller scale. I don't think it can really compare in any way to the Crosstown Shootout. We would get maybe 3,000 fans at an average game for us. When Western-Central week shows up we'd get about 5,000 or 6,000, almost double that of what normally shows up."

As a transfer, Stainbrook had to sit out his first year at Xavier, so he watched his first Shootout from the bench, knowing that he would not play in it. That was the first year after the fight and the game was played on a neutral court at U.S. Bank Arena, with UC winning, 60-45.

"Watching it I was so eager to be able to play the next year," Stainbrook said. "I was able to be on the bench and watch everyone, sort of watch everything. I had an outsider's perspective from a really good angle. It made me want to play so bad. If there was one game that whole season that made me really, really want to get back on the court it would be that game. Every fan I ever talked to, any teammate, any other student, coaches, whatever, that was *the* game."

As the Musketeers and Bearcats prepared for the first game at U.S. Bank Arena, the Shootout was viewed with a measure of caution as the coaches from both schools wanted to make sure there wasn't another fight.

"It was addressed, I believe," Stainbrook said. "It was something that was just sort of glanced over. It was slightly talked about, like, hey guys, you understand what happened last year, everyone knows the implications of it and make sure you keep your emotions in check. It wasn't some big sit-down or seminar. For the most part people understood that there was an issue the year before. The was a little bit of nervousness.

"We did not win that first game and I think that we were a little bit timid. The team in general, we were a young team and the energy wasn't there for us. I think that was caused a little bit by the fight and the fact that we didn't want anything else to escalate. The second year the majority of all that was gone. At that point, they had won the year before and I think we were really upset about that. The coaches were not happy and they reflected that in the practices leading up to that week. At that point, it all went from timidness to a little bit of anger and a lot of energy."

In Stainbrook's first game against UC, he scored seven points and pulled down 11 rebounds. He describes the experience as one of "complete and utter joy."

"Just being able to be a part of it made it so special," he said. "From talking to friends, they made sure that you know that they hate UC. On the court, it's complete and utter hatred, and sometimes it's more hatred for the fans than it is for us. I don't feel any will toward the players and UC in general. I appreciate the atmosphere that they bring, but on the court for those 40 minutes or for however long it takes, it is complete and utter hate."

Stainbrook said he didn't have a relationship with any of the UC players during the two years that he spent at Xavier.

"I just met a couple of them when we used to play in the Deveroes League so you would be acquaintances with them there, but other than that, no," he said. "To be honest, with that kind of rivalry, I don't think I've ever really spent time in Clifton. I've been to OTR, I've been to the Banks, I've been downtown, but I never spent leisure time in Clifton."

After two years at U.S. Bank Arena, the game was moved back to the respective campuses in 2013-'14. The first one was played at UC's Fifth Third Arena.

"Being a senior I remember talking to one guy in particular, Jalen Reynolds, telling him, 'Hey, it's gonna be a hostile environment. They are going to try to do everything to try to get under our skin,'" Stainbrook said. "When it was downtown you had fans on both sides. I wouldn't say that it was packed because U.S. Bank was pretty big, but when you go to UC, it's completely sold out and it's 99.9 percent UC fans. You're kind of walking into enemy territory. There's no going back. It was definitely an environment that was a little more cautious for us because of the fight.

"I think I was the first player for Xavier on the court and everything was empty except for the student section. It's completely full and they see me and they just start booing, they start yelling, everything, and I was just like, oh my god. That will stick out with me for a long, long time. I smiled. I don't let anyone get under my skin that way. It's all fun for me. I love playing basketball. I may be a little weird in this way, but I love going to a road game and winning, seeing everyone very upset walking out. That game sort of seemed like a blur. It went by so quick."

Fifth Third Arena, Stainbrook said, reminded him of "a really giant high school gym."

"I don't mean that in a negative way," he said, "because another place that reminded me of a high school gym that I played in was Cameron Indoor Stadium, when I was at Western and we played at Duke. It might be a larger version of Cameron Indoor. It's not your typical, rounded arena with all nice seats…it's a little bit older and it's very large and boxy, but that doesn't take away from the experience because they pack that place whenever we play them. It feels like people are on top of you. It feels like there's not a bad seat in the gym. You look around and it seems like they're just right there."

Xavier held on to win that game, 59-57, when UC's Farad Cobb missed a 3-point shot in the closing seconds that could have won the game for the Bearcats. Stainbrook scored seven points and grabbed six rebounds.

As Cobb released the shot, Stainbrook said, "The biggest thing going through my mind was 'box out, box out, do not let them get a rebound.' I had that feeling in my chest that if they got an offensive rebound and a put-back that it would have been a very, very tough way to try to come back and try to eke out a win. We had controlled the game for the majority of it and we couldn't let it slip away. At the time, all that mattered was that we won and there was just total pandemonium afterwards. That shot was one that will stick in my head.

"I was on the weak side, I hit someone (to box out) and then I was turning as I saw it going up. I think it was a little bit short, it kind of hit the front rim and went down. It made you a little bit nervous. At first, I was like, you know what, with some of the luck I've had in some games, I would not be surprised if it went in. I was praying to the basketball gods, don't let it happen."

Xavier's Dee Davis scored 16 points in that game to lead the Musketeers, making five of five 3-point shots.

"It was unbelievable," Stainbrook said. " I remember saying, 'Coach, more plays for him, more plays for him.' He stepped up in a huge way. He would always shoot (the three) but it wasn't necessarily his forte. He was more of a floor general who led the team, but he was by no means a deadly 3-point shooter or maybe even an average 3-point shooter.

"That's the one thing that benefited our team my senior year when we went to the Sweet 16 was that at any given moment anyone could go off and when that happened, we were very unselfish in the fact that, 'Hey, I want to score, I want to do this, but guess what, if Dee's playing really well, if Myles (Davis) is playing well, go to that guy.' We're not going to force it but if they're playing well, give them the ball."

There have been no fights in the Crosstown Shootout since 2011. For the most part, the players and coaches from both schools have kept their emotions in check. Stainbrook can remember only one incident when he feared another fight might break out, but his fears were unfounded.

"I think we did a really good job of keeping it under control," he said. "But I remember at UC my senior year (Octavius) Ellis, he either scored a basket or blocked a shot and he started running down the court and looked at their bench and was kind of cutting across his neck or waving his finger. At that point, I was like, they want to start something. I felt like at this moment anything can happen and that's how it's going to be. I was like okay, if that's how it's gonna be, let's get it on. But that's probably the only moment."

Stainbrook ranks the Crosstown Shootout second only to the 2015 NCAA Tournament when the Musketeers went to the Sweet 16 on his list of the most memorable moments from his days at Xavier.

"The NCAA Tournament, when we played in the play-in game my junior year, it didn't feel right," he said. "You're in Dayton, you're 45 minutes away from home, it didn't feel like an NCAA Tournament game. But winning the game against Ole Miss and then winning against Georgia State and then even playing in the Sweet 16, even though we lost against Arizona, those are definitely the top three moments. But the Crosstown ranks right below that. That's the only thing that can even compare to the NCAA tournament, which is a big thing."

Stainbrook is proud of his 2-0 record against the Bearcats and is quick to mention it whenever the topic comes up. And he enjoys the banter between fans from the two schools about which program is superior, especially when UC fans bring up the Bearcats' two national titles to Xavier's none.

"It's always brought up that, 'Hey, we're better right now. You won a championship when you weren't even born,'" Stainbrook said. "That's always the comeback."

CROSSTOWN SHOOTOUT
PHOTO GALLERY

*UC's JaQuon Parker drives for the basket against Xavier's
Jeff Robinson in the 2011 Crosstown Shootout.*

*Xavier students camp out for tickets the day before
the Dec. 10, 2011 Crosstown Shootout at Cintas Center.*

*UC students wait in line for tickets to the Jan. 28, 1999
Crosstown Shootout at Shoemaker Center.*

UC's Farad Cobb finds himself boxed in by Xavier's James Farr, left, and Jalen Reynolds during the 2015-'16 Crosstown Shootout.

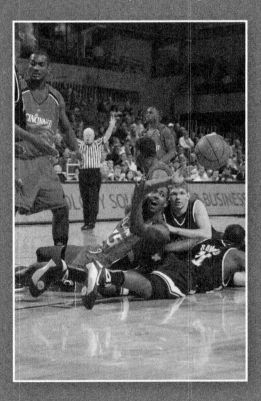

ABOVE UC's Yancy Gates boxes out Kenny Frease during the first half of the 2011 Shootout.

UC's Darnell Wilks and Xavier's Brad Redford fight for a loose ball.

Xavier's David West walks off court after the Musketeers' loss in 2001.

Xavier's Jason Love celebrates Xavier's double-overtime win in the 2009 Shootout.

ABOVE *The UC student section urges the Bearcats to win one for ailing UC head coach Mick Cronin in 2015.*

Xavier's Jalen Reynolds celebrates with a Musketeer fan after XU's win over UC in the Dec. 12, 2015 Crosstown Shootout.

ABOVE *UC's Shaq Thomas heads to the bench in the 2015 Shootout, with Chris Mack yelling in the background.*

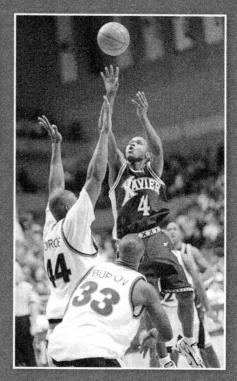

Xavier's Lenny Brown hits the game-winning shot over UC's Rodrick Monroe and Darnell Burton in XU's Nov. 26, 1996 upset of the top-ranked Bearcats.

UC's Bobby Brannen (34) and Charles Williams (20) react to a call during the 1996 Shootout.

*UC's Shaq Thomas goes up for a shot in traffic during
the Dec. 12, 2015 Crosstown Shootout.*

*UC's Cashmere Wright, boxed
in by Xavier's Kenny Frease,
passes to a teammate in 2009.*

*Xavier's Lenny Brown, right,
celebrates with his teammates after
hitting the game-winning shot
against top-ranked UC in 1996.*

Xavier's Jaylen Reynolds grabs a rebound in front of UC's Octavius Ellis in 2015.

UC associate head coach Larry Davis, left, shakes hands with Xavier head coach Chris Mack before the Feb. 18, 2015 Shootout.

Xavier's Matt Stainbrook, UC's Shaq Thomas, left, and Octavius Ellis try to grab a loose ball in 2015.

UC's Bobby Brannen falls to the floor as he and Xavier's Darnell Williams grapple for a loose ball in 1996.

UC's Octavius Ellis blocks the shot of Xavier's Larry Austin Jr. in 2015.

ABOVE UC coach Mick Cronin protests an official's call in the first half of the 2008 Shootout.

Xavier's Kevin Frey goes up for a layup during the Musketeers' upset of top-ranked UC in 1999.

UC's Ryan Fletcher and Xavier's David West contend for a loose ball in 1999.

UC's Nick Williams fouls Xavier's Justin Cage in the first half of the 2004 Shootout.

CINCINNATI PLAYERS

Roger McClendon, the sixth-leading scorer
in UC history, was 1-3 against Xavier.

ROGER MCCLENDON
1984-'88

"To go 0-for-4, I don't know if I could come back to the city."

*R*oger McClendon first met Xavier's Byron Larkin on his recruiting visit to Cincinnati while UC was pursuing both players.

"I actually did create some life-long friendships," McClendon said. "Byron Larkin is one of those people that I recall staying in contact with, but at first, no, there was no love at all.

"We met on a recruiting trip. He was here the same time I was here looking at Cincinnati. It was at a football game. That's how we first met. He was a very humble guy, very intelligent. He was an outstanding player. He wasn't a great outside shooter but he was a great scorer and he got the most out of his game."

McClendon was a McDonald's High School All-American from Champaign, Ill., where his father was a professor in African-American studies at the University of Illinois.

"We moved to Illinois right before I started my high school career," McClendon said. "I was a big-time Cincinnati Reds fan from New York, just because I adopted them. Sparky Anderson, Joe Morgan and Pete Rose, I loved that whole team and had no idea where Cincinnati was on the map."

McClendon decided to attend UC, where he would play for Tony Yates. Larkin went to Xavier to play for Bob Staak. For the next four years, from 1984 to 1988, the two high-scoring guards would be linked as the offensive stars of their respective teams.

At UC, McClendon was the top attraction in a program that was struggling to regain the success of its glory days of the 1960s. A long-range shooting specialist with a willowy body, he took advantage of the inception of the 3-point shot in 1986 to finish his career as the second-leading scorer in school history with 1,789 points behind only the legendary Oscar Robertson. McClendon still ranks sixth on UC's career scoring list.

Larkin was part of a program in a much different situation. The Musketeers had never been a national power in college basketball, although they did win the National Invitation Tournament in 1958, but were on the rise under Staak.

During Larkin's four years at Xavier, the Musketeers made three trips to the NCAA Tournament. McClendon played at UC during the school's 15-year NCAA drought and never made it to the tournament, although he did make one appearance in the NIT in 1985.

Once he arrived in Cincinnati, it didn't take long for McClendon to get caught up in the Shootout. Like many of the players from his era, he got his first taste of the rivalry during the summer playing pickup games that also involved Xavier players.

"When I really started to understand it, it became a part of me," he said. "It was almost eerie in the sense of, while I didn't know the history, I got to know those guys in the summer. I can't describe it, but there was a competitiveness that came over the court when those guys stepped on the court. You'd walk onto the court with the Xavier guys and it was instantly on, even before the first game my freshman year."

McClendon was on the winning side against Xavier only once in four games. That was in 1987, his junior year, when the Bearcats won, 75-73, at Riverfront Coliseum. UC lost by three to the Musketeers during McClendon's freshman year, by four during his sophomore year, and by 18 during his senior year.

By his junior year, McClendon had blossomed into a force on offense, averaging 19.9 points. As the Xavier game approached in late January, the Cincinnati media naturally sold it as a personal confrontation between the two gifted guards.

"We didn't look at it that way," McClendon said. "But for me personally I was in kind of that scoring mode coming out of my sophomore year and going into my junior year. They looked for me to score. I was able to do a lot of one-on-one opportunities and be successful at that, and Byron was already a scorer, so I think it naturally played to the strength of the teams and it played out that way."

Both players lived up to the hype. McClendon put on a dazzling shooting display, scoring 29 points and making 10 of 20 shots from the field, including five of seven from 3-point range, to best Larkin, who scored 24. But the game that would provide McClendon with one of his best memories from his time at UC will always be remembered not for his offensive outburst, but for a game-winning shot by Joe

Stiffend, whose game was decidedly lacking in flash, but who hit a 17-foot jump shot for the winning points just before time expired.

McClendon didn't mind being overshadowed if it meant that he got to taste victory against the Musketeers, and he was happy for his teammate, a player who had overcome long odds to get where he was.

"That was a thrill," McClendon said, "because to go 0-for-4 I don't know if I could come back to the city. I remembered Joe as a player in Illinois. He was unbelievable as a high school player. He was all of 6-3 but most people think he was 6-8. He would dunk on anybody. If it was a 6-10 guy, it didn't matter. He had unbelievable leaping ability. He was very strong, mentally strong. I remember the play, we got it off the rim, kicked it out, one pass, and Joe put it up to win the game at the buzzer.

"It was all in the flow of the game. There was no timeout. The ball went through the hoop, I grabbed it out of the basket. I remember running in trying to see if it was going to come out, trying to see if there would be an offensive rebound so I could tip it in."

Xavier had trailed by five points with 2:23 left, but came back to tie the score at 73-73 on a basket by Dexter Campbell. It was his only basket of the game. McClendon grabbed the ball and tossed the inbounds pass to Lamont Hamilton, who spotted Stiffend running down the side of the court.

Hamilton passed to Stiffend, who dribbled, ducked under Xavier's Kyle Taylor and shot over an onrushing Campbell for the winning basket.

> " What happens is with the electricity of the crowd, as players, what you're training yourself to do is tune everything out and focus on those 40 minutes that you're going to be on the court. That's the only thing you can think about. "

"Joe loved being the hero. He was that kind of person," McClendon said. "He never had a bad day. He was always smiling, always positive. That was great for the team and for the team chemistry. Everybody was very excited for him. He liked being appreciated. I think that was a great shot for Joe in his career."

What made the moment even sweeter was the fact that Stiffend had to contend with a learning disability that made getting through college a struggle.

"I think he had dyslexia," McClendon said. "Growing up in East St. Louis, that's a very tough area with poverty, crime, prostitution, all those kinds of things. For him to come out of there and go through college…he was always a hard worker, but he had to fight that disability all the way through. And he was very tenacious at it. Hats off to him."

McClendon said Tony Yates tried to approach the Xavier game the same way he did every other game, but it was impossible for the players to not get caught up in the atmosphere.

"From the media side, obviously it was going to be a different game," McClendon said, "He tried to take some of the attention off and the hype from the media. But no matter what a coach might say, I think the emotion takes over for a lot of players in that game and you play as hard as you can, like a do-or-die situation.

"What happens is with the electricity of the crowd, as players, what you're training yourself to do is tune everything out and focus on those 40 minutes that you're going to be on the court. That's the only thing you can think about. But the intensity of every rebound and every shot is magnified like a playoff game or an NCAA championship game. I think the fans are what the rivalry becomes all about. The fans are so intense about their team. It's that history."

McClendon lives in Louisville where he is Chief Sustainability Officer for Yum! Brands. His history in the Shootout includes more losses than wins, but he had one night at Riverfront Coliseum when he put his offensive gifts on full display only to see his friend steal the show at the end.

"When I'm sitting down with Larkin and we run into each other," McClendon said, "he can say he's got three and I've got one. But I remember the one."

KEITH STARKS

1987-'91

"It turned out it was Levertis Robinson who elbowed me in the face."

*W*hen he thought he had been elbowed in the face by Xavier's Dexter Campbell, Keith Starks reacted instinctively by taking a swing at Campbell, who responded with what Starks describes as "a half-hearted swing" of his own.

Neither player landed a punch, but each was called for a technical foul. UC was assessed a second technical because some of its players left the bench, ostensibly to become part of a fight that never materialized.

Xavier led by five at the time with 3:56 to play. Larkin capitalized on UC's technical fouls by making three of four free throws. McClendon missed his two foul shots for UC. The Musketeers then went on a 16-2 run to beat UC, 98-80, on Jan. 12, 1998, during Starks' freshman year. If the outcome wasn't disheartening enough for Starks, he discovered after the game that Campbell wasn't the one who had elbowed him.

"It turned out that it was (UC's) Levertis Robinson who actually elbowed me in the face," Starks said.

Oops.

Starks laughs now about what clearly was a case of mistaken identity and says when he sees Xavier players from that era, they laugh, too. But he's not embarrassed by what happened, even though he understands that it led to a lopsided Xavier win.

"This is probably the first time I've brought it up or talked about it in a long time," Starks said. "Would I do it again? Depending on the circumstances and how the game was going and not knowing what I know now, I probably would have done the same thing because at the time they were a lot better than we were and we just wanted them to know that we weren't gonna back down."

That was Xavier's third win in four games against UC as the tide began to turn in the rivalry. The Musketeers would go on to finish 26-4 that season and play in the NCAA Tournament for the second straight year. UC would finish 11-17, its third straight losing season . The Bearcats hadn't been to the NCAA Tournament since 1977.

Just a few years earlier, Starks, a 6-foot-7 forward from Taylor High School west of Cincinnati, believed he was headed to Xavier, not UC.

"Xavier was probably my first choice as a junior in high school," Starks said. "Mike Sussli was recruiting me when he was an assistant coach at X. He communicated with me every day through telephone calls and through letters. If I had committed as a junior, I would have gone to X. It was one of the first schools that really recruited me at an early age. I'm a loyal guy, I'm a family guy and it just felt like I was getting that from Mike Sussli."

But just when Starks had all but decided that Xavier was the place for him, Staak left for Wake Forest and was replaced by Pete Gillen.

"When Pete came in, I didn't have as much contact," Starks said. "The recruiting went a different way."

Starks then turned his attention to UCLA.

"I went out there the summer after my junior year," Starks said. "I fell in love with it and I was gonna commit during the first signing period, but then my grandfather got sick. I grew up with my grandparents, so I decided to stay home. UC started recruiting me at the tail end of that. Since X had fallen off a bit, it was only reasonable for me that if I was gonna stay home, I was going to UC."

Starks was part of Yates' heralded recruiting class that was supposed to turn the UC program around. The class also included Robinson, Lou Banks, Kevin Williams, Marty Dow and Elnardo Givens. But when the NCAA instituted its new academic requirements for freshman eligibility known as Proposition 48, only Dow met the requirements. Yates referred to the players as "The Cavalry" during the year they were forced to sit out.

Starks didn't get to experience his first UC-Xavier game until Jan. 12, 1988. When he walked onto the Gardens floor he already had a strange feeling.

"It was awkward because had things fallen into place at the start of my junior year (in high school) I would be on the other side of the bench," Starks said.

The incident with Campbell plus Xavier's blowout victory made that first Shootout a game to forget for Starks. It was a much different story during his

UC forward Keith Starks took a swing at Xavier's Dexter Campbell
in the 1988 Crosstown Shootout because he thought Campbell
had elbowed him in the face. He later learned that the inadvertent
elbow came from his teammate Levertis Robinson.

sophomore year. Not only did the Bearcats knock off Xavier, 86-76, Starks produced the best Shootout performance of his career with 17 points and nine rebounds.

"Even though it was our home game, we still both played at the Gardens so there was really no advantage to either team other than the fact that we wore different uniforms," Starks said. "I do remember that I played pretty well. I wanted to make amends from the year before. I wanted to come out and show people that I'm not a thug, that I still know how to play the game the right way."

That was the last Shootout for Yates, who was fired at the end of the season after six years at his alma mater.

"I loved playing for Coach Yates," Starks said. "He was a people person. The guys loved him. People ask me what was the difference between Coach Yates and Coach Huggins. In my opinion, it was the approach in practice. Guys were held a little more accountable (under Huggins). Practice was a little more competitive. Nothing against Coach Yates. I love Coach Yates to death. Every time I see him he doesn't forget to remind me that we're third or fourth cousins down the line in our family tree."

Starks scored seven points with five rebounds in Bob Huggins' first Shootout, which ended in a controversial fashion with the play that for a long time was known simply as "The Call" when an official ruled that the ball caromed off UC's Lou Banks before it went out of bounds. In fact, it was knocked out by Xavier's Michael Davenport. The outcome was decided by Jamal Walker's game-winning 3-point shot with seconds remaining in overtime.

"I think that set the tone for the ill will between Huggins and Pete Gillen during Pete Gillen's stay at Xavier," Starks said. "I'm sure their relationship has mended a little bit since then. It's been over 30 years. But I do think that kind of set them down that path because Huggs was irate. He couldn't believe that call was made and how bad that call was."

Huggins was so upset in the locker room immediately after the game, Starks said, that "every other word was an F word. I don't know what was said in-between. I just know every other word was an F-word. He made sure that we understood that it wasn't our fault and then he went back out. My understanding was that he was trying to find (UC athletic director Rick Taylor)."

UC recovered to beat Xavier, 69-56, during Starks' senior year on Jan. 30, 1991, in the first Shootout played in Shoemaker Center. Starks scored 11 points and pulled down eight rebounds.

"All of us who played in that game, we knew what our record was in our four years there and we didn't want to go out and be 1-3 and lose at home," Starks said. "Our game plan was to just go at 'em and be extremely physical with them. We thought they were a little soft from that standpoint. We wanted to go out and dominate the boards and dominate on defense."

Huggins' approach to the Shootout, Starks said, wasn't much different from Yates' in that both coaches badly wanted to win, but both tried not to place too much emphasis on it.

"It was still just one game," Starks said, "but it was a game that was gonna kind of define the city. With Huggs, it didn't matter if it was Bethune-Cookman or if it was Louisville, he wanted to win and he wanted us to play with the same passion and intensity regardless of who the opponent was. It just made it extra sweet from an intensity standpoint that it was gonna be Xavier, just because of how people looked at Xavier in terms of their education and the kind of guys they recruited. We were not, in people's eyes, the best of people from that standpoint. I talk to Xavier people and even now some of them are very adamant that we probably shouldn't have gotten into the University of Cincinnati because of the (Prop 48 status).

"It was a different mindset in how we approached the game. Huggs was a little meaner about it (than Yates), I would say, a little more tense. He made us think that in some people's eyes we weren't good enough to be on the floor or good enough to be in the same city, just kind of playing that good cop, bad cop, with the way that people thought of us, and we responded to that."

Starks, now the varsity basketball coach at Ursuline High School in Cincinnati, played professionally after he left UC in France, Belgium, China, Italy and Switzerland and credits Huggins for making that happen.

"Playing for Huggs, it totally changed my future in terms of basketball," he said. "He gave me the freedom to do a lot of different things, to go out on the perimeter, which helped prolong my playing career after I got out of UC, so I'm forever grateful for that. I love my university to death. I would do anything for them, even to this day, even though Huggs is not there. It changed my life in a way that I was able to keep playing basketball and it's opened other doors because of that."

Starks watches the Shootout religiously every year. If he's coaching a game on the night it's played, he records it on his DVR and watches it later. The rivalry still means a lot to him, but in a different way.

"A rival is a rival and you want to beat them as much as you can, but by the same token it's only a game at the end of the day," Starks said. "I still see Michael Davenport a lot. And I see Jamal a lot and we're very cordial. We high five. We hug each other. We really don't talk about basketball as much as we talk about just how life's going and raising families and things like that."

Starks has a 15-year old daughter, Alexis, a highly-regarded player at Anderson High School.

"Now my daughter is being recruited by both schools," Starks said. "Everything has kind of come full circle."

*Terry Nelson predicted a UC blowout in 1992 and the Bearcats
made him look like a prophet with a 93-75 victory.*

TERRY NELSON

1991-'93

"Xavier doesn't really have a chance."

A few days before the Shootout in 1992, UC forward Terry Nelson boldly predicted that UC would blow out Xavier. He made his comments outside the back entrance to the locker room in Shoemaker Center and had no idea the furor they would cause.

"Xavier doesn't really have a chance," Nelson said. "I feel like we should go in there and blow them out...Just say we should win big because I have that much confidence in our players."

Nelson, a junior college transfer from Long Beach, Calif., was in his first year at UC. He had driven across the country crammed into a tiny Plymouth Sundance to start school the previous summer with Corie Blount and Erik Martin, two other players who had played junior college basketball in California. Before he arrived in Cincinnati, Nelson had never heard of Xavier and knew very little about the city.

The morning his prediction appeared in the Cincinnati Post, Bob Huggins called him into his office and chewed him out for providing bulletin board material to the Musketeers. The Bearcats, who played in their sixth Final Four that season, made Nelson look clairvoyant with a 93-75 victory at Cincinnati Gardens.

Nelson now runs UC's Legends program, which reaches out to former UC athletes. He also does color commentary on UC radio broadcasts. His prediction earned him the nickname, "The Prophet," and made him a media personality in Cincinnati.

The first time he heard about the Crosstown Shootout was while he was playing against Xavier players in a summer league at Purcell Marian High School the summer before his first season with the Bearcats.

"I had heard of Xavier of Louisiana (in New Orleans)," he said. "It was closer in proximity to California and I had family down in Louisiana. That's the only reason I heard of Xavier. All I heard about Cincinnati was WKRP. Then we got here and it's WKRC, the TV station. We didn't know anything about Cincinnati. We just wanted to get out of California. We wanted to get away from gangs and smog and congestion and come out here to try something different.

"When we started preparing for (the Xavier game) I thought it was just a regular game. I was shooting off my mouth and didn't think anything of it until the next day when it hit the paper. That's when I got the call in. Not only was there the chewing out in the morning before practice but when I walked into the gym, every TV station has their tripod ready and their camera guy going. This had never happened before. I realized I shouldn't have said what I said probably. I kind of figured it out when I took a verbal beating from Huggins, but when I got there and I saw all the cameras and everybody was being interviewed asking about my comments, I realized I had started a firestorm."

Huggins' practices leading up to the Shootout were the most intense of the season.

"(Huggins) has a short fuse for mistakes (before that game)," Nelson said. "He wants your attention to be at peak levels the entire three hours. You can't come in and go through the motions for a half hour. He'll just stop, run you, and re-set the clocks. Those practices are tough. You're going to hear everything except the name that your mother gave you. You're going to hear a lot of stuff and you can't take it personally because taking a verbal whipping in practice is nothing compared to what you're going to get in the arena. So he just wants to prepare you.

"The attention to detail had to be perfect or we started it over. Normally we would have a three-hour schedule from drill to drill. Drills are 10 minutes, then you go to the next drill. If this wasn't right, we'd start the drill again. We made sure we went from drill to drill and focused on certain things like boxing out, defending the three, bumping cutters, just little details that would knock them off their kilter just a little bit. They were going to do the same thing but we wanted to make sure we were better.

"The (Gardens) was cold. It was an older floor. (I remember) the excitement, the music thumping, the anticipation of all week long building up to this. If it was nothing else other than the week of preparation and anticipation, it would have been a good game already. But then we hit a couple of shots and Anthony Buford started getting into the face of (XU coach) Pete Gillen. It was just all the in-game stuff that made it a great rivalry.

"You grew up fast in games like that. I'm not the scorer. I'm not Anthony Buford shooting threes. I'm not the glorious one. My job is to make sure their post players don't go off, make sure that they don't have four or five offensive rebounds, double-figure rebounding games, because at any moment when I'm not focused, I can get embarrassed because I'm a 6-6 post player, guarding 6-9, 6-10 guys like Aaron Williams and Brian Grant (both of whom played in the NBA). Both of them had the ability to embarrass you, so if you're not focused, it can really go bad for you.

"What helped us is that they pressed us to start the game, which lowered our stress level because that's all we do in practice is work on the press. So when they pressed us, we carved it like a hot knife through butter and that's how we got our (22-4) lead. But you know in that game no matter what lead we had, they were going to make a run. You can't take your foot off the pedal because they're at home, they have nothing to lose, and like always in a game like that, somebody steps up and makes a name for themselves. It was (Michael) Hawkins that time. He scored 22 points. He was a freshman. He really had a great game."

Xavier cut UC's lead to three points, 56-53, but the Bearcats quickly rebuilt it back to a comfortable margin.

"We just kept pulling away because they kept trying to press us and they were giving us wide open threes," Nelson said. "We were getting dunks. We beat them at what they do best and then Buford got really hot and they couldn't catch up. Every time they made a mistake we capitalized and we played just well enough to make sure that they never put a serious dent into that lead.

"(After the game) Huggins briefed me. We're walking off the court and he puts his arm around me after we shake hands with (the Xavier players). He goes, do me a favor, why don't you retire 1-0 as a prophet? So I knew I couldn't go into the media session saying more outlandish stuff. But it did sort of elevate my status as someone who was not afraid to speak his mind and then we backed it up. But if they were counting on me to score 20 points to back up that statement, it wasn't going to happen

"It was a safe statement for me because I wasn't a scorer. If I shut down Brian Grant or Aaron Williams and I had a couple of charges and a couple of points, then my prediction was true. I had an 'and-one' on a turnaround jump shot. (Made the basket, was fouled and made the free throw). I had a dunk. I missed a dunk. There was a lot of fun within there where I had some moments that really stood out for me. It wasn't about scoring."

The following year, in 1992-'93, UC went to the Elite Eight and lost in overtime to eventual national champion North Carolina. And the Bearcats beat Xavier again, 78-67, at Shoemaker Center.

"The second game was at our place," Nelson said. "We already had the experience of going to the Final Four. We had a lot of big games under our belt. Nick Van Exel was one of the featured players in college basketball. Corie Blount was really starting to make a name for himself. We already had a group of guys that were used to being around one another, Tarrice Gibson, AD Jackson…Curtis Bostic was back, so we were deeper at the forward position and we could easily switch and do a lot of different things that we didn't do in our Final Four year. We were a better defensive team our second year because we were the same size across the board pretty much.

"They wanted to come out and make a statement. But we had so many walk-throughs. We must have had six or seven walk-throughs. Normally we have about four or five, so Huggs was kind of anal about that. We knew everything that they were going to do, almost like it was scripted like a football play.

"I knew Grant was going to catch the ball, take one or two dribbles looking to the middle, and he was going to turn over that left shoulder, so as soon as he caught the ball, I watched him. I saw his shoulder turn. I saw his left leg begin to drop-step. I turned to that side. He turns and hits me. I fall. The ref right behind me calls a charge and Brian just looks at me and says, 'You got me.' We just knew what they were going to do. We were so ready.

"Huggins didn't like Pete, so he wanted to win and he wanted to rub it into Pete. He wanted to give it to Xavier because Huggins is kind of territorial and Cincinnati was his town. He wanted everybody to know Cincinnati was his town, so this game was like validation. Xavier was building their program. They had some great players. It was like power forward university coming in there with all the guys they had and Huggs just wanted to make a statement."

As he looks back on his college career, Nelson said, the two Crosstown Shootouts mean more to him than UC's appearance in the Final four or the Elite Eight.

"I didn't play much in the Final Four," Nelson said. "I started the game, had a couple of quick points, and then Huggs started rotating and stuck with a lineup the entire time. He didn't go through his normal rotations and play the 10 guys that he was normally accustomed to. The fact that we lost that game and that was the end of the season, it didn't sit well, whereas the anticipation for the Crosstown Shootout, all the preparation, the prediction, the rivalry, the intimacy of knowing the players (makes it better). They know you. You know them. And then you come out victorious and then that's bragging rights. Everywhere I go, (people say) that's Terry Nelson from the Final Four team, but within the circles it's like, oh yeah, Terry's 2-0 against Xavier, especially during Crosstown week. Whenever there's a Crosstown Shootout, I'm the most requested person on radio and TV because of the prediction and how it happened. I never get called during the Final Four.

"(The Xavier game) meant more. The Final Four is a team accomplishment and it's a great thing. I remember not so much the game, but all the stuff that we did as a team during the Final Four, hanging out together. We were a loose bunch. We had video cameras and Huggs just let us be who we were, rapping in the back of the bus, creating songs. It was just a fun time traveling together, that whole ride through the tournament. That's what I remember.

"(With the Xavier game) you had your fingerprint on the game. You had to be locked in mentally. I had some big plays in both games. The trash talking was personal, fun but still personal. It's a different level of trash talking when you're playing against Xavier and you're saying, 'Remember what I did to you in the summer league? That's exactly what's going to happen now.' We were trying to get into their head psychologically to get any type of advantage.

"We liked the Xavier guys. They weren't bad guys. They weren't thugs or anything and we weren't thugs. We were just guys that liked each other. It was one of those respect rivalries. When we played in the summer league it was probably the most watched game in the summer league, with a packed, hot gym, so people couldn't wait for the Crosstown Shootout. When you have that rivalry going on within the game, it's intense, it's trash talking and afterwards we were all hitting the club together."

The nature of the rivalry has changed over the years, Nelson said. The players don't hang out together like they did during Nelson's day.

"When we played, everything was downtown, so you went downtown," Nelson said. "That's where everybody met at the Waterfront or Prime Time or whatever. Now Xavier doesn't come to our side. We don't go to their side. We don't go downtown. It's different because you have guys come in and they're a lot like (I was) where they don't really understand the rivalry. They see it on TV. They know it's a big game, but they don't really understand the level of preparation, the level of intensity, the focus that you have to have in this game, playing against somebody who knows you and wants to beat the crap out of you. It's not like they want to win. They want to beat the crap out of you. They want to brag. They want to talk. They want to milk it. I just don't think (the current UC players) get it."

Corie Blount, who played for 11 years in the NBA,
takes great pride in his 2-0 record against Xavier.

CORIE BLOUNT

1991-'93

"There's no way we were going to lose to that little school."

When Terry Nelson made his now-famous prediction he caught plenty of flak from Bob Huggins, but none from his teammates because they had been saying the same thing among themselves all week.

"At the time, we were pretty confident in our team," Blount said. "I remember a couple of reporters were asking me what I thought about what Terry had said. I was like, man, we all agree with him."

Blount was an athletic, 6-foot-10 center who became the Chicago Bulls' first-round pick in the 1993 NBA draft. He played 11 years in the NBA for seven different teams. Even though he's from Monrovia, Calif., he returned to Cincinnati after his playing days and feels a strong allegiance to the Bearcats.

He grew into the Shootout after he understood what it meant to Huggins and the rest of the city.

"Just listening to people you could tell that it was going to be a big game," Blount said. "That's when the buzz kicked in. We were pretty excited about the game after all that buzz. When we found out it was like the key to the city, we were like, oh yeah, we got to get this."

Blount's Bearcats won their first game against Xavier, 93-75, as predicted by Nelson, and the second one, 78-67, during Blount's senior year when he averaged 11.3 points and 8.1 rebounds. But he almost missed his first Shootout when he went down with a sprained ankle in practice the day before.

"I came down on Mike Reicheneker's ankle during a post drill," Blount said. "I knew it wasn't a regular sprain. I came down on it awkward and it hurt like hell. That's when everybody got a little uptight. They kept me up all night, me and Tom (Lemley), the trainer. It was an all-nighter for me, stem and ice back and forth, and then stretching. I would do this cross-fiber rub where he would kind of push the swelling out of the fluid area and then he would ice it. Then he'd come back with the heat. He pretty much did that all night the night before the game. I didn't get any sleep.

"That morning during shoot-around I was able to run a little bit and move on it a little bit. I didn't know how many minutes (Huggins) was going to give me but he asked me could I play. I said, 'Yeah' and he said, 'We'll see how everything goes.' It was like, all right, show me what you can do. I hadn't built that kind of credibility up yet, where I could just say I'm going to play, with him not knowing what I could do."

Blount started the game and played 23 minutes. He scored seven points with five rebounds, and felt very little pain.

"It's amazing," he said. "You don't feel pain until before or after the game. While you're out there, you might feel a little pain, but just from the emotions and everything going through you, want to compete and help your team win."

Having played in junior college before signing with UC, Blount had never been part of a game played at such a fever pitch. He felt it as soon as he walked into the Gardens.

"Their student section was loud," he said. "When we walked in they were all over us during our layup time. You felt the intensity of the crowd, definitely. Both years I could say that, even at our house. It was just an exciting atmosphere. I had never seen nothing like that.

"That was the biggest game of the year for us because of the city. We kind of hung out with (Xavier's) Brian Grant and Aaron Williams and all those guys. When we would go hang out at the club, we knew that the people in the city would respond to the guys who won that game a little more than the ones who lost, so we took that to heart. We thought, man, this is our city. We always thought we were the big brothers. I know in my two years there's no way we were going to lose to that little school. We always treated them like a little school."

Even during his NBA days, Blount never played in a game that matched what he felt in the Shootout. The NBA playoffs are ultra-competitive, but during the course of an 82-game season, NBA teams play each other on multiple occasions. The Shootout is one game every year, winner take all (although the two rivals did play twice a year from 1948 to 1958).

"The thing about the NBA is that on some nights it's just like a regular game,"

Blount said. "You're just showing up to kind of do your job. I guess that's the best way to put it. Of course you're ready to play, but you're not really feeling it from the crowd or feeling it from any individuals in the arena. It's just another game. Every now and then you'd get the New York Knicks rivalry with the Bulls or playing against Miami or something like that. But when it came to that Shootout, I thought the city did a really good job of promoting it, making it like, wow, this is for the city of Cincinnati. It was everywhere. In the city it was pumped up pretty good."

More than 30 years later, Blount is still proud of his 2-0 record against Xavier.

"Whenever we all get together, I'm like ya'll can say what you want, but I ain't never lost to Xavier," he said. "That usually keeps them quiet when they come and try to talk trash to me. We knew those guys. We were pretty much friends with those guys. It was always a talking-shit fest."

But he admits he has a hard time dealing with Xavier's recent success against UC.

"It makes me sick to my stomach," he said. "I have to be honest with you, man, I hate it because I always viewed that game pretty much as who had control of the city. I've got friends who went to Xavier, that played at Xavier, so now all year round I get to listen to 'Man, we whupped your ass this year,' again, again, again. Me and (former XU player) Leroy Greenidge, we've got this little thing going where he would wear my jersey and I would wear his jersey, depending on who lost. I've been avoiding him."

UC All-American Danny Fortson scored 40 points and pulled down 17 rebounds against Xavier in UC's win over the Musketeers during the 1995-'96 season.

DANNY FORTSON

1994-'97

"I had the hot hand that day."

The basket seemed so wide, so inviting, that after he made his first couple of shots, Danny Fortson knew he was going to have a big night.

"You kind of know that feel," Fortson said. "I felt like I was playing for my Pittsburgh AAU team."

Fortson twice scored 60 points or more in AAU competition, but this was a much bigger stage. Now he was scoring almost at will for UC, one of the top programs in college basketball, and he was doing it against Xavier, the Bearcats' crosstown rival. As a 6-foot-7, 260-pound forward, Fortson's strength was scoring around the basket. He rarely shot from 3-point range, but on this night he launched a shot from long range. It didn't go in, but it didn't matter to him.

"That's how good I felt," Fortson said, "that I would shoot a 3-pointer. That should tell you something."

Fortson finished with 40 points and secured 17 rebounds in third-ranked UC's 99-90 victory over the Musketeers at Cincinnati Gardens during his sophomore year on Jan. 17, 1996.

Later that season, Fortson made his first Associated Press All-American team. He was a second-team selection as a sophomore and a first-team selection the following year as a junior. After his junior year, he left UC for the NBA, where he was the 10th overall pick by the Milwaukee Bucks. He played 10 seasons in the NBA for five different teams, ranks fifth on UC's career scoring list with 1,881 points, and averaged 18.8 points during his UC career. Only Oscar Robertson, Ron Bonham and Lloyd Batts averaged more.

Fortson's first points on that memorable night came 41 seconds into the game when he connected on a short jump shot off an assist from Damon Flint. He played 38 minutes and made 14 of his 22 field goal attempts. He was 0-for-1 from 3-point range and 12 of 17 from the free throw line. He committed one turnover with no assists and committed four fouls.

"You're so focused on beating Xavier, you're not really worried about what you're doing personally," Fortson said. "They won't go away. You try to stomp them out and they keep coming back. But I would probably have to say that late in the game I looked up and I thought, I'm doing pretty well. That's when I realized. When you get 30 points, you know you've got 30 points. I felt like I was having a real good game and also I felt like I was doing my job as far as rebounding.

"I remember getting double-teamed. But there's a solution for that with (Bob Huggins). He got crafty and he had me going off a couple of double-screens, and by the time I got to the block the ball was already coming to me so they didn't really have a chance to double-team me like they wanted to. I credit a lot of that to him. He put me in the right position during that game. With Huggs, it's whoever gets the hot hand. He gives everybody an opportunity. Any coach would do that. If you see somebody's got the hot hand, you're going to ride it out. Huggs wants to win. He doesn't care who scores or how it happens as long as you win at the end of the day. I had the hot hand that day."

In all his years in basketball, including his time in the NBA, Fortson said he was never part of anything like the Crosstown Shootout.

"I don't think there's any city in the country that has anything even close to a rivalry with two teams in one city like Xavier and Cincinnati," he said. "It was almost like it was an NCAA Tournament championship game. It was like a Super Bowl. I had never played in anything like that. Maybe a high school state championship, but that wasn't even anywhere near the intensity level of when you played Xavier, no matter how good you thought you were.

"Back in those days, I didn't ever get cold feet and I remember getting a little nervous before the game. I always thought when we played we had a better team than Xavier for those years. It didn't matter who was playing for Xavier, it could be the last player off the bench, and he would come in and hit a 3-pointer. Simple as that. Weird stuff happens when you play them.

"Most of the guys weren't from Cincinnati and at first we didn't take (the rivalry) serious. But then we could see Coach Huggins getting nervous. And he never gets nervous. He'd start to get antsy and yelling at everybody right before that game. We didn't understand it and we didn't take it serious until you get out there on that court and it hit you. You'd see exactly why he was nervous. We knew also if you lost that game there was going to be hell to pay. Somebody was going to pay the price."

Fortson, who lives in the Cincinnati suburb of Glendale, says he doesn't think much these days about his 40-point game against Xavier. In fact, he says, not many people in Glendale know who he is.

"Whenever somebody brings it up, I'll sit back and say, 'What the hell happened?'" Fortson said. "But that was three lifetimes since then, it seems like. You sit there and you say to yourself, 'Yeah, I guess I used to be able get up and down the court and do a lot of different things that a young man would.' Every now and then I get a comment about it from a Xavier fan or a UC fan, which I appreciate very much."

The Xavier game that Fortson remembers even more than his 40-point outburst, although not nearly as fondly, occurred 10 months later on Nov. 26 at UC's Shoemaker Center. The Bearcats were the No. 1-ranked team in the country. Xavier was unranked. UC had won two in a row over Xavier, five of the last seven, and was a 17-1/2 point favorite. But the Musketeers took down the mighty Bearcats, 71-69, on Lenny Brown's shot over Darnell Burton near the foul line as time expired.

"When we lost that game, it put a hole in our confidence level," Fortson said. "We were pretty cocky and arrogant going in and Xavier humbled us. I don't think we could ever recover as a team from that loss because we had the ultimate team, we thought. You lose to the crosstown rival that's not even ranked on your home court nevertheless. We never got a chance to really jell. It just hit us hard. That was a bad loss. If that game had been in the middle of the year, it would have ended differently, but since it was at the beginning of the year, we had new guys like Ruben Patterson. They didn't really understand the rivalry. Our point guard was Charles Williams. He was from Los Angeles. He knew nothing about it. So the guys didn't come with the intensity level that Xavier came with that day."

UC had a two-point lead with 6.7 seconds left when Xavier's James Posey got loose for a layup to tie the score at 69-69. After a timeout, Williams lost the ball out of bounds with 5.4 seconds to play, setting up the final possession for Xavier. Fortson had fouled out and was watching from the bench.

"I saw that nightmare coming," he said. "Lenny Brown, he was a street baller. He was a hell of a player and I know he's done that a million times up there in the projects in Delaware. I saw the killer instinct in his eye, dribbling around. I said, 'This guy's gonna make it.' I knew it. I said, 'He's going to drain this.' Sure enough, damn, I looked at the ball up in the air, and I said, 'That's going in.' It went right in. Swish. And you know what the worst part of that was? I knew the next day at practice was going to be hell.

"Me and Bobby Brannen, my roommate, we didn't even sleep that night because we were scared that we were going to oversleep and not make practice. Huggs made us practice at 5 in the morning or 6 in the morning. He was livid. I don't think he left the office at Shoemaker that night. He stayed there overnight watching film. That's a bad day. That's never good. And you were warned about that beforehand, too, from the older guys."

Fortson, who was 2-1 against Xavier, still watches the game on television occasionally, but not as much as he used to now that Xavier has gained the upper hand.

"Xavier has been beating us pretty good," he said. "It's not a rivalry after awhile when you never win. It's still intense, though. It's not like Xavier runs all over us. We still give them a fight.

"Huggs used to tell us, not to mean any disrespect to Xavier, because I definitely respect the program, but when I was getting recruited here, the saying was that we have Cincinnati on the name of our chest for a reason. Our attitude was we were the only school representing Cincinnati because we've got the city's name on our chest.

"We played against them in the summer time. We never had any problem. We'd see them out every now and then. Jeff Ruby used to have a place called the Waterfront. We'd see them over there. But we always knew when we played them out there on that court when it counts, it's going to be serious because they've got a lot of pride. Of course, they're not going to let us just walk all over them. I definitely respected those guys."

CHARLES WILLIAMS
1996-'97

"I felt my stomach drop."

As the 1996-'97 season began, the UC Bearcats believed they had the ingredients to win a national championship. Danny Fortson returned from the 1995-'96 team that lost in the regional final to Mississippi State, along with guards Damon Flint and Darnell Burton.

UC added junior college All-American Ruben Patterson to that mix, along with Williams, another juco transfer who was recruited to play point guard in place of the departed Keith LeGree. With two future NBA players – Fortson and Patterson – along with one of the best 3-point shooters in the country in Burton, the Bearcats were picked as the pre-season No. 1 team in the country by Sports Illustrated, which featured on its cover a picture of Fortson – with a road map to Indianapolis, the site of the Final Four – superimposed on his bare chest.

Williams, from Chaffey (Calif.) College, was being counted on to make it all work. He made his first start in the second game of the season against Xavier in the Crosstown Shootout at Shoemaker Center. He was bringing the ball up the court with the score tied, looking to set up what the Bearcats hoped would be the game-winning shot.

"I remember Coach (Bob) Huggins specifically talking to me about how he wanted the ball to be in my hands at the end of the game," Williams said. "I was supposed to just bring the ball up and get us into our set. I'm pretty sure it was designed for me to make a play, either drive and score, or drive and kick it out to one of our shooters. We had Darnell Burton and Damon Flint on the floor."

The ball never reached either Burton or Flint because Williams bounced it off his foot and out of bounds, giving possession to Xavier with 5.4 seconds to play. Brown then buried the game-winning shot as time expired.

"I got a little excited," Williams said. "Instead of keeping my composure I decided to race up the floor, which I hadn't done all day. There actually wasn't that much ball pressure when I caught the ball. I rushed for no reason. I felt myself losing control when it went off my foot. My stomach dropped."

Williams said he wasn't as worried about the immediate reaction from the crowd at The Shoe as he was about his friends' reaction back home in L.A.

> **I've always put a lot of pressure on myself to run the point guard position a certain way and I teach it the same way. I don't like my point guard to pass the blame.**

"People look at basketball different (on the West Coast)," he said. "It's more of a business. We compete a different way. The guys I grew up with, it's all about doing it the right way. When I lost it, my first thought was, 'Damn, I'm on national TV and half of L.A. saw me lose the ball.' Sure enough, when I got back to my dorm, remember this was '96, I get back to my dorm and my pager was blowing up with all kinds of calls and my voice mail was full. I knew a lot of people from L.A. were watching and were disappointed. I was more worried about that than anything else."

Williams didn't hide from reporters after the game. He answered every question and accepted the blame. If he had committed a turnover in a similar situation today, he might not have had to answer a single question because most schools close their locker room to the media after games and make available only the players they choose. But Williams believed that accepting responsibility was part of a point guard's job and he willingly accepted it.

"I've always put a lot of pressure on myself to run the point guard position a certain way and I teach it the same way," he said. "I don't like my point guard to pass the blame. If you have the ball in your hands, you need to be a man about it and accept responsibility of being the best player on the floor, the leader on the floor, running the offense the way it's supposed to be run."

Until the turnover, Williams had played well in his first start. He scored 10 points and committed only two turnovers against extreme pressure. He also made

*Charles Williams' turnover in the 1996-'97 game set up
the game-winning shot for Xavier's Lenny Brown.*

six of his eight free throws. Until that memorable turnover he had done everything that was expected of him, but of course that's not what he's remembered for.

"I had a decent game, but it doesn't matter what I did before that," he said. "It's what you do at the end of the game."

Williams didn't sulk in his room after the game. He picked himself up and began to look forward to the next game, which was scheduled four days later against Rutgers.

"I'm pretty sure I went out that night and hung out with my buddies," Williams said. "I remember being out with D'Juan Baker and Kenyon Martin and a couple of other guys. We went out and talked. At that point, I don't think D'Juan was playing that much. We used to talk about what we need to do to get better and redeem ourselves."

But Williams never played another game against Xavier. His last game at UC was on Feb. 25 at Southern Miss. Before the Bearcats' game against Marquette on Feb. 27, problems were discovered with his junior college academic transcript and he was taken out of action while the school, and eventually the NCAA, investigated. It was later determined that UC had acted improperly during the previous summer by arranging for Williams to receive preferential treatment from a professor who had been enlisted to help Williams become eligible. As a result of that and several other transgressions, UC eventually went on NCAA probation. Williams left school and returned to the West Coast.

"I coached community college basketball on the West Coast for three or four years, got a chance to play (professionally) and make some money," he said. "Once my playing career was over and my community college was shutting down our basketball program, I was living in Vegas at the time. I wanted to continue what I was doing with basketball training.

"I came back here to Cincinnati thinking I would only be here a short time just to visit and here I am 12 years later now. I've never been one to run from anything. I wasn't going to run from where it didn't work out for me basketball-wise. I've made the most of my opportunities here in the city because of my opportunity at UC. It's worked out well, in my favor. I run a very good AAU program. I have a lot of kids that I work with. I work with some professional athletes. I can't complain."

Williams doesn't try to hide his infamous turnover. It's part of who he is and he uses it as a teaching tool.

"I talk to the team about my turnover," he said. "I don't talk to them about anything else (at UC). Some of my new players who come into my program will Google me and find out about my basketball experience, but I don't really talk about myself too much about anything from my basketball accomplishments. My whole purpose is to teach the kids and put the focus on them, not myself."

Williams, who lives in the Cincinnati suburb of Blue Ash, says he frequently comes into contact with people who remember him from his UC days.

"People don't talk to me about the turnover," he said. "They talk to me about UC basketball. They say that they liked the way I played or they miss the Coach Huggins era. There's nothing negative at all."

Williams has only recently begun to attend a UC game occasionally and he does that, he says, only because Terry Nelson reached out to him.

"If it wasn't for him, I wouldn't be associated with UC at all," Williams said. "I don't feel anything for UC other than watching the new guys get better, watching Mick with the guys. I don't feel bitter other than I wish the situation would have been handled differently at the end with the suspension. I still have never gotten the true story on a lot of different things that happened. You can't dwell on what's happened in the past. You've got to learn and move on."

Mel Levett ranks beating Xavier as his third most-cherished basketball memory, behind his dunk to knock off No. 1 Duke and his school-record 10 3-pointers in a 42-point performance against Eastern Kentucky.

MEL LEVETT
1995-'99

"This game is for real–for real."

As Danny Fortson personally wreaked havoc on Xavier with his 40-point, 17-rebound performance, Mel Levett had one of the best seats in the house. He was a freshman watching Fortson's dominant performance from the UC bench, having recently met the NCAA's academic requirements for freshman eligibility.

Levett, from Cleveland, played only a few minutes in UC's 99-90 win over the Musketeers at the Gardens, but he got a taste for what the rivalry was all about while he marveled at Fortson.

"I played with Dan in AAU," Levett said. "I had a chance to see his dominance and how big that guy was when he was still in high school. But then to see him two years after, to see how he grew even bigger, it was like you couldn't get around this guy. He had that turnaround soft jump shot. I couldn't believe a guy of his stature would play with such ferocity around the basket. Every shot would come off hard. Every move was a power move. Dan was just great at finessing and at the same time being able to muscle you.

"So watching him in that game and knowing what that game meant to UC, to see him have a big performance, that still stands as one of the biggest Crosstown Shootout games I ever played in. (At one point) he almost pulled the basket over. He got a two-hand dunk off the drop step and he pulled that basket and it wasn't really secure to the ground like it was supposed to be and that back end lifted up pretty good off the floor. He scored 40 and he was dominant but that dunk to me, I was like, uh-oh, that thing is going to fall."

Levett got on the floor late in the game when the Bearcats had the victory secured.

"When you're a freshman, you're too ornery to know what the moment is about," Levett said, "but I found out in those last couple of minutes when I got a chance to play that the intensity was still high. I remember very well getting chased down by little Pat Kelsey because he didn't want to give up that game-ending, high-flying punctuating dunk. I was looking for it. I got out on a little breakaway with a little under a minute left. He wasn't having it, man. He came out of nowhere and he kind of tackled me and we both fell into the basket support. He walked away and the crowd yelled a little bit. That's when I understood, okay, this game is for real–for real. You compete 'til the end. You don't want to see certain things happen that demoralize your team, so you stick your neck out there a little bit."

The Crosstown Shootout didn't always go so well for Levett and the Bearcats during his four years at UC. The following season, Levett's sophomore year, he watched mostly from the bench again, as Xavier took down top-ranked UC on Larry Brown's buzzer-beating jump shot.

"Everybody was rooting us on to really make a nice run that year and that game really threw us for a loop," Levett said. "Coming into that game, Huggs was his normal self around the time of that game, very irritable. He dealt with the media. He went to the crosstown luncheon. He's doing all these things, but he really hasn't had a chance to really get with us yet and really prepare us and we're in our mode of we were kind of feeling good about ourselves. You start to fall into what people are saying, the hoopla and things like that, and I think we got caught up in it a little bit. We prepared for the game, but I don't think we really dialed into the game. Huggs was like a prophet when it came to those type of things and he would tell us the day prior, two days prior, you're preparing to lose. It came to be true. We didn't go out and take care of the ball in that game.

"We didn't make a lot of shots either in that game. Darnell (Burton) and Damon (Flint) weren't hitting from the outside. (The guys on the bench) didn't play as much going into that game as I thought we would. A lot of us on the bench felt like maybe we could go in and stop what was happening or maybe change the atmosphere of the game. But we never really got the chance. I only played a minute to maybe 30 seconds. The bench was very short that game.

"Their guards were on fire. Gary Lumpkin was controlling the ball at the point guard position. They didn't get out of whack. Posey was doing his thing down low running the floor and making shots. They had a chance to win the game at the end and that's what you ask for as a player or a coach. Lenny Brown was in one of those moments that every athlete would love to be. For him to hit that shot in our place, us being as highly ranked as we were, and obviously to go down into Crosstown Shootout folklore forever, I know that guy is still basking a little bit in that glow whenever that question is asked about that game. That will live forever."

Levett's next Shootout was another disappointment. Not only did the Bearcats get blown out, 88-68, at the Gardens, they were physically dominated by the Musketeers.

"That game was rough," Levett said. "It really took a toll physically on me. Afterwards, my whole body just locked up on me, cramps everywhere. I remember spending an hour or two hours with (trainer) Jayd (Grossman). I couldn't take off my uniform. They put me in the shower with my shoes on. I'm standing there just trying to cool and relax. Physically, they ran us. I don't think we were in as great of shape as we should have been as a Bob Huggins-coached basketball team because it showed in our turnovers and ball-handling. They slapped the press on us.

> As a senior you feel like this is my time to leave a mark on the season, with my team in this rivalry. That game was ultimately personal.

"They were high-octane. People around the country, I think, were getting a dose of Xavier basketball at that point, too. I think they were really starting to come along in a lot of people's eyes. That press, with Darnell Williams and Posey...with Brown and Lumpkin they had five guys that could just play so fast...Darnell Williams played over the ball so well out of bounds. That guy was so active. If you watch any Xavier film from back then, him over the ball was just a monster. He followed the ball out of bounds wherever it went and he was so long and long-winded on top of it. That was the other thing about Darnell Williams, that guy could run for days. They got out on a good run on us and they didn't look back. They really poured it on us and we felt it tremendously. I felt it physically but again emotionally it was a bad loss for us."

At that point, Levett was 1-2 against Xavier and the last thing he wanted was to finish his career with a losing record against the Musketeers. He made sure that didn't happen with a 23-point performance to lead the Bearcats to an 87-77 victory his senior year.

"As a senior you feel like this is my time to leave a mark on the season, with my team in this rivalry," Levett said. "That game was ultimately personal. I think the junior year game was personal for them. I felt like knowing these guys and having the opportunity to play in this game the last several years that I could go out there and really let it all out. It was one of those atmospheres where you're feeling it. The crowd's into it. You've got a good sweat going. There are no goosebumps. You're just ready to go out and explode. Athletically I was able to go out and take advantage of Brown in a couple of situations. We didn't pull away until kind of late in that game with some good shots and again I was able to knock down a couple of shots.

"But the two rebounds at the end of the game are what I remember most. It was like volleyball being played on the rim and I'm kind of just watching and thinking to myself, when are you actually going to go jump and get the ball? Finally I just go and I grabbed the ball and it was probably the second highest I ever jumped in a UC uniform. I jumped a lot and I had done some really nice things but that first rebound was the second-highest I ever jumped. The second rebound was the first-highest I ever jumped. Those last two rebounds of that game to put that game away, it was one of those moments like, hey, give me this, this is mine. This game is over."

Levett had more than his share of special moments at UC. He finished his career with 1,119 points, tying him for 34th in UC history and his dunk with one second left gave the Bearcats a 77-75 victory over top-ranked Duke in the Great Alaska Shootout on Nov. 28, 1998. He ranks that as his top UC memory, followed by his school-record 10 3-pointers in 14 attempts to score a career-high 42 points in UC's 106-54 win on Dec. 20, 1997, over Eastern Kentucky, which he ranks 2A, and his 23-point game against Xavier, which is 2B.

But he will always be remembered by UC fans for his dunks, even though he developed into a fine shooter by his senior year and had more of an all-around game than his nickname, The Helicopter, would indicate.

"I got that name from one of my AAU coaches in the eighth grade," Levett said. "I was really starting to jump at that point, starting to get really strong with it. We got a fast break and I cocked it and windmilled it. I remember the look of astonishment on everybody's face. I was kind of surprised myself like, wow, I really got it all the way around and did that.

"Everything was just kind of in a blur for a second. I remember my coach (assistant coach Tom Erzen), he was pointing at me as I was running down the court, going, 'You're no longer Melvin, you are now The Helicopter,' and it caught on from there. When I got down here to UC it kept growing with the folks here.

"My thing about it is, man, if they give you a nickname they obviously like you. I went from the Helicopter to Levettation, the Melivator, to the Grim Leaper. That was all the fans, man. I'm appreciative for that because that's what made Melvin Levett's name still stick out for some people. Coming out of high school, dunking was my forte. Dominique Wilkins was my favorite athlete at that point. I patterned my game a little bit after him."

It's no surprise, then, that when Levett caught a pass from Kenyon Martin and began to drive to the basket for the game-winning shot against Duke he knew exactly what he was going to do with the ball.

"It was just a matter of how hard I was gonna dunk it," he said.

Levett, who teaches language arts in the Winton Woods school district, hopes to get back into coaching after a brief stint as the head coach at Colerain High School. He loved everything about the Crosstown Shootout. He relished the competition with the Xavier players during the summer, enjoyed seeing them around town, and appreciated the respect the players had for each other and still do. He fed off the electricity generated by the fans and he took full advantage of his last chance to come up big his senior year after the Bearcats were so soundly beaten during his junior year.

"You go down with some of the greatest players at both universities that have ever played in that game," Levett said. "To be named with a few of those guys and to be able to win a couple of those match-ups, to see some of the dramatics that took place, to see still how big it is today, to be able to walk around the city and have somebody mention something from the Shootout or just mention UC basketball, and they know you from that rivalry, it's special to have your name submitted to that."

Kenyon Martin was the National Player of the Year in 2000 and the first player selected in the NBA draft, but he won only once in four tries against Xavier.

KENYON MARTIN

1996-2000

"You learn to dislike them."

*F*ans never saw the best games between UC and Xavier, according to Kenyon Martin, because they were played during the summer with no fans around, no media, and best of all, no officials.

"Us going over there playing pickup ball and them coming over to us playing pickup ball, those games were a lot better than what everybody saw," Martin said. "We talked shit. There were no rules. There were no media there to make sure it didn't get out of control or to make sure there were no fights. We never got in a fight, but those games were a lot better in the summertime because there ain't no rules. There were fouls and all that stuff, but it ain't the NCAA environment. If you call a foul, go and take the ball out. I'll foul you as hard as I want to."

It's understandable that Martin prefers to remember the pickup games rather than the real games because he was 1-3 against the Musketeers, 1-2 in the games in which he actually played.

The 6-foot-9, 230-pound center was the National Player of the Year in 2000 and the first player taken in the NBA draft that summer. His No. 4 is one of three retired numbers in UC history along with Oscar Robertson's No. 12 and and Jack Twyman's No. 27. Robertson and Twyman are both members of the Naismith Memorial Basketball Hall of Fame.

Led by Martin, the Bearcats were ranked No. 1 in the country for most of his senior year. But their quest for a national championship was derailed by a broken leg that Martin suffered in UC's first game of the Conference USA tournament in Memphis against Saint Louis, ending his college career. He averaged 18.9 points, 9.7

rebounds and blocked 107 shots, then a school record, during his final season at UC.

Martin didn't play in the Shootout during his freshman year because the Xavier game was scheduled in November at a time when Martin was still struggling to achieve the test scores he needed to be eligible. He watched as the Bearcats, who were also ranked No. 1 that season, fell to Xavier at Fifth Third Arena.

Before that game, he didn't know much about the Shootout or what it meant to the fans of both schools.

"I didn't have an idea until the game actually started and then losing against them," Martin said. "It was a big deal about us losing to them of all schools. Then after that you start to realize the intensity of it, the rivalry every year. Everybody starts gearing up for it in the city."

Martin's first few months at UC were so difficult that he flew back home to Dallas a few weeks after he arrived with no intention of returning.

"I was in Cincinnati two weeks after I graduated," Martin said. "I hadn't been away from home for that long without going back. Then the team went to Europe on a tour, but I couldn't go because I was ineligible. I was the only one in Cincinnati. I had nobody to talk to, nobody to be around, so I picked up and went home. Then (Bob Huggins) came back from Europe and he was looking for me. He called my mom and my sister and asked them if I was in Dallas and they said I was. He told them there's a plane waiting for him at the airport and they told him he's on his way."

What changed his mind?

"Huggs," Martin said. "He wasn't asking me to come back. He told me get my ass on the plane. My mom and my sister, especially my sister, they were a big influence on my life. They let me know what the situation was, the magnitude of it. Being able to go to school for free and play Division I basketball outweighed the fact that I was homesick. If I wouldn't have went back I don't know what the path would have been from there. It was definitely the right decision.

(Huggins) wasn't hard on me (after I went back). He understood I was homesick. I wasn't the first person to get homesick."

But even after he returned to Cincinnati, Martin still had to pass the test or he would have to sit out the entire season. He finally got the news that he passed on Dec. 30, 1996 on his 19th birthday. The Bearcats were in Puerto Rico at the time playing in a holiday tournament.

"I was elated," Martin said. "I was taking the SAT over and over and over and over and not having a chance in hell of passing it, so they presented me with the ACT. I took it twice. They combined my scores and I did it. I didn't have goals of making it to the NBA or being the No. 1 pick. None of that existed in my life, man. I was fortunate enough to be athletic enough to get a Division I scholarship.

"I played hard. I had that, so all I had to do was be coached on basketball, on schemes and positioning, playing the game the right way. I didn't know what to expect. I'm being blatantly honest. I was along for the ride. I was blessed to get a scholarship, very blessed and fortunate, so anything after that, I didn't have a clue. I wasn't a McDonald's All-American."

Martin fouled out in his first Shootout on Dec. 13, 1997. He played only 15 minutes and scored two points with four rebounds. The Bearcats lost to the Musketeers, 88-68, at the Gardens.

"It was taking some guys some time to get used to being in that kind of situation," Martin said. "But you know those rivalries can go either way. It can be a close game or it can go the total opposite. My first two years unfortunately it went the other way."

Martin recorded his only win against Xavier in his junior year, 87-77, at Shoemaker Center. He scored eight points with eight rebounds and blocked six shots. But he still says he could have done more.

"I was happy with the win," Martin said, "but as far as my personal play, I thought I could have done more even though we won. I'm glad that we won, of course. I hate to lose and I'm all about winning, but I could have done better that game. I remember not being satisfied with my overall play."

The worst of his four games against Xavier came during his senior year in 1999-'00. Again the Bearcats were ranked No. 1 and again they were upset by the Musketeers. It was a bitter pill for him to swallow.

"Me and Huggs got into it on the bench," Martin said. "They were pressing us and our guards couldn't get the ball up the court. He was yelling at me, telling me to go get the ball. I told him that ain't my position. I didn't recruit these guys that can't get the ball up the court. We were just going back and forth. He walked off. I told him to put me back in the game. He looked back at me and put me back in the game. He understood the situation. I told him the honest to God truth.

"We had three freshmen on our team that we depended on and they didn't meet the intensity. You've got to be as a whole to beat them, to be in that kind of environment. You need everybody. We had freshmen that we really depended on to give us playing time and scoring. I think the intensity of the game got to them

"They had beaten us twice. I was 1-2 against them, so I was thinking I could leave 50-50. For that not to come into fruition, I was like, now I got to deal with this, now we got to hear this around the city. If you keep losing, it only makes it worse, but we bounced back. That was the important thing. Had we not bounced back after that Xavier game it would have been bad, but we bounced back as a unit.

"We thought we were more talented than they were. We thought we were the better team, but the better team, the more talented team, don't always win. And they proved that. That one hurt. I went home. I went to my apartment and wasn't seen.

I didn't have much to say. I probably was obligated (to talk to reporters) but I didn't have much to say. I had a few (disappointing) things while I was at Cincinnati, never beating Temple, that's one of them. That eats at me. We played them three or four times and never beat them. That irks me bad. And then of course the conference tournament, that goes without being said. Everybody knows the devastation of that."

Martin said he never placed more emphasis on the Xavier game than any other game.

"I don't get up for certain opponents," he said. "I get up for everybody. That's what made me who I am. I treat everybody the same. Win, lose or draw, if we're gonna play, I'm gonna battle. Whether you're ranked or not ranked, I want to embarrass you."

As he looks back now, he takes pride in being part of the Crosstown Shootout, just as he takes pride in his 15-year NBA career, especially when he considers where he came from.

"It's movie-worthy, it's book-worthy," he said. "If people look at the way I grew up and my mentality about basketball and not ever dreaming about being in the NBA and not being eligible right away, not being a McDonald's All-American, having to sit out, not starting his freshman year, averaging three points, shooting 35 percent (actually 31.3) from the free throw line and to be the consensus National Player of the Year, c'mon man.

"I came from poverty, inner-city poverty. We never had a car growing up. We had to catch a city bus to go to the grocery store, at times not having electricity in the house, having to use the neighbors' electricity with an extension cord, things like that, being homeless at times, real-life situations, man. In my childhood, I saw my father once when I was nine or 10 years old. I think I turned out all right, man, I turned out pretty good. I have values and I stand for something. I think my mom and my sister did an excellent job of helping me become the man that I am and trusting Huggs with their brother and their son and him doing right by me. I can't ask for much more."

With that type of background, a 1-3 record against Xavier, while being bothersome, is not something to get too worked up about.

"I didn't like the Xavier guys," he said, "because of the rivalry we had with them. You learn to dislike them. I had never had that. I learned to really dislike somebody you don't know. I liked the fact that the fans really buy into it. Most of the people that are from Cincinnati have ties to either university or both. There's families divided during that time, people at work are divided. I like that part of it. You get to talk noise to your neighbor or your co-worker and everybody gets together to watch the game."

STEVE LOGAN
1998-2002

"A milestone moment for me."

One of the most humiliating experiences in Steve Logan's UC career occurred during the Crosstown Shootout. But it turned out to be a moment that helped catapult him to first-team All-American status his senior year.

It happened at Shoemaker Center during Logan's junior year in 2000-'01. The 17th-ranked Bearcats led by 15 points in the first half and seemed well on their way to a victory over their crosstown rivals, but the Musketeer, behind 23 points and 13 rebounds from David West, came back to trail by only one, 67-66, with 32.2 seconds left. That's when Lloyd Price stole the ball from Logan and made a layup to put the Musketeers ahead, 68-67, in what became a 69-67 Xavier win.

"It was a milestone moment for me," Logan said. "After (Price) ripped the ball away from me and laid it up, my game personally took a turn for the best. Once again, the rivalry was high. We just lost to Xavier, so we didn't want to lose two years in a row. We prepared well, we made some mistakes, but you've got to give Xavier a lot of credit. They came over there ready to play. We played a good game, but at the end of the game I made a crucial mistake. It was a national TV game, an embarrassing moment for me. After that play, I turned into a different player for the best."

Logan, who scored eight points in the game, said he had been warned about Price.

"We studied their players," he said. "Coach (Bob) Huggins was great at breaking down film and dissecting players' advantages and weaknesses. Lloyd Price, he had some long arms and he was very active. We knew we couldn't play with the ball around him, that it would be hard crossing (with the dribble) because his arms were so long. I made a mistake crossing the ball over in front of him to try to get by him and that led to the layup. The rest of it is history.

"A lot of things were going through my mind. First of all, we just lost to Xavier two years in a row. Second, it was because of me. All the way up to that game I had been really struggling, having a mediocre year.

"Bob Huggins chewed me out, but at the same time he directed me on how I was supposed to play. He was down on me a little bit and I understood why. Me and Coach Huggins had a lot of moments where we disagreed, but actually at this point in my career, being a junior and hearing what he had to say, I agreed with him. Even though he chewed me out, I understood where he was coming from. I don't remember the exact words, but some of the words weren't pleasant. Coach got his point across."

In the Bearcats' next game, at UNLV, Logan scored 22 points. He made nine of 14 shots from the field, four of six from 3-point range, in UC's 90-72 victory.

"I was on fire," he said. "He started me that next game, which actually boosted my confidence. He still trusted me even though I made a crucial mistake against Xavier and we lost our biggest rival game."

Logan, a 6-foot guard, went on to average 17.6 points that season and was named Conference USA Player of the Year. The following season, he averaged 22.0 points with 5.3 assists, was named C-USA Player of the Year for the second straight season and became an Associated Press first-team All-American.

Perhaps it's a stretch to say that Logan wouldn't have achieved any of that if he hadn't been so motivated by the mistake he made against Xavier. But he really believes that turnover was the turning point in his career.

"I didn't want to lose the game and get the ball stolen from me," Logan said, "but I used that to put fuel on the fire for me to go out there and just play how I know how to play and excel after that moment. I had a great year. I didn't look back after that game."

Logan was a product of the Cleveland playgrounds who was signed by Huggins even though the UC coach had reservations about him. Not only was Logan small, he had a tendency to gain weight and Huggins sometimes referred to him as a "fat kid" during his first two years with the Bearcats.

But thanks to some prodding by then-UC assistant coach Cronin, Huggins decided to take a chance on Logan. He responded by scoring 1,985 points during his four-year career, leaving him second on UC's career scoring list behind Robertson. Sean Kilpatrick, another UC first-team All-American, surpassed him in 2014 with 2,145 points, bumping Logan to No. 3.

*All-American guard Steve Logan says a turnover he
committed against Xavier turned his game around.*

Logan's first brush with the Crosstown Shootout occurred during the summer before his freshman year.

"I remember it like it was yesterday," he said. "We had an open gym at Cincinnati. At the time, Lenny Brown, Gary Lumpkin, (James) Posey and those guys were at Xavier. They brought five or six guys over to play in open gym. Those guys were diving on the floor, yelling and screaming. I never seen guys diving on the floor at open gym. It just was unbelievable. That's how much it meant to them. That's how I realized how big that game was.

"I loved it because it's something that I came from. I grew up playing ball on the playground, man. If you lose a game early in the morning at the playground you might not get back on for a couple of hours. That brought that same similarity to what I came from, the hard work, bustin' your butt, playing hard. We had Kenyon Martin, Pete Mickeal, Ryan Fletcher, Michael Horton. We played all day. There was a couple of fights, but there wasn't nothing crazy where we wouldn't play again. That's what was exciting about it."

Logan's UC teams went 2-2 against the Musketeers. The Bearcats beat Xavier, 87-77, during his freshman year, then lost 66-64 his sophomore year when the Bearcats were ranked No. 1 in the country.

"That's how big that rivalry is," Logan said. "They didn't care that we were No. 1. They weren't going to just lay down. They played us better than anybody all year. That was at the old Gardens. The crowd was right on you. It was a tough atmosphere. Those guys came out full force and they would bring it. I realized what type of game you have to play to beat those guys. We had to play a perfect game and we didn't and we lost with the No. 1 player in the country (Kenyon Martin) at the time. (Xavier's) Kevin Frey hit some big shots. He played a hell of a game."

Logan saved his best Xavier game for last when he scored 22 points to lead the Bearcats to a 75-55 blowout over the Musketeers in his senior year.

"Experience kicked in for that game," Logan said. "We had an experienced team in terms of being in battles together. We were all on the same page. I was having an unbelievable year. We just came out there and took the game from them."

Logan, who lives in Cleveland, runs a non-profit organization called 'Logan's Elites,' which is designed to teach life skills and basketball to young men and women.

"It's an honor to play in the Xavier-Cincinnati rivalry," he said. "Both programs are very good programs, in academics and sportsmanship. It just means a lot to play in a game like that.

"Even though we don't get a lot of recognition for that game, that's one of the biggest rivalries in college basketball. Besides North Carolina and Duke, that Xavier and Cincinnati rivalry is in the top two or three by far."

LENNY STOKES

1999-2003

"My teeth started chattering."

The plan was for Leonard Stokes and Lionel Chalmers to play together in college. Stokes was from Buffalo; Chalmers from Albany. They had played together in the backcourt on their AAU team in New York state, became friends and were going to attend Providence to light up the Big East Conference.

"That was our dream," Stokes said.

But it didn't work out that way. Before he could commit to Providence, Stokes made an official recruiting visit to UC and was blown away by what he saw.

"When I came to UC, it was such a family environment, with the city, the fanfare, I had never seen anything like that," Stokes said. "I said, 'Wow, man this is eye-opening.' The UC fan base was unbelievable. Everywhere we went people knew who we were and I was (just) on a visit. It's not like I had done anything yet. It's still like that to this day. I played 13, 14 years ago and we still go places and everyone comes over. It's real unique. I tell my friends it's just so different here in Cincinnati, the level of respect and commitment from the blue-collar, everyday working individuals who love UC basketball.

"I told Lionel, I think I'm gonna go to UC. UC wasn't recruiting Lionel. They had respect for him as a player but (Kenny) Satterfield was on their radar. It just kind of broke up the dynamic. He said, 'That's fine,' and we just decided to go our separate ways."

But not as separate as they might have thought at the time. Both players ended up in Cincinnati after Chalmers signed with Xavier and both became 1,000-point scorers. Stokes finished with 1,318 points, which ranks 21st in UC history.

*Lenny Stokes says the Crosstown Shootout can
"make or break" a team for the rest of the season.*

They've remained friends – they both have a daughter named London – and kept in contact during their college careers, but not during the days leading up to the Crosstown Shootout.

"His parents would come to town (for the Shootout)," Stokes said, "and they'd say, 'Hey, Lenny, let's go to dinner.' I'd say, 'Listen, I don't want to hear from you guys until after that final buzzer when we beat Xavier.' That was the message, but there wasn't any malice. The game would be over and me and Lionel's parents, we'd joke and talk about the game. We were best friends other than the week of the Crosstown Shootout until that final buzzer went off."

Stokes' first Shootout was on Dec. 18, 1999 at Cincinnati Gardens.

"We're No. 1 in the country with Kenyon (Martin), Pete Mickeal, (Ryan) Fletcher, Jermaine Tate, all of those guys, and you've got me, Kenny Satterfield and DerMarr Johnson. We're all freshmen and played at high levels in high school and Huggins is telling us this is the most important game you're gonna be involved in and this is a rivalry.

"We're kids at that point so we're all looking at each other when we get back to the dorm, like what is he talking about? We played in front of 10,000 people in high school so this can't be much different. We just didn't know. When we got to the game, Cincinnati Gardens was the loudest place I ever played in in my life, louder than the Shoe. The ceilings were lower. There was a more intimate crowd on top of you. That was one of the only times we used signs to call the plays because it was that loud.

> ❝
> **I was nervous. I couldn't hear anyone. We were yelling in each other's ears and you still could barely hear at certain peaks of that game.**
> ❞

"My teeth started chattering. I was nervous. I couldn't hear anyone. We were yelling in each other's ears and you still could barely hear at certain peaks of that game. I played for a couple of minutes, but I remember coach (Rod) Baker coming to the end of the bench and saying, 'As soon as this game is over, run to the locker room.' Everyone stormed the court. After that experience, you know what the game is like. That is when you learn the history, when you get spanked and you're like, these guys beat up on us and it was a big deal. Then you understand how to approach it, to take the game seriously."

The Bearcats lost their No. 1 ranking after that game, but then reeled off 16 wins in a row. They reclaimed the top spot after beating Tulane on January 12.

"I think that loss (to Xavier) kind of woke us up halfway through the year that we can be beaten," Stokes said. "I think that rejuvenated us for the second half of the year. We lost to Temple (on Feb. 20) at home, but that Xavier loss let us know, hey, you guys aren't invincible, and we kind of locked in and got a little more focused after that game."

UC finished that season with a 29-4 record and lost only two more games the rest of the way. The first was in the Conference USA tournament in Memphis when Martin, the national player of the year, broke his left leg. The Bearcats' last game of the season was a 69-61 loss to Tulsa in the second round of the NCAA Tournament.

But they got revenge in 2001-'02 when they rolled past the Musketeers, 75-55, in the first Shootout played at Cintas Center. UC out-rebounded Xavier by 20. It was Stokes' only win in four games against Xavier.

UC had lost its season opener to Oklahoma State, but by the time the Xavier game came around on Dec. 14, the Bearcats had won six in a row. At the time, neither team was ranked, although UC would be ranked as high as No. 4 as the season progressed.

"We beat up on Xavier pretty bad in that one," said Stokes, who scored 15 points. "Everyone was expecting that game to be a battle, but we won that game big-time. We knew we had lost to them two years in a row. We had veterans on that team. We had a year to mature and we just said to ourselves, 'We're not gonna lose this game.' We went in with that mindset. We locked in and we were on a hot streak as a team. That year that was the farthest I went in the NCAA tournament. We went to the Sweet 16."

The Bearcats lost to Xavier, 50-44, during Stokes' senior year. Before that game, UC forward Jason Maxiell told reporters he thought Xavier's David West was soft. West responded by dominating UC with 23 points.

"I think David West took that game personally," Stokes said. "Before the game they lined us up to sing the anthem and when we all were going to shake hands, David West just ran to other locker room, so I knew he was kind of focused and locked in on that game. That was bulletin board material when Maxiell said that. You see that with the young guys. They have words that they shouldn't say at times. I played against him for three years and I never thought that David West was soft. I knew he was a load."

Stokes learned during his four years at UC that the Shootout was important not merely for bragging rights, but because it could have a profound impact on the rest of your season.

"When you lose to Xavier," he said, "those losses either propel you or they'll suppress you. The teams that I've been on, it always pushed us, it always motivated us. We would say, 'Let's get refocused, let's get readjusted and let's push.' As players, we always had respect for those guys – David West, Romain Sato, Lionel Chalmers, Lloyd Price – all of those guys were NBA-caliber guys. We all had mutual respect for each other and we all had respect as friends during the offseason."

Stokes lives in the Cincinnati suburb of Kenwood and is Chief Executive Officer of Smart Growth Construction. He was sitting behind the UC bench at Cintas Center when the fight erupted in 2011 and he was appalled by what he heard and saw during the game.

"I was sitting next to Whit Babcock, who was our AD when that happened," Stokes said. "Some of what those guys were yelling back and forth, I was like, wow, we would never do that to each other. We would compete and we would talk trash if a guy made a shot or you were knocking a guy down and he didn't score, but it was competitive more than enemies. It was a lot over the top.

"I don't think unless you live in Cincinnati you understand how big (the Crosstown Shootout) is. It makes or breaks teams at times. I don't think words can really drum up how big of a game it is. We're the University of Cincinnati so we've got Cincinnati across our chest. I think you've got a lot more people who take pride in that and I think Xavier was always viewed as more of a little brother just by attendance and national exposure. I think they took that game, I hate to use those terms, but I think in their eyes that game was their Super Bowl for years because we were always No. 1 and they were not viewed as that and they would come in and take that game a lot more seriously, a lot different than we did."

UC forward Eric Hicks, who grew up in North Carolina, was convinced that nothing compared to the Duke-North Carolina rivalry – until he played in the Crosstown Shootout.

ERIC HICKS

2002-'06

"We thought we were gonna punish them."

*W*hen you grow up in North Carolina, as Eric Hicks did, there's one college basketball rivalry that trumps all others.

"I was more of a Duke-Carolina guy," Hicks said. "I'm from Greensboro. I'm used to that being the biggest rivalry, so when I actually came up here people were saying it's just like Duke-Carolina. I was just like, yeah, yeah, yeah. You've got to be in it one time and then you get a taste for it and the buildup for it. I tell people (from North Carolina) that they've got to come up here and see it and they'll see that it's on the same level. The only reason Duke-Carolina gets more publicity is because both of them are always Top 25. But the rivalry, in my opinion, is up there with it. I mean, the city shuts down and the winner gets to talk so much trash and that's what Duke-Carolina is."

Hicks, a 6-foot-6 forward who played at UC from 2002 through 2006, ranks second in school history with 256 career blocked shots and 28th on the career scoring list with 1,231 points. He was a first-team all-Big East Conference selection as a senior, but he was just 1-3 against Xavier.

"Man, that was tough," Hicks said. "My senior year, I played bad. My sophomore year, I really thought we had that one. That team, I thought that was a Final Four, national championship team because we were loaded at positions. Who's got two shooting guards like Tony Bobbitt and Field Williams? We made it to the NCAA Tournament but we underachieved. My second year I think I was running my mouth because our team was a lot better and then Lionel Chalmers turns around and hits a lucky shot (in a 71-69 Xavier win). We had a really good team – we went

226 * INSIDE THE CROSSTOWN SHOOTOUT

10 deep – we really just thought we were gonna punish them."

Hicks did punish the Musketeers in that game with 10 points, nine rebounds and eight blocked shots, but it wasn't enough.

Regardless of whether the game is played at UC's Fifth Third Arena or Xavier's Cintas Center, Hicks said, the crowd noise is overwhelming.

> **When you're in a crowd like that you don't really hear what people are saying. All you hear is (crowd noise). You really don't get to hear nobody say, 'Your mama's ugly.' You don't get to hear none of that.**

"When you're in a crowd like that you don't really hear what people are saying," Hicks said. "All you hear is (crowd noise). You really don't get to hear nobody say, 'Your mama's ugly.' You don't get to hear none of that. The coaches, when they draw up plays, literally have to yell. That was my first time experiencing that many people in that type of environment. Coaches can do all that yelling until they turn red but at the end of the day all I can do is look at them and shake my head. Yeah, yeah. I don't know what you just said."

The Bearcats finally broke through with a 65-54 victory in Hicks' junior year, with Hicks scoring 16 points and pulling down 14 rebounds.

"Me and (Jason Maxiell) were like, man, if we don't beat them this time, we're sorry," Hicks said. "We felt like we were the bigger, stronger, better team. If you look at it, we had more of an experienced team and we were dealing with a young Xavier team. We were looking at getting to the Sweet 16 or Elite Eight. Let's be honest, we had me, James (White), Armein (Kirkland), Jihad (Muhammad), Max, Roy Bright…if we can't beat them, we need to hang it up.

"That was (Keith) Jackson's last year (at Xavier). He was so pissed about that. Jackson told me the young guys came out scared on his team, but I just felt like we had their number. You know how some of those games you just know you're gonna win, well that was one of them. We controlled the game for the most part, the whole game."

But in Hicks' senior year, Xavier won again, 73-71, in overtime, in Andy Kennedy's season as UC's interim head coach, when White missed a 3-point shot at the buzzer that would have won the game for the Bearcats.

Hicks' fondest personal memory from the Shootout occurred "when Romain Sato tried to dunk on me and I blocked it. He was going to tear the rim down and I went and blocked it. We ended up losing the game, but that really felt good. He was a really good player, very athletic. I think they went up four and he was going to try to show off. I told him to get that shit outa here. That was my thing."

Since leaving UC, Hicks has played professionally in Belgium, Poland and Russia. And he has gotten to know some of the Xavier players much better than he did when they were playing against each other in the Shootout. There might be a little trash talking as the players re-live their glory days, he said, but there's no animosity.

"When you get older and more mature, it ain't like I'm still mad at you," Hicks said. "I'm an adult now. Those are special memories. I'll take those to my grave. To be a part of it, to play in it, a lot of people cannot say that."

Connor Barwin, a UC football player who joined the basketball team
when it was short-handed, played in 34 games over two seasons.

CONNOR BARWIN

Basketball, 2005-'07
Football, 2005-'08

"If Xavier had a football team, we'd whup their ass."

*C*onnor Barwin played four years of football at UC, three as a tight end, one as a defensive end. He was a first-team All-Big East Conference selection, led the league in sacks, and helped the Bearcats win a Big East championship that resulted in a trip to the Orange Bowl. He also played two years on the basketball team, which was short-handed in the aftermath of Huggins' firing.

But despite all of his athletic achievements at UC, Barwin-who now plays defensive end for the NFL's Philadelphia Eagles-says he's remembered most for a few words that he uttered at halftime of the Dec. 13, 2008 Crosstown Shootout at Fifth Third Arena. After football coach Brian Kelly addressed the sellout crowd during a ceremony honoring the football team, he handed the microphone to Barwin.

"If Xavier had a football team," Barwin shouted, "we'd whup their ass!"

He got the response from the crowd that he was hoping for when the UC fans roared with approval.

"From playing in (the Shootout) a couple of years, I guess I felt like I could say something like that," Barwin said. "I thought about it before I went out there, but I hadn't decided if I would say it or not. In the moment, I decided it would go over fine or it would be something that would get the crowd back in the game. If I remember, that game wasn't going too well."

It wasn't. The Bearcats trailed Xavier, 39-25, at the time. Barwin's fiery words didn't do much to improve the situation because UC ended up losing, 76-66, but the otherwise disappointed fans were able to walk away with a moment they would long remember.

By then Barwin's college basketball career was over. In two seasons, he played in 41 games, averaging just over 10 minutes per game and scoring a total of 45 points. His role was to play defense, rebound and give the starters on those undermanned teams a breather.

"I just tried to keep my guy from getting the ball and rebound as hard as a I could," Barwin said. "I usually played against a bigger guy and I tried to push him away from the basket."

The Crosstown Shootout, he said, "was by far the most intense rivalry I had ever played in up to that point. I would still say it's right up there as one of the most intense rivalries I ever played in."

> **"**
>
> **I'm sitting at the end of the bench thinking this is the greatest thing that ever happened to me. I'm sitting at courtside, it's Big East basketball, we're playing Syracuse.**
>
> **"**

Barwin always loved basketball and was a solid player at Jesuit High School in Detroit, but he had no intention of playing basketball when he arrived at UC. Just before he began his freshman year on the Bearcats football team, though, Bob Huggins was fired. Before the 2005-'06 basketball season ended, interim head coach Andy Kennedy needed bodies. Barwin ended up being one of those bodies.

"(Quarterbacks coach) Dan Enos recruited me to play at UC," Barwin said, "but I hadn't been given a scholarship yet. I was being recruited by MAC schools, no Big East schools, no BCS schools. (Head coach) Mark Dantonio said he wanted to come and see me play basketball. I probably had the best high school basketball game of my career. I think I had like 20-some points, I had a few dunks, I was making jump shots I usually don't make.

"Fast forward, I played football my freshman year. I believe there were one or two guys who decided not to come to UC because Huggins was fired. And then Armein Kirkland tears his ACL against Connecticut (in January). I'm at home and I believe one of the football coaches called me and asked me if I wanted to play (basketball). Or maybe Andy Kennedy called me, and I was like, of course. I actually had hernia surgery a couple weeks earlier. I guess Andy Kennedy had called Mark Dantonio and said we just need a couple of bodies to get through practice. We've only got like eight guys."

Dantonio gave Kennedy two possibilities-Barwin and linebacker Angelo Craig-who also joined the team, but didn't see the amount of playing time that Barwin did.

"I just connected right away with Corie Blount," Barwin said. "Andy Kennedy told me to go out and shoot around a little bit with Corie. I think Corie went back to AK and said you can tell he's played basketball a lot. Three days later, Andy Kennedy threw me into the Syracuse game.

"I'll never forget. I'm sitting at the end of the bench thinking this is the greatest thing that ever happened to me. I'm sitting at courtside, it's Big East basketball, we're playing Syracuse. Andy Kennedy walks over with a big-ass grin on his face and says, 'Are you ready to go?' In all my sporting life, I was never more nervous as when I walked to the scoring table to check myself in. I didn't even know if I was going to the right spot. I had no idea. Then 30 seconds into when I get in, there's a loose ball and I dive on the court and the crowd started cheering and we're in the bonus so I get to go shoot a free throw and I'm just as nervous as I've ever been."

Barwin missed the free throw but made two of them later in the game. He finished with two points, one rebound and one steal in eight minutes. That was on Jan. 14, 2006. Five days later, he got his first taste of the Shootout at Cintas Center, where the Bearcats lost, 73-71, in overtime.

"The first year Andy Kennedy kind of said, 'Okay, we've got the Crosstown Shootout coming up,'" Barwin said. "He didn't have to say much. You could just see the intensity from that kind of senior-dominated team leading up to that game. It was an unbelievable game. I think I played a little bit and got a couple of rebounds. We ended up losing though. Eric Hicks was not happy to have lost that game his senior year. The next morning we had a shoot-around and Eric isn't there yet. People are kind of getting nervous about what's going on. And Andy Kennedy grabs a couple of guys and says Eric's calling a team meeting in the locker room. Eric was still in his street clothes from the night before and he absolutely lit into a number of guys. I had never seen somebody take a loss as bad.

"Eric was a good player and extremely passionate. He played with his emotions on his sleeve. People had to physically hold him back. I was in the corner as a freshman just taking this all in. I was like, holy shit, is this what college basketball is all about? I never saw anything like that ever again. I realized how intense this rivalry was."

He got another indication a year later when Mick Cronin prepared for his first

Shootout as the Bearcats' head coach. UC had just beaten Temple and Xavier was next up on the schedule.

"As soon as we got in the locker room, Mick didn't even mention anything about the (Temple) game," Barwin said. "He couldn't have cared less about what just happened in the game that we just played. It was probably his finest moment when I played for him in that speech he gave us directly after the game before we played Xavier.

"He was so excited about preparing for that game, about the emotional connection he had for that game. He just went on and on about what it means, trying to explain to a crop of new guys that were on the team that year. I wish I could remember exactly what he said, but it was like a wild moment for me. He grabbed everybody's attention in that locker room."

Four days later, the Bearcats upset Xavier, 67-57. Barwin – who played six minutes, didn't take a shot and committed four fouls – says UC won because of Cronin.

"Without a doubt I think it was Mick," he said. "His words carried so much. And then in that rivalry it seemed like whoever was supposed to win, didn't win. We had no pressure on us at all. We went out there and won. I think Mick willed us to the victory that year. We obviously weren't as talented as them and they might have had a little bit of a letdown playing us because we were so bad that year.

"You always loved the kind of energy that was in that game," Barwin said. "You kind of felt the connection with the city and how important the game was. There's no professional basketball teams in the city, so it just resonates with everybody there. In Cincinnati, there's a lot of people who have lived there a long time so you have these lifers that are Xavier fans and there's lifers that are UC fans. How close the schools are, the reputations of the two schools and how they were kind of opposites a lot of years played a part in it – public and private school, that kind of stuff, and having so many people that are connected to that game. They've been watching it for 20 or 30 years and their dad used to watch it. I remember the kids from Cincy that played football for Cincinnati. Half of them were like, yeah, we go to Cincinnati, but our parents raised us to root for Xavier in the Crosstown Shootout. That helps you understand how deep-rooted this game was in people's families."

Barwin calls his two years on the UC basketball team "one of the most memorable experiences I've ever had playing sports."

The first year was special "because probably I shouldn't have been on that team. It was two great coaches (Kennedy and assistant coach Frank Martin) who knew they were getting fired and really didn't care and then there was this very talented senior-dominated team playing their first year in the Big East Conference. They were a bunch of great guys to play with and I'm an 18-year-old kid. ESPN thought we still had Huggins so we were on ESPN every night, playing all over the country. It was really unbelievable. Playing for Andy, it was just more fun for me. Andy loved me. Frank used to get on me a little bit, which I appreciated. Eric Hicks, all those guys, Chadd Moore, Jihad, they were all great older guys.

"(The following year) I remember having so much respect for Mick Cronin because I didn't know how he did it. I mean, we were not good, but he never let down for a second. If I ever go into coaching, I learned a lot from him that year because he was on us like he expected us to win every single night. I would sit there and watch everything and think, I don't know how he does this every night. He knows we're not very good. But he stayed on us every night. We were terrible, so it was hard, but it was a lesson for me. I learned a lot watching Mick and his intensity and how he got after it every single day."

Barwin didn't return to the basketball team after his sophomore year, but it wasn't because Kelly told him he couldn't.

"The third year, Mick's second year, he said to me, 'You know we don't necessarily need you now, I've got my recruits here, but if you still want to play you can still play,'" Barwin said. "Mick was very focused, and he should have been, on building his team and developing his players. Looking back on it, I kind of wish I would have played that third year just because it was so much fun and I learned so much.

"Brian never told me not to play. Mark and Brian were smart people. In their view, they always told me if you're competing that's better than anything we can have you do, to compete at that level. But I didn't want to play on the team if I wasn't going to play. That first year I averaged about 10 minutes a game. That was enough to really keep me involved in the game. I didn't want to practice and not play in the game. That second year with Mick I didn't think I would have played that much. Now that I think about it, I wish I would have played that third year. I would have found a way that Mick would have had to put me in the game.

"It was really fun because whenever you do something that you're probably not supposed to be doing, you really appreciate it more and that's what basketball was for me. And obviously the Crosstown Shootout was a big part of that."

Deonta Vaughn, the fourth-leading scorer in UC history, scored a game-high 24 points in his first game against Xavier, a 67-57 UC win.

DEONTA VAUGHN

2006-'10

"It doesn't get no better."

*I*n the middle of December, 2006, Deonta Vaughn and his UC teammates were still trying to get their footing under very strange circumstances. It was Mick Cronin's first year as the Bearcats' head coach and he was in the early stages of trying to restore a program that had been torn asunder by Bob Huggins' departure in 2005.

Cronin had been forced to scramble to put together a roster that he filled with junior college players, two holdovers from the team under Kennedy the year before, and one UC football player.

The only true freshman on the roster was Vaughn, a 6-foot-1, 190-pound guard from Harmony Community Prep in Cincinnati. Vaughn had grown up in Indianapolis and had a standout high school career. He committed to Indiana but was unable to qualify academically to play as a freshman and went to Harmony.

"Coach Cronin was recruiting me for Murray State," Vaughn said. "I ended up going to a prep school because I didn't have the credentials to go straight to IU. Once I didn't go to IU and coach Cronin saw that I was still available and he knew what kind of player I was, he came down and talked to me like a man and told me he's been watching me throughout the year and he knows exactly who I am. From there, Cincinnati was always one of my top schools to go to."

Vaughn turned out to be a godsend for Cronin and the Bearcats. He averaged 14.5 points as a freshman and finished his career as the third-leading scorer in UC history behind Robertson and Logan with 1,885 points. He currently ranks fourth. He shares the school record for 3-point field goals (313) with Sean Kilpatrick and holds the record for 3-point field goal attempts (913).

But all of that would come later. As his first Shootout approached, Vaughn was as clueless as the rest of his teammates, most of whom knew very little about Xavier or the rivalry.

"I knew about it because of me being at the prep school that's in Cincinnati," Vaughn said. "I just knew that the whole city of Cincinnati was talking about how big of a rivalry it was and how important it was for each team. But I think I was just more excited to play for the University of Cincinnati than the rivalry thing. I didn't totally understand how the game was. I didn't get to go to the game and see how big of a rivalry it was while I was at Harmony. I didn't know until the week of the game how important it was and how huge it was.

"It was crazy because we had a new team that was just trying to get the program back on its feet and you've got players that have never played in it. It started out a little nervous for us, but throughout the week we were like, it's just another game, man, we're going to come out and we're going to play and we're going to do what we have to do. They tried to make me say like I knew about the rivalry thing, but like everybody else I was new to it too. I didn't know how the atmosphere was. I heard about it, but actually being there with it was something totally different."

A steady stream of former UC players visited practice in the days leading up to the game. "Steve Logan, Terry Nelson, Curtis Bostic, and Oscar (Robertson) mentioned it a couple of times, and Melvin Levett," Vaughn said.

But it wasn't until he set foot on the floor at Fifth Third Arena on game night that Vaughn began to understand what they were talking about.

"When you go on the court, everybody's going to have their first jitters because it's something very important to your school or your city or just to you in general," Vaughn said. "When you ain't never been there, there's gonna be a lot of jitter bugs, but after we shook off the jitter bugs we were ready to roll. The atmosphere is like being in the NBA championship with two championship caliber teams going against each other in the same city only five minutes away from each other.

"I remember just being in the atmosphere with the lights and the fans just going crazy when we scored or when I hit a shot, people that were anticipating the whole game. I wanted to come out and establish myself as a player because I came in underrated and I wanted everybody to know that I'm here to play ball and there ain't nobody gonna be in my way and keep me from doing what I got to do. Once I got rolling, I just put it in my head that you're just out here playing ball with your boys or somebody you know at the park."

Vaughn scored 24 points to lead all scorers. He made only two of 10 shots from 3-point range, but he was 9-for-20 overall, made all four of his free throws and pulled down five rebounds in a 67-57 UC victory. His first basket came on a layup 1:03 into the game. He didn't score again until he made a jump shot with 8:40 left in the first half. That basket pulled the Bearcats within three points. By the end of the first half, he had scored 11 points and UC had a 3-point lead that it never relinquished.

The Bearcats entered the game with a 6-2 record and had beaten Temple four days earlier. Playing on their home court was an advantage, especially with a brand new team, but few expected UC to win against a Xavier team that was 7-2 entering the game.

"We had a great conversation before we went out," Vaughn said. "We said we're gonna go out there and leave it all on the floor and see what happens. I think after that it really opened up to (the Xavier players) who we were as a team and not to take a team lightly even though they've got first-year players."

But the Bearcats did not beat Xavier again during Vaughn's time at UC, leaving him with a 1-3 record in the Shootout. As a sophomore, Vaughn scored 10 points on 3-for-11 shooting in a 64-59 UC loss. He scored 27 points as a junior, but the Bearcats lost by 10. And as a senior, he scored 13 points in an 83-79 double-overtime loss at XU's Cintas Center, the only double-overtime in the history of the rivalry. Vaughn missed a layup with 11 seconds left in the second overtime that would have pulled the Bearcats within one point. Jason Love then made two free throws to give the Musketeers a four-point lead with 10 seconds to go. UC would not score again. Vaughn's goal of finishing 2-2 against the Musketeers went unfulfilled.

"I just remember it was in the back of my head, 'Damn, we had 'em," Vaughn said.

But he'll always have the memory of that unlikely win during his freshman year.

"We had a nice little get-together as a team," Vaughn said. "We went out to eat and we felt real good as a team. That's one of my best times being there because of the fact that we did beat Xavier as a new team and you've got a freshman that came in and led them in scoring for that game and tried to carry them. It was just great for me because I accomplished so much throughout that time as a freshman. For me to score 24 points as a freshman in that atmosphere with the adrenaline rushing through your body and help your team win, it doesn't get no better."

As the season wore on, things got a lot worse for the Bearcats. They went 11-19, which was their first losing season since 1987-'88, and lost 16 of their last 18 games playing in the ultra-competitive Big East Conference.

"It was very hard because a lot of us weren't used to losing," Vaughn said. "And we knew that other teams had everything over us. I just think that we looked at it like we've got another year to get better. As a small team, an undersized team, and with the cards that we were dealt, I think we did pretty good as a team."

JaQuon Parker was one of the toughest UC players during the Mick Cronin era.

JAQUON PARKER

2009-'13

"We wanted nothing to do with those guys."

The day before he played in his first Crosstown Shootout, JaQuon Parker was sitting in the UC locker room with fellow freshmen Lance Stephenson and Sean Kilpatrick talking about how little the game meant to them.

Parker was from Virginia, Stephenson and Kilpatrick from New York. What did they care about playing Xavier? They were much more interested in the games against Big East behemoths Syracuse, UConn, Georgetown and others.

Then they heard the booming voice of UC forward Yancy Gates, who had grown up in Cincinnati and was heavily recruited by Xavier. He knew what the game meant to the city.

"Gates stopped us and he was like, no, man, this game means everything," Parker said. "We really need to win this game. We don't like them. They don't like us. It's that real. That's when I first found out how important that game was to the people of Cincinnati. That's the first time you'd see Big Gates get real serious like that, like you all better take this game serious. We need to win this game. Coming from Big Gates, Big Gates looking down on you, I'll take this game serious, buddy."

Parker's first Shootout was an 83-79 double-overtime UC loss at Cintas Center on Dec. 13, 2009 when the Bearcats were ranked 19th nationally and Xavier was unranked.

"It was much different than any game I ever played in," Parker said. "We're used to people getting to the arena probably like five, 10 minutes before the game, but that game was filled up 30 minutes before the game. When we went out for warmups, it was filled up, people holding posters and talking all that crazy stuff about you.

"Especially playing over there, it just feels like that place is caving in on you, all these people in there. You know they hate you. You've got to try to put it out of your mind, but they're going nuts over there, so you've got to try to do what you can do. It literally seemed like the floor was shaking. Say you were to shoot an air ball, they never let you live it down. Then you've got that in the back of your mind the whole time. It's tough. It was just as intense (at Fifth Third) but this time you felt like everybody's for me now, I can go out there and play. But still it's a different type of intensity."

Unlike the old days, the players from UC and Xavier do not hang out with each other during the off-season. Parker didn't know any of the Xavier players. They kept their distance, even if they happened to run into each other in public.

"We wanted nothing to do with those guys," Parker said. "You stay over there and we'll stay over here. It was like that. Sometimes you think like I really don't want to play those guys, I really don't care about this game, but then once they win, they're kind of bragging about it, they're going on about it, doing their thing to the Oscar Robertson statue. The fans dress him up. They put a Xavier jersey on him. They put him in all Xavier stuff and take a picture of him. It didn't make me mad, but I was like, man, that's disrespectful. We've got to go out and win this game. It's really important."

The following season the Bearcats rolled to a 66-46 victory at Fifth Third Arena. Xavier won during Parker's junior year at Cintas Center in the game that will be remembered for the fight that broke out with 9.4 seconds left.

Parker played only 15 minutes in that game because he was bothered by a groin injury. He didn't participate in the fight, but saw it up close and was shocked by what he saw.

"I think (Mark) Lyons hit a shot in the corner," Parker said. "He said something really crazy toward everybody on our bench and I think that's when it really popped off. It escalated from there. I didn't throw no punches. I was just trying to help my guys out, like, move them back, just break it up. We don't need this. Yancy and Dion (Dixon), it was their senior year. I don't want to mess with this during their senior year. I was just trying to pull people off people and try not to get hit myself. I haven't seen anything like that before. It was crazy."

Mick Cronin was furious in the locker room after the game.

"He was just disappointed in us that we did that," Parker said. "He coached us better than that. He teaches us as people not to ever do anything like that. He made guys take off their uniforms. He said, 'You don't deserve to wear this Cincinnati stuff. Take it off. You're embarrassing me, embarrassing the program, embarrassing the school.'

"We kind of felt like, man, why did we do this? Was that worth it? Everybody was calling us thugs. Man, we ain't really about that. It was just something that happened in the heat of the moment. We were embarrassed. We were disappointed in ourselves."

There was also the immediate concern that Gates, who had landed a punch just below Xavier center Kenny Frease's left eye, might be suspended, or worse, kicked off the team.

"That was the thought," Parker said. "He was going into the locker room and he was upset. He was like, man, I messed up my senior year. Now I don't know what's going to happen. So we kind of thought it was going to be over for the year. We thought his senior year is over. It's done with. He's gone."

As it turned out, Gates was suspended for six games. Suspensions were also handed out to Octavius Ellis, Cheikh Mbodji and Ge'Lawn Guyn. All four were required to apologize for their actions during a press conference two days later. Gates became so emotional he cried.

> **It just feels like that place is caving in on you, all these people in there. You know they hate you.**

"He was hurt," Parker said, "one, because we lost the game and that we lost in that way, and that he did that type of thing. That ain't him. Big Gates is a lot of things, but he is a gentle giant. My three years here with Gates, I never seen him threaten one person. He just ain't that type of guy."

UC's next game was at Wright State four days later. Because the Bearcats were forced to play with a four-guard lineup due to the suspensions, no one knew what to expect. Not only did the Bearcats win, 78-58, they played a wide-open style and made 14 of 32 3-point shots. That victory was the first of 10 in their next 11 games that would launch them all the way to the NCAA Tournament's Sweet 16.

"We only had about six or seven people," Parker said. "We were like, we're literally all we've got. We couldn't even practice. We were playing three on three all the time. That really brought us together. Let's do this for everybody who said our season is dead. We're doing this for that. That's when we went to the four-guard offense and it worked for us. We were all playing for each other. That year we were the most in tune with each other because we needed everybody. We bonded that much better. We ain't taking nobody for granted. We're all here. We're all together. If somebody would shoot a free throw, we'd put our arms around each other, like, we're here for you."

When Gates returned, there was concern that his presence might upset the delicate balance the Bearcats had discovered, but Gates fit seamlessly into the new style.

"I remember him coming in, and he was like, I ain't trying to change nothing," Parker said. "I'm just trying to fit in. You all keep on doing your thing. You all have got something good going."

The following year the Shootout was played on a neutral court at U.S. Bank Arena and the Bearcats won, 60-45, leaving Parker with a 2-2 record against the Musketeers. By then, he fully understood what "Big Gates" had been talking about that day in the locker room four years earlier.

"It means a lot to the fans," Parker said. "They really go hard for this game. I think our fans want us to win this game more than we want to win this game. Most of us are from out of town. We're coming in and we don't really know how deep this thing is. About your sophomore year, you really find out. You're like, man, I really want to knock these guys off. We want to beat them. But your freshman year you don't know what you're getting into, really, until you see Coach Cronin going extra hard in practice.

"It's a lot of fun (playing in that game) because every mistake you make can be capitalized," Parker said. "The game is so intense. You've got to go in there and basically try to play perfect."

CASHMERE WRIGHT

2009-'13

"Those games show who you are as a player."

*H*aving lost two of his first three games against Xavier, Cashmere Wright was determined to go out with a win over the Musketeers during his senior year in 2012-'13, the year after the Bearcats were blown out in the game that was stopped prematurely because of the fight.

"I came into the locker room that week and I told (my teammates) this is my senior year and I'm not losing to them," Wright said. "That's not gonna happen, especially after last year."

While the powers that be from both schools were determined to avoid another ugly incident, Wright saw the situation much differently.

"Everybody talks about the fight but what I bring up to people is that we lost by 20," Wright said. "Not only did we embarrass ourselves in the fight, we embarrassed ourselves playing basketball. During practice that week, I told them we're not losing. I don't care what everybody else has to say about it. There's no way they're gonna beat us."

The Bearcats followed his lead and hung a 60-45 defeat on the Musketeers in the first of two games that were played at U.S. Bank Arena after the game was moved from campus sites in an attempt to calm things down. Sean Kilpatrick was the star for UC with 25 points, but Wright scored 15 points, with six rebounds and four assists, statistically the best game he would play in the Shootout during his UC career.

Even though the fight was fresh on everybody's minds, Wright said, it wasn't something the players talked about as they took the floor for the Shootout the following year.

After losing to Xavier during his junior year, Cashmere Wright
told his teammates they were not going to lose to the Musketeers
again in his final game against them. "That's not gonna
happen," he said. UC followed his orders, winning 60-45.

"We were labelled because of what was in the public eye," he said. "That's what it looked like and it was bad and we understood. But we knew as players who we were, so why change who you are as a player to try to make other people feel comfortable with you? You've got to be comfortable in your own skin and that's what we did. Tu Holloway was gone. Mark Lyons wasn't there. (Kenny) Frease wasn't there, so really the people who were in the fight from their side weren't there so there was no reason for either side to bring it up."

As well as he played in his final Shootout, Wright doesn't consider that his best performance against Xavier. He prefers the game he played during his sophomore year when he scored 10 points and recorded four assists in UC's 66-46 win over Xavier. Yancy Gates dominated that game with 22 points and 14 rebounds, so it was easy to overlook Wright's contribution, but Wright has never forgotten it.

"As a point guard you've got to realize who's scoring the ball and where they're coming from," he said, "and you've got to get it there. Then I guarded Tu (Holloway) and he had eight points maybe."

Wright still marvels at Gates' performance in that game because he knew how much it meant to him.

"He grew up around that game," Wright said. "To actually be part of it had to be big for him. You prepare so much for that game and for everything to click right in that particular moment in that type of game and him being from Cincinnati, it was just an amazing thing to watch."

Wright, from Savannah, Ga., ranks 22nd on UC's career scoring list with 1,317 points and is the Bearcats' career leader in steals with 198. He had seen the game only on television before he arrived in Cincinnati. He was looking forward to playing in it, but tore his ACL on the first day of practice his freshman year, causing him to miss the entire season and push back his first Shootout experience by a year. But he could tell from being around the program how much the game meant to the Bearcats, to the city, and to Mick Cronin.

"I didn't know how close the schools were or how much the schools didn't like each other, the whole thing about that game," Wright said.

He watched his first UC-Xavier game from the bench, but remembers being impressed at how quickly Fifth Third Arena filled up long before tipoff, something he hadn't seen yet.

"That was the first game where we had the crowd beforehand," he said. "It was pretty full. I didn't really understand it and then there was the electricity in the building. It just ramped up a whole lot. You saw it from everybody, each coach, because Cronin was from Cincinnati and the Xavier coach was from Cincinnati, too. So for both sides you could just see the magnitude of the game just crank up."

Unfortunately for Wright, the Bearcats lost to the ninth-ranked Musketeers, 76-66. The following year, Wright's redshirt freshman year, they lost again, this time in double-overtime, 83-79, at Cintas Center. Wright scored only four points in 32 minutes. That was followed by the game that Gates dominated his sophomore year.

Then came Wright's junior year and the fight. Unlike many of the players and coaches, Wright said he didn't see it coming. Now when he looks back on it, he realizes how silly it was, even as he understands how it could happen in a game that's played at such high intensity.

"At the end of the day, it's a game," he said, "you play hard, you play with everything you've got but it's a game. But you understand that emotions happen in a basketball game because of the type of people you're playing with. The crazy thing is that we actually played against each other more than people knew. But like I said, when you get in those games, everything around that game builds up. It gets emotional. You don't want to lose that game. We were embarrassed over how that game was going."

As the fight unfolded, Wright was mostly a bystander. At first he did his best to prevent it, but once it got going, he knew better than to wade into the middle of it.

"I was trying to break it up, telling people, all right now, but I'm six foot tall," Wright said. "I can't go out there and stop a person 6-9 and try to break up a fight. That's not my thing, man."

The repercussions were immediate. The visibly upset Cronin made his players peel off their jerseys as they entered their locker room and let them know how disappointed he was in them. The players didn't argue.

"He's a coach and we represented the University of Cincinnati and he felt like we were embarrassing him as a coach and the university," Wright said. "That was his way of saying that. Emotions were high, but after you calm down you understand what he did and why."

Wright entered UC in the same class with Gates and they were very close. It was hard for him to see his friend go through that experience and to hear the things people around town were saying about him because he knew they weren't true.

"If you meet him and talk to him, he's pretty cool," Wright said. "He's laid back. If you're a basketball player you've got to become, I won't say an alter-ego on the court, but you need to become a different person and he's that way. His emotions got involved and people saw that persona and they judged him. If you really don't know him, all you're judging is what you see in one incident. He felt like people thought of him being like just a beast, not a nice person. He hated it. But he's just a regular person. He's not trying to get in trouble. He wants to have fun just like everybody else."

The immediate problem for the Bearcats was to try to find a way to win without Gates. Their solution was to use a four-guard, free-flowing offense and it worked like a charm, with UC winning 10 of its next 11 games.

"We reinvented ourselves, but I think we reinvented ourselves to a strong point," Wright said. "Everybody don't remember that we were actually struggling before that anyway."

In fact, with Parker out of the lineup due to a groin injury, UC had lost two games before the Dec. 10 Shootout, to Presbyterian and in overtime to Marshall. He was back at full strength for the Wright State game, the first one after the fight. He joined Wright, Kilpatrick, Dion Dixon and Justin Jackson in the starting lineup.

"So all we were really missing was Yancy," Wright said. "Other people looked at it like we were down. We lost Yancy, but we gained JaQuon. It allowed us to spread our offense more. We started doing very well."

In the end, Wright said, the fight might have actually helped the Bearcats.

"Everybody hated us," he said. "They felt like we were the bad boys of college basketball. To a point, that kind of works for you because now people look at you and they're scared. We played in the Big East and people were looking at us like they kind of showed fear against us. They looked at you a whole lot differently. With how we played defense in the first place, we got comfortable and just did our best out there."

Since graduating from UC, Wright has played professionally in Holland, Greece and Poland. He will always remember what it was like to play in the Crosstown Shootout.

"I don't know how it is at Xavier, but at Cincinnati it's like all-out war that week," Wright said. "Every decision you make matters. Everything that happens in that game, whether you're at home or you're away, the crowd goes crazy, so you realize two swings in the wrong direction and the whole game can go the wrong way for you.

"You've got to keep very calm, remember everything that's been taught to you, remember what you've got to do and still be free enough to play basketball. That's what you're doing. That's basketball. I loved it personally. Those games show who you are as a player. Of course I miss it, but I'm always a part of it because I'm still a UC alum."

A radio interview that UC All-American Sean Kilpatrick did before the 2011 Crosstown Shootout was cited by Xavier players as a reason for the fight at the end of Musketeers' 76-53 victory over the Bearcats.

SEAN KILPATRICK

2010-'14

*"If you can get through the Xavier game,
you can get through any game."*

*H*igh-profile college basketball players from major programs do so many media interviews that after awhile they take them for granted, just another task in a busy day. So when UC sophomore guard Sean Kilpatrick was handed a phone the day before the Crosstown Shootout in 2011-'12 and was told that he was to be interviewed by Andy Furman of WQRT-FM in Cincinnati, Kilpatrick expected to hear the usual banal questions about the game.

Instead, Furman asked, "Are you better than (Xavier guard) Tu Holloway?"

"I'll let the fans decide," Kilpatrick said.

Furman persisted.

"I need to know," he said. "No one's listening. Just between you and me."

"Yes, I am," Kilpatrick said.

"Would Tu Holloway start for UC?" Furman asked.

"Would he, with the players we have now?" Kilpatrick said. "I would say no."

When the interview was finished, Kilpatrick didn't think much about it. He went about his business and later went to a Friday's in Hyde Park.

"I thought I did everything right," Kilpatrick said. "Two to three hours later, my Twitter feed was blowing up more than usual. I'm thinking, what the hell is going on? Why is this happening? The next thing you know you go to Google and you see that I said something that I wasn't supposed to say.

"And I was like, I just did this interview about two hours ago and now they're saying that I said something that I wasn't supposed to say to stir the pot between UC and Xavier? The next thing I know I got a call from Coach Mick Cronin and I got a call from my dad. Like I told Coach Cronin, I'm doing what's right, not only what's right, but I'm doing what I believe in. I'm going to ride with my teammates before anything. That's the type of person I am.

"I didn't know who Andy Furman was. I still don't know who Andy Furman is. I didn't know what he did. Of course, when he did the interview…he asked the question, any player at that time would agree with me…You don't want your teammates to look at you as if you're a sellout. You can't put a kid into a situation like that and mix his words up and try to make them into saying something that he's really not trying to say. And I think that's what Andy did to me. I don't have no grudge towards him or anything like that, but Coach Cronin still might."

The next day Xavier blew out UC, 76-53, at Cintas Center. The brawl at the end of the game attracted national attention and threatened the very existence of the Crosstown Shootout. It all started with a radio interview that caused the Xavier players to feel slighted. As Holloway said in the post-game press conference, "We got disrespected a little bit before the game, guys calling us out."

That was news to Kilpatrick, who insists he wasn't trying to say anything derogatory toward the Xavier players. Five years later, he harbors no ill will toward Holloway. And never did.

"Still to this day, I can see him and we'll talk like nothing happened," Kilpatrick said. "We walked past that time in our lives. We were both in the D-League at one point and he's still there. He's someone that I support because it's bigger than what the Xavier and Cincinnati Shootout is. With him taking it the way he did, it was fuel for him to get pumped for the game and I can't blame him for that. He's a competitor. I think that's good for the sport."

Cronin's reaction after the game was swift and pointed.

"He was furious," Kilpatrick said. "He said, 'How could you embarrass the university like that?' I mean, we embarrassed our families on TV, the university, our president at the time. We embarrassed our AD. We embarrassed our coaches. When you're dealing with a situation like that, it's only right that you make your team take off the jersey that they're playing for. We didn't do a great job of representing our school."

Four UC players were suspended, leaving UC shorthanded for their next game at Wright State, which they won, sending the Bearcats on a run of 10 wins in 11 games.

"I think we responded in the right way and we had a mindset that it was basically us against the world because they looked at us like we were a whole bunch of thugs," Kilpatrick said. "I didn't think everyone was with us, especially our fans. They did a great job with us after awhile, but they still had some negative comments to say.

When we played against Wright State, we just said, 'You know what, everyone's against us anyway so we have nothing to lose. Everyone's counting us out to not make it to the tournament.' What happened is we just turned our whole season around with those games."

The following season, Kilpatrick's junior year, the game was moved to U.S. Bank Arena in downtown Cincinnati. Kilpatrick scored 25 points-his best performance in four Crosstown Shootouts-in a 60-45 UC win.

"There was a lot of weight on my shoulders," Kilpatrick said, "being able to grab a win in that type of setting. After that, the fans from Cincinnati started to come to a lot more games and were more behind you. Once you lose that Xavier game-and I had the experience of being on both sides of the spectrum-once you lose that game, it's different because your fans start looking at you like, yeah, you won this game but you lost the Xavier game and you don't want to hear anything like that, especially from your own fans.

"There was still the same type of intensity, but there was a different feel to it because now you were more like in an NBA arena and you have to refocus differently knowing that it wasn't going to be the same as it was at Cincinnati or the same how it was at Xavier. The atmosphere was a lot different. You get more of a college atmosphere when you play it on campus so I liked it better on campus, especially my campus. The crowd in U.S. Bank arena was more divided, one half was Cincinnati and the other half was basically Xavier.

"What I was telling the young guys is that this week is going to be crazy, but you also have to remember that we're playing for something bigger than the Xavier and Cincinnati game. I think everyone had a different mindset going into that game. It was really big for us, being able to kind of put the cherry on top with winning that game for the city as well."

There was very little awkwardness among the players before the game, even though it was the first time they had played against each other since the fight. It helped, Kilpatrick said, that both teams toured the Freedom Center together down the street from U.S. Bank Arena about a week before the game.

"It was great that they did that," Kilpatrick said. "It was better for us to sit down and hash everything out then and there and see both teams as coming together and basically bring peace to the city as well. I think it was a smart idea. For the game, it was still that competitive spirit but everyone wanted to compete in the right way, in the right form.

"What they did was they put us in groups. It was like five to six people in one group. You'll have like three of our guys and three of theirs and some groups were uneven because the teams weren't even. Everyone had to interact with each other. You had some of the assistant coaches that were with our group. It was good because you never get to see most schools like that.

"I've only been in that game five years of my life, so me being able to see them like that for the first time in my career at the University of Cincinnati, I think it was good because everyone blows that game and that week out of proportion. It's still a game at the end of the day. You're still trying to go somewhere in life, and not only that, you don't want to embarrass your family members and you don't want to embarrass the school that you play for."

During Kilpatrick's senior year, the Bearcats lost to Xavier, 64-47, leaving him 2-2 against the Musketeers. After that game, the Bearcats ripped off 15 straight wins and advanced to the NCAA Tournament for the fourth straight year. That's when he realized that there's value even in losing to Xavier.

"You've got to look at it this way," he said. "It makes you turn bad things around in a positive way. You've got to look at it for both teams like if you can get through the Cincinnati game or you can get through the Xavier game, you can get through any game. We took it as a positive and said this is how it's got to be from now on. There's no more slippage. You can't sit here and take things like this anymore because now it's very important because now all these wins have to get racked up. I think it humbled a lot of guys when we played them and we did things the right way."

Kilpatrick, who now plays in the NBA for the Brooklyn Nets, had one of the finest careers in UC history. His 2,145 points rank second on UC's career scoring list. He was a first-team AP All-American as a senior in 2014 when he led the American Athletic Conference in scoring.

Playing in the Crosstown Shootout, he said, "was an experience that you would probably never really be able to describe. You have to be on the court to feel it. You could sit in your seat and feel the goose bumps that you get like what a national championship was. That's what it felt like as a player. Me being able to be a part of that was something that was really historic for me."

Kilpatrick said he doesn't think about the fight much anymore unless someone asks him about it. He has heard the theory that one reason the fight occurred was that the refs lost control of the game, but says that's not unusual. It's up to the players to police themselves.

"The refs lose control of that game every year," Kilpatrick said. "That's something that's going to happen when you're dealing with two teams like that that are competitive and when you're dealing with two great coaches like that. The refs are going to lose control of that game. I don't think that they had any kind of control of it from the jump, but I didn't see anything happening like that. No way."

FARAD COBB

2014-'16

"If I make this shot, it'll change my whole life."

During his two years at UC, Farad Cobb made 127 3-point shots, but he's still haunted by the 3-point shot he missed during his first Crosstown Shootout.

The Bearcats had taken a 55-53 lead against Xavier on a Gary Clark basket with 1:09 left. After a 3-pointer by Xavier's Dee Davis gave the Musketeers a one-point lead, Troy Caupain made two free throws to put UC back on top, 57-56, with 19 seconds to play. All the Bearcats needed was one defensive stop to win the game.

Instead, Clark committed a major mental mistake by fouling Xavier's Trevon Bluiett, who made two free throws with 11 seconds remaining to put the Musketeers ahead, 58-57. UC had one more chance to win, but Cobb's 3-point shot with four seconds left rimmed out. Myles Davis rebounded for Xavier, then made one of two free throws with one second left to make the final score 59-57.

"That's one of those shots, like, man, if I make that shot, it'll change my whole life," Cobb said. "But it didn't happen like that."

Cobb arrived at UC after making 46.3 percent of his 3-point shots during his one season at Northwest Florida State College in Niceville, Fla. It didn't take long for him to get a feel for the Crosstown Shootout.

"When I first got on campus a fan came up to me and was like, I don't care what else you do while you're here, just beat Xavier because I hate 'em," Cobb said. "Then I started to hear more about it as I was here. I was like, whoever Xavier is, they must not like them so much. We've got to win that game."

He got his first chance to play against the Musketeers on Feb. 18, 2015 at UC's Fifth Third Arena.

"I haven't experienced anything like that," he said. "It was bigger than I projected it to be. That whole week, we didn't have any other games. Coach (Cronin) made his schedule so we just focused on them. It was just exhausting and stressful. There's a lot of pressure going into that game. You stay up all night going over the scouting report. Going into that game you can't wait to get on the court because you want to get it over with and see what happens. You don't want to think about it no more.

"The first time we played them I came off the bench. (Before the game), the Bearcat (mascot) came out of the ceiling. They'd never done that before since I've been here. Then you see all this fire and everybody was on their feet before the game. You're a little nervous. When I checked in, I was just like, okay I'm here now. Then you just kind of go into your natural game after that."

The Bearcats fell behind early because of a 3-point shooting onslaught by Xavier's Dee Davis, who made four treys in the first half and finished five-for-five from beyond the arc.

"He was shooting 18 percent (from 3-point range) going into that game so they told us to let him shoot it," Cobb said. "Not that anybody's to blame, but he ended up going five-for-five from three in that game. If we had just played him and not the percentages..."

The Bearcats trailed by eight points with just over eight minutes left when they began a comeback that eventually put them ahead, however briefly. Cobb wasn't supposed to take the final shot for UC, but it worked out that way. He had a clear look at the basket. All he had to do was knock down a shot he had made so many times before during his career.

"The play was for Troy to come down and make a play, but he came down and they doubled him so he passed it," Cobb said. "I pump-faked Dee Davis and lined it up, but I missed it. I thought it was good too. It was definitely a good look. It hit the side and kind of bounced off. It definitely had a chance to go in. I was just like, damn, man, everybody's gonna be depressed around here. I just felt like I would have automatically been in the Bearcats Hall of Fame for beating Xavier at the buzzer.

"I stayed up the whole night, me, Shaq (Thomas) and a couple of other guys talking about the game and about the scouting report. There was a lot of stuff we could have done. We just stayed up thinking about that stuff and how you can't get it back. You have to kind of put it in the past, but you still think about it. You can't just erase it from your memory. That game doesn't stop you from going to the NCAA tournament or anything like that. You just want to win for yourself and the fans so you can say we beat Xavier."

Cobb would get another shot at the Musketeers during his senior year, this time

Farad Cobb would like to see UC and Xavier play
twice a year as they did during the 1950s.

at XU's Cintas Center. Xavier, which had one of its best teams that season, was the clear favorite. The Bearcats were ranked 23rd in the country, but Xavier, unbeaten and ranked No. 12 through nine games, took control of the game early, jumping out to an 18-6 lead in the first eight minutes on the way to a 16-point halftime lead.

UC came back to get within five points midway through the second half, but Xavier pulled away for a 65-55 victory, its third straight over UC and fourth in the last five games. That Xavier team eventually was ranked as high as No. 5 in the country, but Cobb still believes the 2014-'15 Musketeer team was better because of center Matt Stainbrook.

"I just feel like the big guy, Stainbrook, the big white dude inside, I feel like he was a great passer and he was a problem in the post," Cobb said. "He was the whole scouting report. They had basically the same team (in 2015-'16) except for him and Dee Davis at the point. I just felt like from looking at the scouting report, the team the year before was better. No one ever got in a rhythm in that game. We were never able to close the gap to get it where we could control the game for whatever reason."

As he looks back, Cobb regrets that he never got the chance to know the Xavier players better.

"I don't know them," he said, "but I've talked with them. I've met them around Cincinnati, like Jalen Reynolds and James Farr. Those are pretty much the only two that when we see each other we'll nod to each other and have a quick conversation."

When he was told that the players from both schools used to play against each other in pickup games during the summer, Cobb said he wished that were still the case.

"I don't know why that stopped," he said. "I would love to do that because when we play in the games, I don't like them. I don't like Xavier. But outside of the game, at the end of the day, it's just basketball. I think we should have been doing that. Instead of us playing each other all the time in open gym, we could have been playing them just to have some different people."

Cobb would also like to see UC and Xavier play twice every year, as they did back in the 1950s, once early in the season and again in the second half of the season.

"If you just win one time, that's just a good night," he said.

As it is, Cobb will have to live with his two losses to the Musketeers and the bad memories from the first one.

"I always think about that shot," he said, "like, what if that would have went in? I'm pretty sure that there's some fans that probably hate me because I was the one who took the last shot."

MEDIA

Andy MacWilliams, right, the former Xavier play-by-play announcer, was a big part of the fabric of the Shootout because of his rabid devotion to the Musketeers.

ANDY MACWILLIAMS

UC play-by-play voice, 1980-'82
Xavier play-by-play voice, 1983-'97

"No. 1 in the country, No. 2 in their own city."

When the name of the rivalry between UC and Xavier was changed from the Crosstown Shootout to the Crosstown Classic after the 2011 brawl, it seemed artificial, diluted, even silly.

By then, Cincinnati sports fans had grown accustomed to the Crosstown Shootout. But it hadn't always gone by that name. Former Xavier radio play-by-play voice Andy MacWilliams says he was the first to use that term in the days leading up to the 1984-'85 game, which Xavier won, 55-52.

Before he christened it, MacWilliams said, "The game was just the UC-Xavier game. Coming off that long UC domination, it really wasn't much of a rivalry."

But in 1984-'85, both teams had talented freshman guards, Byron Larkin for Xavier and Roger McClendon for UC.

"We got the vibe from the UC camp that Yates had his first real good recruiting class and it was time for UC to sort of put Xavier back in its place as a nice little program over there," MacWilliams said. "Tony was going to bring in the Chicago kids and the big recruits and it was time for Xavier to crawl back into the hole and be second fiddle. Everybody was picking UC, but I predicted a Xavier victory in that game. That's the game, during the buildup, when I started calling it the Crosstown Shootout and everybody sort of glommed onto it. It was no brilliant deal. It just seemed logical. I just labeled it."

Years later, when the game was re-named to eliminate the word 'Shootout,' MacWilliams was upset.

"That sort of hurt," he said. "They tried to sterilize it. There was a lot of sentiment at that point to have the game go on a hiatus. The knee-jerk reaction was not to play the game and then they tried to sterilize it."

The Crosstown Classic era lasted only two years. Both games were played downtown at U.S. Bank Arena in 2012-'13 and 2013-'14 before it was returned to the school's respective campuses and again was called the Crosstown Shootout.

MacWilliams never played or coached in the game, but he was a big part of the rivalry's fabric. He called three Shootouts as UC's play-by-play voice and 14 more as Xavier's play-by-play voice from 1983 until 1997 when he had to give up the job because of problems with his voice. Specifically, MacWilliams' condition was spasmodic dysphonia, defined as involuntary movements or spasms of one or more muscles of the larynx. In effect, MacWilliams' voice would sometimes desert him in mid-sentence.

"I couldn't perform the way I wanted to," MacWilliams said. "Doing the Xavier games was a special deal. It became a big part of the way I was identified so it was a hard thing to give up. But the radio business has become so much more corporate that it was probably a blessing in disguise on some level."

MacWilliams, who works as a financial advisor for Morgan Stanley, remains involved with the Xavier program. He writes for 'MusketeerMadness.com,' attends all of Xavier's home games, and makes an occasional road trip with the team.

It's doubtful that many people know that he first used the moniker, "Crosstown Shootout," but many remember his classic call in the Nov. 26, 1996 game when Xavier upset UC, the No. 1-ranked team in the country, 71-69, on a last-second shot by Lenny Brown.

After Brown hit the shot, MacWilliams screamed, "The UC Bearcats are No. 1 in the country, No. 2 in their own city!"

"My son, Bryan, was a freshman at Xavier," MacWilliams said, "and we talked the night before on the telephone. Skip (Prosser) had gone into siege mentality and he had the players believing they could win the game. I told my son, 'Skip, you and I and the players are probably about the only people that think they can go over there and win.' And Bryan said, 'Dad, you've got to come up with a special line when they pull the upset,' so we kicked around a bunch. He actually came up with it. I just happened to remember it.

"I don't think UC was totally geared up at that point. Nobody gave Xavier any credit. Skip's recruiting class the previous year had been unbelievably good. James Posey was a Prop 48 and nobody knew how good he was going to be. Lenny Brown, Gary Lumpkin, Darnell Williams, all those guys. UC was definitely not prepared for what those guys produced."

The score was tied at 69-69 and UC had the ball when point guard Charles Williams dribbled it off his foot out of bounds to return possession to Xavier for Brown's final shot.

"It was right in front of me," MacWilliams said of Williams' turnover. "I couldn't believe it. He wasn't even being pressured. He's bringing the ball up and he dribbled it off his foot. I think (WLW radio's) Seg Denison scooped up the ball. He was sitting beside us. I thought, 'This is a gift from heaven.' They inbounded it at quarter court there. Darnell Burton let Lenny back him down in the lane and Lenny hit that floater."

MacWilliams was also behind the mic for the Handshake Game, Xavier's 82-76 overtime win over UC at the Gardens, when Bob Huggins refused to shake Pete Gillen's hand after the game.

"I'd never seen Gillen that upset," MacWilliams said. "He was redder than a beet. He walked by us and slammed his fist on the table, almost knocked us off the air. He was so pissed off. That's the bile, the visceral hate. The Shootout was like at a record level after that. And then Gillen leaves to go to Providence and I felt like I was left as the only vestige. Everybody was on my ass. It was pretty crazy."

MacWilliams didn't try to curtail his enthusiasm for Xavier or his emotions when he was doing the games. When Xavier trailed UC by seven in overtime in the Jan. 31, 1990 game, MacWilliams went on a rant about UC's Prop 48 players. Xavier then came back to win.

"I got a little bitter on the air," MacWilliams said. "I sort of ripped Huggins and those guys. Xavier came back to win it in a miracle finish and Huggs heard what I had said on the air. The next morning I'm doing the morning sports and the sports director said, 'Huggins and (UC athletic director Rick) Taylor want you to report to their office with the tapes to review what you said,' and I said, 'Those guys don't pay my paycheck. They can have all the tapes they want. I'm not going up there on their turf to be bitched out. Xavier won the game. The hell with it.' It wasn't all that rational, what I said (on the air)."

By his own admission, MacWilliams got carried away again on Jan. 29, 1992 when UC blew out Xavier, 93-75, after UC's Terry Nelson predicted the Bearcats would do just that.

"People on the Xavier side of the equation had gotten into the habit of actually winning the game and being competitive and Huggs brought that really good '91-'92 team over to the Gardens – the Final Four team – and just blew Xavier's doors off and deservedly so," MacWilliams said. "They were really good. I lost my cool in that game when they went up 20 or 25 and said it was a damn embarrassment. Not too professional, but entertaining. My attitude in doing those games was, if I can't get excited about it, who is?"

MacWilliams and Huggins didn't get along well, but he gives Huggins credit for fueling the rivalry when he first arrived in town in 1989. He remembers driving back from the airport with Joe Sunderman, his broadcasting partner, and listening on the radio to the UC-Minnesota game, Huggins' first as the UC coach and the first game the Bearcats played at Shoemaker Center.

"They're playing Minnesota and he has that Steve Sanders or whatever his name was, the football wide receiver... and Minnesota is ranked," MacWilliams said, "and that Sanders guy hits a shot at the buzzer to beat them. I go, 'This is going to be interesting. This guy must be a hell of a coach if he can do that with walk-ons.' He has Lou Banks and Levertis Robinson and some quality guys, but he's starting a wide receiver on the football team and he beats Minnesota. He's going to get this up and running. It's going to be interesting. And it certainly was."

The Shootout has been up and running at full speed ever since.

"I'm showing my basketball prejudice but I think it's right up there with Opening Day," MacWilliams said, "somewhere in that range as a premier sports event. With a couple exceptions it's a fairly healthy way of showing the contrast between the David and Goliath stuff. With the exception of the fight and a couple of other incidents, it's been a pretty healthy rivalry. We all get along on some level."

JOE SUNDERMAN

Xavier player, 1974-'79
Xavier radio announcer, 1980-present

"The epicenter of college basketball in the entire country."

*J*oe Sunderman, the play-by-play voice of Xavier radio broadcasts, was in a private box "a million miles up in the air" at Riverfront Coliseum the night in 1980 when Bob Staak's Musketeers upset UC.

"I was thrilled to see it," Sunderman said, "happy for my friends that were on the team, happy for the school. The match-up was good that night for Xavier and they took advantage of it. It was a great moment for Xavier at that point when they were turning the program."

Sunderman was just one year removed from his own playing career at Xavier. He had signed with the Musketeers and coach Tay Baker after graduating from Cincinnati's La Salle High School in 1974, choosing Xavier over Miami (Ohio). He spent five years at Xavier because he had to sit out one year because of knee surgery.

He never won a game in four tries against the Bearcats, losing by nine his freshman year, by seven his sophomore year, by five his junior year and by two, 60-58, in his senior year. In his final game against the Bearcats, Xavier had scored 10 straight points to take a 58-53 lead with 4:28 left. The last points of that run came on a breakaway dunk by Nick Daniels after an outlet pass from Sunderman, but Daniels received a technical foul for hanging on the rim. The Musketeers didn't score again.

UC's Eddie Lee made a free throw after the technical, then added a field goal to make it 58-56. After Xavier's Keith Walker missed two free throws, Lee tied the score with a 20-foot jump shot. The winning points came on a jump shot by UC's Puffy Kennedy with 1:40 left.

"I didn't like the call truthfully," Sunderman said of the technical foul on Daniels. "It's a memory though. You do remember those games, that's for sure. Other games they fade into the past but those games because they're Cincinnati-Xavier, you do remember those games. I definitely would have liked to have won one, I'll tell you that."

Although he was thrilled to see Xavier knock off the Bearcats that night in 1980 Sunderman doesn't buy the theory that one victory, no matter how memorable, catapulted the Musketeers to the success they've enjoyed since then. He believes the transformation began several years earlier when Xavier officials laid the groundwork to become a charter member of the Midwestern City Conference.

"When I went to Xavier, I figured it was a great education in a great city," Sunderman said. "I thought, 'Why can't this be a very good basketball program?' Of course until you arrive you don't know what it takes and what that requires and the assets and the administration getting behind the program in a big way, a meaningful way. The biggest move Xavier ever made was getting into a league where they could play teams they could handle, so you could have the joy of winning a tournament or the league.

"I think it started when Jim McCafferty and Tay Baker knew they had to get Xavier into a league. I give those guys credit. I was told when I was being recruited that I would be in a league by my sophomore or junior year. It took longer than that but it needed to be done because independents were dying. No matter what league you're in, that creates great excitement and the ball gets rolling."

Sunderman has been the play-by-play voice for XU basketball since 1997, the year MacWilliams was forced to give up the job because of issues with his voice. Before that, Sunderman was the color analyst, beginning in 1980-'81, working with MacWilliams. His first experience doing play-by-play came without any warning on Jan. 26, 1991 when the Musketeers lost to South Florida.

"It happened suddenly," Sunderman said. "We were playing at South Florida and Andy came up on the bus ride on the way to the arena with the players and basically said 'You'll have to do everything.' I said, 'What do you mean, do everything?' He said, 'I can't work.' That was my first experience where he had voice problems. I suddenly went from doing the color to doing the play-by-play and the color. It was a sudden adjustment. I think as a result it was easier than if they had said, 'Hey, in two weeks, you're going to do the play-by-play.'"

MacWilliams returned to finish the season, but eventually Sunderman was given a choice. He could do the play-by-play or WLW radio could hire someone

*Joe Sunderman never beat UC in four tries as a Xavier player,
but he has described many wins in the Crosstown Shootout
as the Musketeers' popular radio voice.*

else to do play-by-play and Sunderman could return to doing the color. He chose play-by-play.

"Walt McBride worked with us for a half season, then they made a move to get Byron Larkin and Steve Wolf to help with the games," Sunderman said. "And Byron has been my partner ever since. It just made a lot of sense at the time. I'm glad I did it. It was the the tragedy of Andy losing his voice because he was a great announcer. It was just unfortunate."

As a broadcaster, Sunderman clearly makes known his allegiance to Xavier, but he doesn't let his rooting interest get in the way of calling the game. His calls are clear and easy to follow and he makes sure he gives the score frequently. Occasionally he criticizes an official's call, but the criticism flows both ways, sometimes in Xavier's favor, sometimes not.

"You're still a fan of the team," Sunderman said. "But you're trained to be objective. You detach yourself from it and try to see how others are reacting to it more so than yourself. At the same time, if you're the local broadcaster and you're not doing a national broadcast, I think it's absolutely fine to let fans know who you want to win the game. It's part of the deal. I believe Marty Brennaman sure wants the Reds to win.

"I do have a lot of pride in the program, pride in the school and pride in the city. They have progressed almost every single year in some facet of the school itself and in the athletic program. It's been a thrill to be a part of it, around it, watch it. I am very happy to be associated with Xavier. It's the greatest decision I made in my life going there."

Sunderman's first game against UC as a player was on Feb. 26, 1975 at Cincinnati Gardens. UC won, 66-57.

"I was a freshman," Sunderman said. "I actually started the game. I remember the seniors and their intensity about it was different. They didn't need to say anything. You could just feel it. But I think you get ready for every game the same. If you start making adaptations you're going to screw yourself up. You try to play as hard as you can every night. You don't make any exceptions. There's no question, though, that when you're around the game for awhile, you learn the intensity of the crowd, the emotions involved in the city. It's definitely different.

"It's one of the biggest sporting events in the city. The best part is that both programs have done very, very well. Everybody has a dip now and then, but all in all, what a city to live in if you like college basketball. First of all you have Cincinnati and you have Xavier and then if you start driving around you've got Louisville and Kentucky and Indiana. You can go on and on. I think this is the epicenter of college basketball in the entire country."

Sunderman feels especially proud on the nights when UC and Xavier both play home games and have sellouts at the same time. It doesn't happen often, but when it does, 23,000 people just 3.5 miles apart are cheering their respective teams.

"That's amazing," Sunderman said.

But he doesn't consider it amazing that Xavier has risen to the point where it's now a perennial Top 25 team and NCAA Tournament participant or that the Musketeers in recent years have beaten the Bearcats more often than not.

Asked if that would have been his wildest dream when he was playing at Xavier, he said, "That was my dream. That wasn't a wild dream."

"I enjoy Xavier winning any game," he said. "That game, though, because I do have neighbors and friends and you know you're going to talk about it for the next week and a half and you've spent a week and half prior to it talking about what might happen, it's certainly much more enjoyable to talk about if your team wins. There's no question about that.

"Going back to the 1980 Xavier win, that certainly did energize the Xavier community. There were points in time when I think Xavier realized, 'Hey, we can do this if we put some effort into it.' I do think that is one of the points and there were many, many points… getting into a league, Pete Gillen, there were a lot of markers."

Sunderman won't declare unequivocally that the Shootout is the best college basketball rivalry in the country, but he's sure it's the best intra-city rivalry.

"I think it took awhile for the country to notice," he said. "There can't be any that are more intense. The schools are just a few miles apart. The city is divided for a day. I've never seen anything like it. I can't imagine. Just the fact that we grow up with each other. Kids in school are discussing it whether they're in the first grade or they're in high school."

UC play-by-play voice Dan Hoard, left, shown with his long-time partner Chuck Machock, says he has trouble sleeping after a loss to Xavier.

DAN HOARD

UC play-by-play announcer, 2000-present

"One of the best rivalries in sports."

*A*s the play-by-play voice of the Cincinnati Bengals, UC football and basketball, Dan Hoard broadcasts more than 60 games every year, but he said nothing means more to him than the Crosstown Shootout.

"I love doing that game," Hoard said. "It's one of the highlights of my year even though the outcome (for UC) has not been great (lately). It's one of the best rivalries in sports. It's the best intra-city rivalry in college basketball. It's a privilege to do."

He would enjoy it more, though, if his team won a little more frequently. Since he took over as the radio play-by-play voice in 2000-'01, UC has gone 5-11 against the Musketeers. Four of those losses were by two points and two were in overtime. And that doesn't count UC's loss to Xavier in 1996 when the Bearcats were ranked No. 1 in the country and the Musketeers were unranked. Hoard did that game on television on Channel 19 as the color man with current Reds TV voice Thom Brennaman.

"I had not been in Cincinnati for very long," Hoard said. "Thom was still trying to squeeze in as many UC games as he possibly could with his busy schedule on Channel 19 and I replaced Kevin Frazier at the station, so until I started doing the play-by-play of the games, they plugged me into Kevin's old role with Thom. That was the first Shootout I ever saw, the first one I ever did, and it's one of the most famous ones ever."

Hoard is a Syracuse University graduate, but says he feels more allegiance to UC than he does his alma mater.

"On the day (of the game) I don't like Xavier at all, no question about it," Hoard said. "I've said many times, and I hope Mick (Cronin) and (Bob Huggins) don't take offense at this, but if (my son) were good enough to play major college basketball, of all the coaches I've ever met, dealt with, listened to, watched, I would want him to play for Skip Prosser. That's my respect for Skip Prosser. I just thought he was the total package.

"But yeah, the day of that game I despise Xavier, absolutely, so much so that there was a specific Shootout when I went over the line, in my own opinion. Was it Jordan Crawford that played there? Something about his body language in that game was annoying me. I was pretty critical of him in that game and it was really homer-ish and after the game I thought to myself, you know what, that was weak. That was just a bad job as a broadcaster and I've tried to never say anything like that since, whether it's the Shootout or any other game I'm doing. It was too much of a homer take on a game.

"You don't need to do that. I mean, anybody listening to the UC broadcast that night knows that I want UC to win and Crawford was a great player. Who cares about the expression on his face? Why should that annoy the other team's announcer? I'm sure that if I was on the other side there would have been plenty of UC guys over the years I would have felt the same way about."

During the rest of the season, when the local bragging rights are not on the line, Hoard says, he does not hate the Musketeers, although he certainly doesn't root for them.

"It's impossible as a UC broadcaster not to look at Xavier kind of through a UC prism," he said, "so naturally you always want UC to be doing better than Xavier. But I don't mind if they do well as long as UC is also doing well, ideally better."

Every year before the game Hoard remembers what he said about Crawford and uses it as a reminder to keep the broadcast on a professional level.

"I remind myself no matter how heated it gets, no matter how excited or depressed I might get depending on how the game is going, don't go over the top," he said. "In terms of pre-game preparation, I always make sure that I do a little research reminding myself of some of the history and making sure I have some extra anecdotal material on games in the past and things like that."

The most memorable Shootout that Hoard ever did was the infamous 2011 game.

"It's the only boxing play-by-play I've done," he said. "I used to get laughs at banquets. I would say, so many people were focused on the fight on the court that nobody picked up on the fact that I jumped out of my seat, sprinted down press row and cold-cocked Joe Sunderman, which obviously didn't really happen because he would have kicked my ass, being bigger and stronger than I am. Or he's so nice he probably would have said, 'Oh, let me turn my cheek so you can hit the other side.'

"I remember at halftime of that game, passing (Xavier athletic director) Mike Bobinski in the hall when I was going back to get a Coke. I always liked Mike and we had a great relationship during the years that he was at Xavier and he said something to me during halftime of that game along the lines of 'I hope the officials get this thing under control or we could have some trouble' and I said the same thing. Both of us sensed that grey clouds were moving in but I don't think anybody thought that it was going to go as far as it did."

When the fight broke out, Hoard tried not to take sides. His goal, he said, was to simply be as descriptive as he could.

"When there are big moments as a broadcaster, that's the approach to take," he said. "That's the Marty Brennaman approach and I think that's what the great announcers try to do, not that I'm putting myself on that list."

After the game, instead of interviewing Cronin for his post-game show on the floor as he usually does, Hoard went to the UC locker room. That's the first time anyone heard Cronin talk about how angry he was at his players and how ridiculous the venom between the two schools had become.

"They didn't want him to come out," Hoard said. "So before he did his incredible news conference, he did a one-on-one interview with me and was just as gracious in that interview as he was in the news conference. That's when I really knew that he was speaking from the heart because I'm talking to him probably 10 minutes before he went into that news conference, so this has just happened. He hasn't had time to compose what he wants to say."

Beyond that game and the 1996 game he did on TV, Hoard can't come up with any other games that stand out from UC's standpoint.

> **It's impossible as a UC broadcaster not to look at Xavier kind of through a UC prism. So naturally you always want UC to be doing better than Xavier.**

"Ironically the ones that really stand out are the heartbreaking losses, partly because there have been more of those," he said. "The UC wins that I've done have all been relatively lopsided. They have not won a nail-biter game in the entire time that I've been doing the games."

Why has Xavier been so dominant in recent years?

"The circumstances have varied," he said. "I do buy into the notion that there was probably a time when the game mattered more to them than it did to UC. I don't think that's the case anymore, but I do think that was true for awhile. Then obviously they were up while UC was down immediately after Huggs was forced out so that helped them continue to win most of the time. And then there have just been some crazy finishes where their shot went in and UC's didn't. So there is an element of luck involved. There is no better example than Dee Davis a couple of years ago. He did not miss a 3-point shot. He went into the game hitting 23 percent or whatever it was. He was a better shooter than he had displayed up until that point but he wasn't as good as he was in that game. He couldn't miss."

Whatever the reason, every UC loss to Xavier is tough for Hoard to take.

"It annoys me for 24 hours as a UC broadcaster and fan," he said. "Yeah, it hurts. I might stare at the ceiling that night for a few hours after the game or stay up and watch a movie I've seen a million times as I go around the horn on my TV remote. That definitely happens."

CHUCK MACHOCK

UC broadcaster, 1992-present

"I always thought that Xavier plays it with more emotion than we do."

When Chuck Machock first arrived at UC to play basketball in 1955, no one had thought to give a name to the rivalry between UC and Xavier.

The Bearcats had not yet established their superiority over the Musketeers in a series that was only 19 games old. UC held a modest 11-8 edge, but it was starting to turn more strongly in the Bearcats' favor, with UC having won four of the last five games. It was a big game, but nothing close to the magnitude it has today.

Beginning on Feb. 13, 1957, the Bearcats won 22 of the next 24 games to take a commanding lead in the local rivalry. During that time, they also won two national championships and played in five Final Fours.

Machock played against Xavier as a member of UC's freshman team. He also played against the Musketeers his sophomore year on the varsity before becoming a student-coach, but he estimates that he was on the floor for all of about 20 seconds.

"It wasn't a big, big thing," Machock said of the rivalry. "We won most of the time and it was two games (per year). It was like Dayton is playing Cincinnati tonight. That's about what it occupied."

No one would have predicted that it would grow into the Crosstown Shootout, that it would become the sporting event of the winter in Cincinnati and probably the second-biggest sports day of the year behind only the Reds' Opening Day. And surely no one would have predicted that the day would come when the Musketeers would turn the tables and have their own run of domination, as they are enjoying

Chuck Machock, the Bearcats' long-time color analyst,
says his favorite game in the Crosstown Shootout was UC's 93-75
win in 1992 after Terry Nelson predicted a blowout.

now with wins in eight of the last 11 games.

After he graduated from UC, Machock embarked on a coaching career that eventually took him to jobs as an assistant coach at West Virginia and Ohio State and a brief stint as the head coach at Central Florida before he returned to his alma mater in 1989 to serve as a volunteer assistant under his friend, (Bob) Huggins, who had worked as an assistant under Machock at Central Florida.

By that time, Xavier had broken through against UC. (Pete) Gillen was the head coach and a UC win over the Musketeers could no longer be taken for granted.

"You've got a Catholic school and a public school in this town and they'll fight tooth and nail every year," Machock said. "You know that and I know that. And it's the biggest game of the year and always will be to one of those two schools. It's bigger to Xavier. It's a big game for UC, but not a bigger game than what we play (normally). They've accomplished more in the last 20 years than the Cincinnati Bearcats have, even though Bob Huggins was here and they had great basketball teams. If you look at the record, Huggs would get beat by one, Huggs would get beat in overtime, Huggs would get beat at the buzzer. I think once since I've been here UC has won that close game at the end. They have not beaten Xavier in a close game in a long, long time. I think it's a meaningful game for Xavier and always will be because it's Goliath. They're always David and we're always Goliath and we always get our asses kicked just like he did in the Bible. You can't go against that one."

Machock coached at UC under Huggins from 1989 through 1992, the last time the Bearcats went to the Final Four. After that, the NCAA said volunteer coaches were no longer allowed. At that point Machock, who also worked as an investment counselor, slid over to become part of UC's radio team, providing color commentary alongside first Paul Keels, then Jim Woods, and for the last 16 years with Hoard.

With Machock doing color commentary on the radio, he was able to remain part of the UC program while serving as a confidant for Huggins. They had the same approach to the game and the same sense of humor. To spend time with them on a UC road trip was to be treated to story after story about their days together. Some of them were hilarious, some weren't really all that funny, but there was no doubt about the joy they brought to the faces of both Huggins and Machock.

"I love him and he loves me," Machock said.

Machock was on the UC bench for Huggins' first game against Xavier and watched the Bearcats lose, 90-88, in overtime, in part because of a controversial officials' call. Huggins chased the official off the floor after the game.

"He went nuts a lot back then," Machock said.

Machock's favorite Crosstown Shootout was the 1992 game in which the Bearcats blew out the Musketeers, 93-75, after Nelson predicted a UC blowout win.

Machock enjoyed the lopsided win but he could have done without Nelson's pre-game bravado.

"We just whipped them," Machock said. "It was like 28-4 or something like that to start the game. It was when we had (Corie) Blount and (Herb) Jones and those guys. We beat them so bad the way we said we'd beat them when that stupid kid of ours had to say something. Hell yes, I agreed, but you don't say that. I've coached long enough to know that you shut your mouth."

As much as he loves to see UC beat Xavier, Machock takes pride in having supplied the Musketeers with one of the best guards in the school's history. He recruited Stan Kimbrough out of Cleveland to play for him at Central Florida. When things didn't go well in Orlando and he decided to leave, he told Kimbrough and several other players that he would help them find another school to transfer to.

"Stan had a hell of a game against Xavier when we came up and played them," Machock said. "So Stan says, 'I like Xavier. I would go to Xavier.' I said, 'Okay.' The coach was (Bob) Staak, who I knew real well. I got along with him extremely well. He was a great guy."

> **" I wouldn't say anything negative about Xavier. They're a bunch of Catholics doing a hell of a job. I'm a Catholic. "**

Kimbrough ended up at Xavier, but never played for Staak, who left for Wake Forest before Kimbrough arrived. But he thrived under Pete Gillen, scoring 1,596 points in three years to rank 14th on the Musketeers' career scoring list. He averaged 18.8 points his senior year when he made 41.7 percent of his 3-point shots.

Machock said Huggins never made beating Xavier a priority like he did with Louisville and Memphis.

"I think they always take Xavier lightly," Machock said of the Bearcats. "I really do. He did not make it a point that we'll come and get these guys. He was not that way with Xavier. He was that way about a lot of teams, but he never really made a big issue with those games."

He believes Xavier's approach is just the opposite.

"They wanted to try to prove to everybody that they were better than UC and for my cents worth, I think they took that game as the game of the year for them every damn year," Machock said. "They wanted to beat us and that's what they did. I ran into (Xavier president) Fr. (Michael) Graham once at dinner and all he could do was brag about how Xavier had Cincinnati's number. Huggs didn't like that. He grew to hate Xavier and Pete Gillen.

"He liked Skip Prosser a lot and he's got a reason to. I can tell you when I was in that assistant coaching part time, Skip would call me and he would ask me about Miami because we always played Miami. He would ask me, 'If we did this what would happen then, and how would you handle this?' So I grew to be pretty good friends with Skip."

Machock says it bothers him to see Xavier dominating the series in recent years.

"But that's where it stops," he said. "I'm being as honest as I can. I always thought and still do that Xavier plays it with more emotion than we do. But hold grudges? I don't hold grudges because it doesn't do any good. It doesn't help us win or lose. But do I want to see Cincinnati beat them every game? Absolutely. I wouldn't say anything negative about Xavier. They're a bunch of Catholics doing a hell of a job. I'm a Catholic. I've never missed Mass on Sunday in my life when I was in a position to go. I went to Catholic grade school and high school. That's a big part of my life."

Win or lose, Machock looks forward to the Shootout every year, not just for the competition he analyzes on the radio, but for the chance to mingle with the Xavier radio team of Joe Sunderman and Byron Larkin.

"I go down before every game," he said, "and I mean this, knowing that it's going to possibly get to a bad situation, I always have a little joke time with both of their announcers because I think they're great guys. Those are two good people, two very, very good people."

Mike DeCourcy, shown here after the 2012 Final Four in New Orleans, said the 2011 fight took some of the luster from the Crosstown Shootout.

MIKE DECOURCY

UC beat writer for the Cincinnati Enquirer, 1996-2000
National columnist for the Sporting News, 2000-present

"Until 2011, it was one of my favorite days of the year."

*B*efore he was hired to cover UC for the Cincinnati Enquirer in January 1997, Mike DeCourcy knew all about the Crosstown Shootout, but only from a distance. He had read about it. He had heard about it. But he had never seen it.

DeCourcy covered the Memphis Tigers for the Memphis Commercial Appeal in those days and the Shootout wasn't on national television back then.

"It was always kind of an annoyance for a basketball person that lived elsewhere to be unable to see it," DeCourcy said. "I was among the really excited people when they finally took it national because I knew what that would mean for people like me who at that point lived elsewhere."

During his first year at the Enquirer, DeCourcy just missed covering one of the biggest games in the history of the rivalry-the November 1996 game when the Musketeers upset top-ranked UC-because he took over the beat too late in the season. So his first experience covering the Shootout was during the 1997-'98 season when Xavier beat UC, 88-68, at Cincinnati Gardens.

"That was when X started so great," DeCourcy said, "and they just tore that Cincinnati team to pieces and then Cincinnati put themselves back together over the course of that year and Bobby Brannen had that great year and then they lost (to West Virginia) on that Jerrod West shot (in the second round of the NCAA Tournament)."

DeCourcy covered the game three times as the UC beat writer, then continued to cover it on a yearly basis after he went to the Sporting News. He estimates that he has covered 15 or 16 Shootouts altogether.

"The thing that struck me the most the first time I watched it was going into the arena and knowing that I was in a building that was in the middle of Cincinnati, so therefore there were probably a half a million (UC) fans that were within driving distance of that arena at the Gardens and there were maybe 50 in the building," DeCourcy said. "And that continued going back and forth from one building to the other.

"The fact that you would go into the building and there would be almost no 'enemy penetration' of the other team's building, to me, was just staggering because you would think that it would be easy for a Xavier fan to get into the Shoe or for a Cincinnati fan to get into the Gardens. Maybe it was, but no one did it and I don't know if that was because they didn't feel comfortable with it or just because the fans from one school to the other made such a concerted effort to unify.

"I think that said more about the rivalry than anything else that happened in all the time that I was going to the games with that unity of purpose among the fans. And that's what made it more unique than anything. I've gone to probably eight to ten Carolina-Duke games and there aren't as many seats at (Duke's) Cameron (Indoor Stadium) as there are at the Gardens or as there are at Cintas or as there other in the Shoe, but you would still see more Carolina fans at a Duke game at Cameron, not that many, but more than you would see at the Shootout.

"There are probably more similarities between those two rivalries because of the proximity. No one else at that heated of a rivalry has that level of proximity. I think it's eight miles between Duke and Carolina and it's three and a half between Xavier and Cincinnati. I think that makes it extraordinary."

DeCourcy has great respect for the Crosstown Shootout, but he ranks it behind Duke-North Carolina.

"The difference between the two rivalries is that for Cincinnati and Xavier they are Top 25, Top 30 teams. That's what they've become in modern college basketball," he said. "Duke and Carolina are among the three or five best and I think that's what elevates Duke and Carolina over (the Crosstown Shootout and Kentucky-Louisville).

"Louisville and Kentucky people want to claim that they have the best rivalry because they hate each other more, but I don't think that's necessarily the key ingredient. For me, the level of competition is the first ingredient in a rivalry, the fact that they are playing for national championships and have for 25 or 30 years and the fact that their competition is incredibly even. You go back a certain period of years and it's almost point for point even if you add up all the scores. That's how balanced they have been.

"I don't think that the rivalry between Cincinnati and Xavier has been quite that way. There have been more swings. This team really has it and then that team really has it and it goes back and forth, so it's been a little less balanced than Carolina and Duke. The other thing about the Shootout is that over the last 15 years or so, if you had to on balance say they have been great games, they really haven't. There have been a lot of fairly one-sided games in that rivalry.

"The problem with the Louisville-Kentucky rivalry that the people from Louisville and Kentucky won't acknowledge is that it doesn't have history. For a lot of people who are in the fight it does because some of them or a lot of them are younger than me now, so they don't remember that it wasn't played forever. It started up again in (1983). And so I don't think in that way it measures up as well because it doesn't have the history of some of these rivalries. Some of these rivalries have been played 100-plus times whereas the Louisville-Kentucky rivalry is still below 50, but because Kentucky and Louisville are so intense and because their programs

> "
> **One of the best things about Cincinnati for me was that it got college basketball in a way that very few cities do.**
> "

at this point are at such a high plane, I would probably say that rivalry is higher. But for history and for the locality of it, I think that the Crosstown Shootout certainly is in the top five."

Another thing that struck DeCourcy about the Shootout while he worked in Cincinnati is the wall of separation between the two schools. There was – and still is – very little crossover of fans between UC and Xavier, even when they're not playing each other. If UC is in the NCAA Tournament and Xavier isn't or if Xavier is in the Sweet 16 after UC has lost in an early round, very few UC fans begin to pull for the Musketeers and vice versa.

DeCourcy cites the 1997 NCAA Tournament when UC and Xavier both were sent to Auburn Hills, Mich., as an example.

"They weren't playing each other, but if they both won there then they would play in the Sweet 16 and I remember thinking at the very least they'll want each other to win so that they could play each other in the next round," DeCourcy said. "And there was none of that. I still remember Xavier fans in blue watching Cincinnati and Iowa State and sitting there with their arms folded. There was absolutely no pulling for Cincinnati at all even though they were from the same town and even though if they both won they would get a chance to play each other. There was no unity at all. I thought you're from the same town, can't you set that aside now? No, not at all, not in the least little bit.

"So I think there is definitely that feeling among a majority of fans on both sides that if they're not doing well they do not switch any allegiance at all. Or if they're watching the tournament and their game is over and Xavier is yet to come, they don't say, 'Okay, I hope they win as well.' I never felt that there was any of that crossover at all.

"I have a picture (from Auburn Hills) of this guy with grey hair and a baseball cap sitting across the way from me with his arms folded across his chest that I can't get away from. I'll never forget that. He was wearing blue. That was during the UC game and I remember the guy sitting there and being completely disengaged. He wasn't leaving, but he was not rooting for the Bearcats."

DeCourcy loved covering the Shootout while he worked for the Enquirer and even after he moved to the Sporting News while continuing to live in Cincinnati, but the fight at the end of the December 2011 game cast a pall over it for him.

"Until 2011 it was one of my favorite days of the year," said DeCourcy, who now lives in Indianapolis. "I would go into that building and I would be so thrilled. You'd start with the party at the Skyline Chili downtown, which I tried to make as many times as I could. You'd get the feel that this is basketball in Cincinnati and isn't that great? Cincinnati is a wonderful basketball town. I really loved living there for that reason. One of the best things about Cincinnati for me was that it got college basketball in a way that very few cities do, especially cities of its size. So it would start there and then I'd walk into The Shoe or I'd walk into Cintas and it would be my favorite 40 minutes. It was intense and the fans were so into it and I'd know both (coaches) and I'd know the players really well, as well as I'd know anybody's team once I was doing the national stuff.

"For me it was just one of the best days of the year. Whoever won, whoever lost, it was great for basketball in the city where I lived and I really looked forward to that. But to be honest, 2011 ruined it for me. It damaged it certainly. I went to the first one at U.S. Bank and it just wasn't the same for me. Going there was a letdown and being there was a letdown. It just did not feel the same. I haven't been to one since because of television obligations but 2011 was such a disappointment for me because that wasn't what it was supposed to be about."

DeCourcy remembers formulating his column as the 2011 game unfolded and focusing on a sportsmanship angle involving Xavier's Tu Holloway, who would play an instrumental role in the fight.

"Xavier was up 20-something and Xavier got a rebound of a shot that Cincinnati missed with about 15:45 left and they got a run-out and Tu Holloway pulled the ball out," DeCourcy said. "I thought, okay, I'm going to write about that, that he had this chance to rub it in but he did the right thing. That's was what was in my head. Then all of a sudden it took a complete 180 from that and he went over toward the bench area and things started to really get bad. From that standpoint, that moment in the rivalry is something that I think they're still working to repair. It needs to recover from that.

"I think it's on its way back because Chris (Mack) has Xavier in such a great spot and Mick (Cronin) is doing a great job at Cincinnati and the coaches are staying even though people are trying to get them away. And putting it back on campus for me was essential. It wasn't important. It was essential.

"I think (the Shootout) was damaged because it went over a limit that it didn't need to go over. That fight was inorganic to me. If someone had thrown an inadvertent elbow and started a fight you could live with that, but this was so totally unnecessary that I think it really took a lot of what made the rivalry special away.

"Then obviously the reaction to it, to move the rivalry off campus, I'm not saying it was necessarily an overreaction , but it wasn't something I would have done. I think it was a mistake and I think that took more of the beauty of the rivalry away. I think a great rivalry is one in which both sides really want to win and really feel pain about losing, but when it's over you act like an adult about it and I didn't think that happened there. I think the rivalry is in the process of recovering from that. The way the games have been contested the last few years there have been no problems and they've moved beyond that, so they are taking the steps that they need to take to heal it. But I don't think it's whole yet."

CROSSTOWN SHOOTOUT
BOX SCORES 1980-2016

Xavier 77, Cincinnati 69
Feb. 4, 1980 – Riverfront Coliseum

CINCINNATI				XAVIER			
SUTHERLAND	1	0	2	MASSA	6	0	12
AUSTIN	7	2	16	HANLEY	9	0	18
JONES	7	1	5	ANDERSON	7	1	15
LEE	10	6	26	K. WALKER	4	9	17
GAFFNEY	0	0	0	HICKS	3	4	10
JOHNSON	0	0	0	HOLLINS	2	0	4
SCHLOEMER	0	0	0	DOW	0	1	1
HOLDEN	1	0	2	A. WALKER	0	0	0
BENTLEY	2	1	5	**TOTALS**	**31**	**15**	**77**
TOTALS	**29**	**11**	**69**				

HALFTIME: XAVIER, 37-21. ATTENDANCE: 11,237

Cincinnati 79, Xavier 72
Feb. 18, 1981 – Riverfront Coliseum

CINCINNATI				XAVIER			
AUSTIN	6	6	18	BAILEY	4	2	10
JONES	8	1	17	JENKINS	4	0	8
HOLDEN	5	0	10	CONDON	0	0	0
JOHNSON	2	2	6	HICKS	8	5	21
KENNEDY	7	8	22	WOLF	2	0	4
BENTLEY	0	0	0	HOLLINS	1	1	3
WALLER	1	0	2	HANLEY	7	0	14
DUARTE	2	0	4	ANDERSON	3	0	6
SCHLOEMER	0	0	0	FLEMING	1	0	2
GAFFNEY	0	0	0	SHIMKO	2	0	4
DORRIS	0	0	0	**TOTALS**	**32**	**8**	**72**
TOTALS	**31**	**17**	**79**				

HALFTIME: UC, 40-29. ATTENDANCE: 12,864

Xavier 53, Cincinnati 51
Jan. 27, 1982 – Riverfront Coliseum

CINCINNATI				XAVIER			
HUGHES	1	1	3	BAILEY	7	0	14
JONES	4	7	15	SHIMKO	2	1	5
WILLIAMS	2	0	4	JENKINS	2	1	5
JOHNSON	0	0	0	WOLF	2	2	6
SCHLOEMER	2	2	6	HICKS	6	3	15
GAFFNEY	1	0	2	FLEMING	1	2	4
CAMPBELL	1	0	2	KELLEY	1	2	4
MCMILLAN	0	0	0	JOHNSON	2	0	4
AUSTIN	8	1	17	**TOTALS**	**22**	**9**	**53**
DORRIS	1	0	2				
TOTALS	**20**	**11**	**51**				

HALFTIME: XAVIER 34-29. ATTENDANCE: 7,863

Cincinnati 73, Xavier 58
Jan. 26, 1983 – Riverfront Coliseum

XAVIER				CINCINNATI			
BAILEY	1	0	2	DORRIS	2	2	6
SHIMKO	2	0	4	HUGHES	3	0	6
JOHNSON	2	3	7	JONES	4	0	8
HICKS	5	5	15	MCMILLAN	2	7	11
FLEMING	4	0	8	GAFFNEY	10	2	22
JENKINS	2	2	6	CAMPBELL	1	2	4
LEE	1	0	2	JOHNSON	2	10	14
WOLF	2	0	4	DUARTE	0	0	0
HANLEY	3	1	7	MCNALLY	0	0	0
JONES	0	0	0	WILSON	0	2	2
KELLEY	0	1	1	NIEMANN	0	0	0
HARRIS	1	0	2	KECMAN	0	0	0
DREW	0	0	0	**TOTALS**	**24**	**25**	**73**
TOTALS	**23**	**12**	**58**				

HALFTIME: 29-29. ATTENDANCE: 12,597

Xavier 72, Cincinnati 63
Jan. 26, 1984 – Cincinnati Gardens

CINCINNATI				XAVIER			
SZCZEPANSKI	2	2	4	BAILEY	1	2	4
DALE	4	0	8	SHIMKO	4	4	12
DORRIS	5	2	12	JENKINS	9	2	20
WILSON	4	2	10	LEE	7	1	15
TIGGS	1	0	2	FLEMING	1	1	3
MCMILLAN	4	4	12	GREENIDGE	3	0	6
NIEMANN	1	0	2	HARRIS	0	3	3
STIFFEND	2	4	8	MCBRIDE	4	1	9
PHIFFER	2	1	5	**TOTALS**	**29**	**14**	**72**
TOTALS	**25**	**13**	**63**				

HALFTIME: XAVIER, 32-24. ATTENDANCE: 7,826

Xavier 55, Cincinnati 52
Jan. 30, 1985 – Riverfront Coliseum

XAVIER				CINCINNATI			
HARRIS	4	1	9	HENRY	4	0	8
MCBRIDE	7	1	15	HUGHES	3	0	6
JOHNSON	0	0	0	HELM	0	0	0
LEE	3	5	11	MCMILLAN	3	3	9
LARKIN	5	2	12	MCCLENDON	9	2	20
DONNELLY	1	0	2	THOMPSON	1	1	3
GREENIDGE	3	0	6	STIFFEND	1	2	4
KELLEY	0	0	0	SHORTER	0	0	0
KELLEY	0	0	0	WILSON	1	0	2
BOWMAN	0	0	0	**TOTALS**	**22**	**8**	**52**
NOBLE	0	0	0				
TOTALS	**23**	**9**	**55**				

HALFTIME: XAVIER, 28-27. ATTENDANCE: 16,342

Xavier 80, Cincinnati 76
Jan. 23, 1986 – Cincinnati Gardens

CINCINNATI				XAVIER			
HENRY	7	6	20	HARRIS	3	0	6
HUGHES	3	4	10	MCBRIDE	6	7	19
GLOVER	0	1	1	JOHNSON	6	4	16
WILSON	0	2	2	LEE	3	6	12
MCCLENDON	6	4	16	LARKIN	8	8	24
PHIFFER	0	0	0	WILLIAMSON	0	1	1
SHORTER	0	2	2	GREENIDGE	0	0	0
STIFFEND	4	1	9	RAMEY	0	0	0
HELM	8	0	16	DONNELLY	1	0	2
TOTALS	28	20	76	TOTALS	27	24	80

HALFTIME: XAVIER, 38-29. ATTENDANCE: 10,376

Cincinnati 75, Xavier 73
Jan. 29, 1987 – Riverfront Coliseum

XAVIER				CINCINNATI			
TAYLOR	4	0	11	PHIFFER	4	0	10
CAMPBELL	1	0	2	STIFFEND	3	2	8
HILL	1	3	5	JACKSON	6	5	17
KIMBROUGH	4	3	13	MAY	3	0	6
LARKIN	8	8	24	MCCLENDON	10	4	29
K. WILLIAMSON	5	4	14	SHORTER	0	0	0
RAMEY	0	0	0	RUEHL	0	0	0
BARNETT	1	2	4	HAMILTON	0	0	0
KOESTER	0	0	0	FLYNN	1	3	5
TOTALS	24	20	73	TOTALS	27	14	75

3-PT. SHOTS: 5-13 (TAYLOR 3-5, KIMBROUGH 2-5).

3-PT. SHOTS: 7-11 (PHIFFER 2-2, MCCLENDON 5-7).

HALFTIME: CINCINNATI, 38-32. ATTENDANCE: 14,678

Xavier 98, Cincinnati 80
Jan. 12, 1988 – Cincinnati Gardens

CINCINNATI				XAVIER			
BANKS	5	0	10	BARNETT	4	5	14
STARKS	3	0	6	STRONG	2	4	8
GLOVER	4	0	8	HILL	7	4	18
ELLISON	7	3	18	LARKIN	8	10	26
MCCLENDON	6	0	13	KIMBROUGH	5	6	17
SHORTER	0	0	0	WALKER	4	2	10
GIVENS	1	1	3	DAVENPORT	0	0	0
RUEHL	1	0	2	BUTLER	0	0	0
ROBINSON	3	1	7	PARKER	0	0	0
WILLIAMS	2	0	4	CAMPBELL	2	1	5
JACKSON	3	2	9	KOESTER	0	0	0
MAY	0	0	0	TOTALS	32	32	98
FLYNN	0	0	0				
YATES	0	0	0				
TOTALS	35	7	80				

3-PT. SHOTS: 2-8 (BARNETT 1-4, KIMBROUGH 1-3).

3-PT. SHOTS: 3-9 (ELLISON 1-2, MCCLENDON 1-4, JACKSON 1-1).

HALFTIME: CINCINNATI, 41-39. ATTENDANCE: 10,313

Cincinnati 86, Xavier 76
Feb. 1, 1989 – Shoemaker Center

XAVIER				CINCINNATI			
DAVENPORT	1	4	6	BANKS	10	8	28
HILL	7	0	14	STARKS	4	9	17
STRONG	2	4	8	GLOVER	4	6	14
WALKER	3	3	9	GIVENS	4	2	10
KIMBROUGH	6	0	15	TATE	4	1	9
PARKER	4	3	14	FLYNN	2	4	8
MINOR	3	4	10	CARSTARPHEN	0	0	0
RAEFORD	0	0	0	WILLIAMS	0	0	0
BUTLER	0	0	0	HUGHES	0	0	0
TOTALS	26	18	76	TOTALS	28	30	86

3-PT. SHOTS: 6-29 (KIMBROUGH 3-11, PARKER 3-9).

3-PT. SHOTS: 0-3.

HALFTIME: CINCINNATI, 37-32. ATTENDANCE: 8,638

No. 25 Xavier 90, Cincinnati 88 (OT)
Jan. 31, 1990 – Cincinnati Gardens

CINCINNATI				XAVIER			
ROBINSON	9	3	21	DAVENPORT	6	1	16
BANKS	10	5	26	HILL	7	6	20
STARKS	3	1	7	STRONG	3	5	11
TATE	8	5	22	WALKER	7	4	21
SANDERS	3	0	7	GLADDEN	7	2	18
GIBSON	0	0	0	PARKER	0	0	0
HUGHES	0	0	0	BRANTLEY	2	0	4
JOINER	2	0	5	WILLIAMS	0	0	0
WARD	0	0	0	WILSON	0	0	0
TOTALS	35	14	88	BUTLER	0	0	0

3-PT. SHOTS: 4-9 (BANKS 1-2, TATE 1-2, SANDERS 1-3, JOINER 1-1)

3-PT. SHOTS: 8-20 (DAVENPORT 3-8, WALKER 3-7, GLADDEN 2-4).

HALFTIME: 38-38. ATTENDANCE: 10,112

Cincinnati 69, Xavier 56
Jan. 30, 1991 – Shoemaker Center

XAVIER				CINCINNATI			
DAVENPORT	4	0	11	JONES	7	0	14
BRANTLEY	1	1	3	REICHENEKER	0	0	0
WILLIAMS	2	0	4	BOSTIC	3	0	6
J. WALKER	2	2	6	JACKSON	0	2	2
GLADDEN	8	3	22	BANKS	4	5	13
GRANT	3	0	6	STARKS	4	2	11
T. WALKER	2	0	4	ROBINSON	4	5	13
WILSON	0	0	0	WILLIAMS	0	0	0
EDWARDS	0	0	0	GIBSON	4	0	10
POYNTER	0	0	0	TOTALS	26	14	69
TOTALS	22	6	56				

3-PT. SHOTS: 6-17 (DAVENPORT 3-9, GLADDEN 3-3).

3-PT. SHOTS: 3-9 (STARKS 1-5, GIBSON 2-3).

HALFTIME: CINCINNATI, 25-20. ATTENDANCE: 13,176

Cincinnati 93, Xavier 75
Jan. 29, 1992 – Cincinnati Gardens

CINCINNATI				XAVIER			
NELSON	2	2	6	WILLIAMS	4	1	9
JONES	11	1	26	BRANTLEY	3	0	8
SCOTT	1	0	2	GRANT	2	5	9
BUFORD	8	9	29	GENTRY	1	5	7
VAN EXEL	4	7	15	GLADDEN	5	2	14
MARTIN	3	2	8	POYNTER	0	0	0
GIBSON	0	0	0	KNOP	0	0	0
REICHENEKER	0	0	0	HAWKINS	7	3	22
BLOUNT	3	1	87	WALKER	1	0	2
JACKSON	0	0	0	EDWARDS	0	0	0
TOTALS	32	22	93	WILSON	1	2	4
				SYKES	0	0	0
				TOTALS	24	18	75

3-PT. SHOTS: 7-14 (JONES 3-3, BUFORD 4-6)

3-PT. SHOTS 9-20 (BRANTLEY 2-2, GLADDEN 2-7, HAWKINS 5-9).

HALFTIME: CINCINNATI 49-34. ATTENDANCE: 20,242

No. 6 Cincinnati 78, Xavier 67
Jan. 27, 1993 – Shoemaker Center

XAVIER				CINCINNATI			
HAWKINS	3	3	10	NELSON	2	2	6
WILLIAMS	3	2	8	BOSTIC	3	1	7
GRANT	5	0	10	MARTIN	4	10	18
GENTRY	2	2	6	GIBSON	3	1	8
GLADDEN	9	0	25	JACKSON	2	1	6
SYKES	1	2	4	BLOUNT	5	2	12
WALKER	1	2	4	DURDEN	0	6	6
MACK	0	0	0	VAN EXEL	4	4	15
EDWARDS	0	0	0	GREGOR	0	0	0
TOTALS	25	7	67	HARRIS	0	0	0
				TOTALS	23	27	78

3-PT. SHOTS: 10-19 (HAWKINS 1-3, GENTRY 2-3, GLADDEN 7-9).

3-PT. SHOTS: 5-15 (GIBSON 1-3, JACKSON 1-2, VAN EXEL 3-7).

HALFTIME: CINCINNATI, 38-31. ATTENDANCE: 13,176

No. 22 Xavier 82, No. 19 Cincinnati 76 (OT)
Jan. 19, 1994 – Cincinnati Gardens

CINCINNATI				XAVIER			
WINGFIELD	0	2	2	WALKER	6	3	16
BOSTIC	4	3	11	SEARS	3	0	6
HARRIS	1	0	2	SYKES	5	4	14
WRIGHT	1	2	4	GENTRY	2	2	6
DURDEN	7	0	18	HAWKINS	0	0	0
FLINT	2	0	4	ANDERSON	0	4	4
GREGOR	1	0	2	HARVEY	0	0	0
BURTON	4	10	20	MASSEY	8	1	20
JULSON	5	2	12	GRANT	4	8	16
JACOBS	0	1	1	EDWARDS	0	0	0
TOTALS	25	20	76	TOTALS	28	20	82

3-PT. SHOTS: 6-21 (DURDEN 4-9, BURTON 2-9).

3-PT. SHOTS: 6-21 (WALKER 1-3, GENTRY 2-5, MASSEY 3-7).

HALFTIME: XAVIER, 41-31. ATTENDANCE: 10,121

Cincinnati 87, Xavier 80
Jan. 9, 1995 – Shoemaker Center

XAVIER				CINCINNATI			
JOHNSON	2	6	10	FORTSON	7	2	16
SEARS	4	4	13	BURTON	2	2	7
SYKES	3	2	8	LONG	2	0	4
HAWKINS	9	2	23	LEGREE	1	4	6
MASSEY	9	0	20	DURDEN	13	2	33
ROSE	2	0	4	JACOBS	3	0	6
ANDERSON	0	0	0	WRIGHT	0	0	0
BRIT	1	0	2	BRANNEN	0	0	0
HARVEY	0	0	0	FLINT	0	0	0
TOTALS	30	14	80	BOSTIC	2	5	9
				GREGOR	3	0	6
				TOTALS	33	14	87

3-PT. SHOTS: 6-26 (SEARS 1-2, HAWKINS 3-9, MASSEY 2-13).

3-PT. SHOTS: 7-13 (BURTON 2-5, DURDEN 5-8).

HALFTIME: CINCINNATI, 41-33. ATTENDANCE: 13,176

No. 3 Cincinnati 99, Xavier 90
Jan. 17, 1996 – Cincinnati Gardens

CINCINNATI				XAVIER			
FORTSON	14	12	40	JOHNSON	5	1	11
BRANNEN	0	0	0	WILLIAMS	11	2	24
LONG	2	0	6	CARR	1	2	4
FLINT	5	16	19	BROWN	4	4	12
LEGREE	4	4	13	LUMPKIN	5	4	14
GREGOR	1	2	4	KELSEY	0	0	0
LEVETT	0	0	0	ANDERSON	0	0	0
DAVIS	0	0	0	HARVEY	1	8	11
BURTON	6	2	19	MURRAY	0	0	0
JULSON	0	0	0	PAYNE	1	1	3
MONROE	0	0	0	BRIT	5	1	11
TOTALS	32	26	99	TOTALS	33	22	90

3-PT. SHOTS: 9-16 (FLINT 3-4, LEGREE 1-2, BURTON 5-6).

3-PT. SHOTS: 2-16 (HARVEY 1-2, BRITT 1-3).

HALFTIME: CINCINNATI, 40-34. ATTENDANCE: 10,118

Xavier 71, No. 1 Cincinnati 69
Nov. 26, 1996 – Shoemaker Center

XAVIER				CINCINNATI			
JOHNSON	2	5	9	PATTERSON	6	1	13
WILLIAMS	1	2	4	FORTSON	7	4	18
BRAGGS	3	4	10	JULSON	0	0	0
BROWN	7	1	19	FLINT	3	4	10
LUMPKIN	5	0	13	WILLIAMS	2	6	10
POSEY	4	6	11	BURTON	3	1	9
ANDERSON	0	0	0	BAKER	0	0	0
PAYNE	0	2	2	MONROE	2	0	4
CARR	0	0	0	LEVETT	0	0	0
TOTALS	22	20	71	DAVIS	0	0	0
				TOTALS	24	19	69

3-PT. SHOTS: 7-18 (BROWN 4-8, LUMPKIN 3-8).

3-PT. SHOTS: 2-11 (BURTON 2-4).

HALFTIME: 31-31. ATTENDANCE: 13,176

No. 10 Xavier 88, Cincinnati 68

Dec. 13, 1997 – Cincinnati Gardens

CINCINNATI				XAVIER			
LEVETT	7	2	19	JOHNSON	2	3	7
BRANNEN	1	3	5	WILLIAMS	3	0	6
MARTIN	1	0	2	BRAGGS	4	6	14
BAKER	0	3	0	L. BROWN	7	8	23
HORTON	1	1	3	LUMPKIN	6	8	23
JACKSON	0	0	0	KELSEY	0	0	0
MYRICK	2	2	6	TURNER	0	0	1
FLETCHER	5	6	17	MCAFEE	0	0	0
PETRUS	6	1	13	A. BROWN	0	0	0
TOTALS	**23**	**17**	**68**	PAYNE	2	0	4
				POSEY	4	2	10
				BUTLER	0	0	0
				TOTALS	**28**	**26**	**88**

3PT. SHOTS: 5-15 (LEVETT 3-6, FLETCHER 1-2, PETRUS 1-1).

3-PT. SHOTS: 4-17 (L. BROWN 1-5, LUMPKIN 3-8).

HALFTIME: XAVIER, 50-35. ATTENDANCE: 10,100

No. 5 Cincinnati 87, Xavier 77

Jan. 28, 1999 – Shoemaker Center

XAVIER				CINCINNATI			
FREY	2	0	4	TATE	3	4	10
POSEY	3	6	13	MICKEAL	4	1	9
HARRIS	0	0	0	MARTIN	4	0	8
BROWN	7	2	1	HORTON	4	2	10
LUMPKIN	7	8	25	LEVETT	7	7	23
MCAFEE	1	2	5	MITCHELL	0	1	1
PRICE	3	2	8	LOGAN	5	5	17
TURNER	0	1	1	MYRICK	0	0	0
TOTALS	**23**	**21**	**77**	FLETCHER	4	1	9
				MCGHEE	0	0	0
				TOTALS	**31**	**21**	**87**

3-PT. SHOTS: 10-22 (POSEY 1-5, BROWN 5-9, LUMPKIN 3-6, MCAFEE 1-3).

3-PT. SHOTS: 4-13 (LEVETT 2-9, LOGAN 2-4).

HALFTIME: CINCINNATI, 34-29. ATTENDANCE: 13,176

Xavier 66, No. 1 Cincinnati 64

Dec. 18, 1999 – Cincinnati Gardens

CINCINNATI				XAVIER			
TATE	0	0	0	FREY	4	4	12
MICKEAL	7	3	17	PRICE	2	2	7
MARTIN	7	2	16	WEST	1	3	5
JOHNSON	2	1	6	MCAFEE	4	6	17
LOGAN	2	2	7	WILLIAMS	3	8	16
SATTERFIELD	3	2	8	MCINTOSH	0	0	0
STOKES	0	0	0	BROWN	4	1	9
FLETCHER	4	2	10	BUTLER	0	0	0
TOTALS	**25**	**10**	**64**				

3-PT. SHOTS: 4-11 (JOHNSON 1-3, LOGAN 1-4, FLETCHER 2-2).

3-PT. SHOTS: 7-17 (PRICE 1-3, MCAFEE 3-7, WILLIAMS 2-5, BROWN 1-1).

HALFTIME: XAVIER, 39-31. ATTENDANCE: 10,100

Xavier 69, No. 17 Cincinnati 67

Dec. 14, 2000 – Shoemaker Center

XAVIER				CINCINNATI			
FREY	4	5	15	DAVIS	5	0	10
PRICE	2	5	9	STOKES	7	0	16
WEST	4	15	23	LITTLE	0	0	0
SATO	5	1	14	SATTERFIELD	8	7	25
MCAFEE	2	1	6	MCELROY	0	1	1
CHALMERS	1	0	2	WILLIAMS	0	0	0
YOUNG	0	0	0	JONES	1	0	2
BROWN	0	0	0	LOGAN	3	0	8
BUTLER	0	0	0	CRAWFORD	0	0	0
TOTALS	**18**	**27**	**69**	GROVE	2	0	4
				TOTALS	**26**	**8**	**69**

3-PT. SHOTS: 6-23 (FREY 2-5, SATO 3-10, MCAFEE 1-4).

3-PT SHOTS: 7-24 (STOKES 2-5, SATTERFIELD 3-9, LOGAN 2-7).

HALFTIME: CINCINNATI, 40-33. ATTENDANCE: 13,176

Cincinnati 75, Xavier 55

Dec. 14, 2001 – Cintas Center

CINCINNATI				XAVIER			
DAVIS	6	0	12	FREY	3	1	7
MCELROY	7	0	14	SATO	6	2	15
LITTLE	3	3	9	WEST	4	1	9
STOKES	7	1	15	CHALMERS	8	0	19
LOGAN	7	4	22	YOUNG	0	1	1
BARKER	0	0	0	WILLIAMS	0	0	0
CRAWFORD	0	0	0	BROWN	1	0	2
MAXIELL	1	1	3	JACKSON	1	0	2
TOTALS	**31**	**8**	**75**	BARONAS	0	0	0
				TOTALS	**23**	**5**	**55**

3-PT. SHOTS: 5-10 (STOKES 1-2, LOGAN 4-8).

3-PT. SHOTS: 4-14 (SATO 1-3, CHALMERS 3-6).

HALFTIME: CINCINNATI, 39-30. ATTENDANCE: 10,250

No. 16 Xavier 50, Cincinnati 44

Dec. 7, 2002 – Shoemaker Center

XAVIER				CINCINNATI			
SATO	5	0	12	STOKES	6	1	13
WEST	10	2	23	MAXIELL	4	0	8
MYLES	3	0	6	JOHNSON	1	0	2
CHALMERS	2	1	5	WILLIAMS	1	0	2
FINN	1	2	4	BARKER	0	0	0
YOUNG	0	0	0	LAND	0	0	0
COLEMAN	0	0	0	HICKS	0	0	0
JACKSON	0	0	0	BOBBITT	0	3	3
CAUDLE	0	0	0	FLOWERS	1	0	2
TOTALS	**21**	**4**	**50**	KIRKLAND	2	0	4
				TOTALS	**18**	**4**	**44**

3-PT. SHOTS: 4-23 (WEST 1-4, CHALMERS 1-5, SATO 2-9).

3-PT. SHOTS: 4-22 (4-13).

HALFTIME: XAVIER, 25-20. ATTENDANCE: 13,176

Xavier 71, No. 10 Cincinnati 69
Feb. 3, 2004 – Cintas Center

CINCINNATI			
WHITE	1	0	2
MAXIELL	4	7	15
JOHNSON	2	2	6
F. WILLIAMS	1	1	3
NICK WILLIAMS	5	4	14
MOORE	1	0	2
HICKS	3	4	10
BOBBITT	6	0	17
KIRKLAND	0	0	0
WHALEY	0	0	0
TOTALS	23	13	69

XAVIER			
CAGE	0	5	5
DOELLMAN	3	1	10
MYLES	4	2	10
CHALMERS	8	1	20
SATO	4	9	18
FINN	3	1	8
COLE	0	0	0
CAUDLE	0	0	0
TOTALS	22	21	71

3-PT. SHOTS: 6-18 (DOELLMAN 1-6, CHALMERS 3-6, SATO 1-3, FINN 1-3).

3-PT. SHOTS: 10-19 (F. WILLIAMS 1-3, N. WILLIAMS 4-6, BOBBITT 5-9).

HALFTIME: XAVIER 37-32. ATTENDANCE: 10,250

No. 21 Cincinnati 65, Xavier 54
Feb. 10, 2005 – Shoemaker Center

XAVIER			
CAGE	2	6	10
DOELLMAN	2	6	10
CAUDLE	2	1	5
FINN	1	1	3
BURRELL	5	2	12
DUNCAN	2	1	5
THORNTON	1	1	3
ODA	0	0	0
JACKSON	2	2	6
TOTALS	17	17	54

CINCINNATI			
HICKS	6	4	16
KIRKLAND	4	3	12
MAXIELL	6	3	15
WILLIAMS	2	0	5
WHITE	1	2	4
MOORE	1	0	2
LUCAS	0	0	0
MUHAMMAD	3	1	7
BRIGHT	1	2	4
TOTALS	24	15	65

3-PT. SHOTS: 3-14 (FINN 1-2, BURRELL 2-5).

3-PT. SHOTS: 2-13 (KIRKLAND 1-5, WILLIAMS 1-4).

HALFTIME: CINCINNATI, 28-22. ATTENDANCE: 13,176

Xavier 73, Cincinnati 71 (OT)
Jan. 19, 2006 – Cintas Center

CINCINNATI			
HICKS	5	1	12
WHITE	7	1	16
MCGOWAN	5	0	11
MOORE	0	0	0
DOWNEY	8	2	22
MUHAMMAD	3	1	10
TOTALS	28	5	71

XAVIER			
THORNTON	7	6	20
CAGE	3	3	9
DOELLMAN	2	3	7
FINN	3	0	7
BURRELL	9	2	20
DUNCAN	2	2	6
RAYMOND	0	0	0
WOLF	0	0	0
CAUDLE	2	0	4
TOTALS	28	16	73

3-PT. SHOTS: 10-24 (HICKS 1-1, WHITE 1-6, MCGOWAN 1-2, DOWNEY 4-6, MUHAMMAD 3-7).

3-PT. SHOTS: 1-18 (FINN 1-8).

HALFTIME: CINCINNATI, 37-30. ATTENDANCE: 10,250

Cincinnati 67, Xavier 57
Dec. 13, 2006 – Fifth Third Arena

XAVIER			
DUNCAN	4	4	14
CAGE	5	3	14
DOELLMAN	2	0	4
LAVENDER	2	0	5
BURRELL	0	0	0
GRAVES	0	0	0
BROWN	3	2	8
RAYMOND	2	2	6
WOLF	0	0	0
COLE	3	0	6
TOTALS	21	9	57

CINCINNATI			
MCGOWAN	2	2	8
WILLIAMSON	6	4	18
SIKES	1	1	3
VAUGHN	9	4	24
WARREN	3	6	12
GENTRY	0	2	2
CROWELL	0	0	0
BARWIN	0	0	0
ALLEN	0	0	0
TOTALS	21	19	67

3-PT. SHOTS: 6-25 (DUNCAN 2-3, CAGE 1-4, LAVENDER 1-6, RAYMOND 2-4).

3-PT. SHOTS: 6-25 (MCGOWAN 2-5, WILLIAMSON 2-5, VAUGHN 2-10).

HALFTIME: UC, 32-29. ATTENDANCE: 13,176

No. 17 Xavier 64, Cincinnati 59
Dec. 12, 2007 – Cintas Center

CINCINNATI			
WILLIAMSON	3	3	9
HYRCANIUK	3	0	6
GENTRY	1	1	3
VAUGHN	3	2	10
WARREN	5	0	10
SIKES	0	0	0
DAVIS	3	0	9
WILKS	1	0	2
BISHOP	2	2	8
MCCLAIN	1	0	2
TOTALS	22	7	59

XAVIER			
DUNCAN	5	0	11
BROWN	5	7	17
RAYMOND	1	0	3
LAVENDER	4	2	12
BURRELL	2	4	10
GRAVES	0	0	0
ANDERSON	3	1	7
LOVE	2	0	4
TOTALS	22	14	64

3-PT. SHOTS: 8-18 (GENTRY 1-1, VAUGHN 2-5, DAVIS 3-5, BISHOP 2-4).

3-PT. SHOTS: 6-26 (DUNCAN 1-7, RAYMOND 1-4, LAVENDER 2-8, BURRELL 2-5).

HALFTIME: XAVIER, 29-25. ATTENDANCE: 10,250

No. 9 Xavier 76, Cincinnati 66
Dec. 13, 2008 – Fifth Third Arena

XAVIER			
BROWN	5	8	20
ANDERSON	7	3	17
LOVE	1	5	7
RAYMOND	1	1	3
JACKSON	4	4	15
REDFORD	1	0	3
MCLEAN	0	1	1
FREASE	1	2	4
HOLLOWAY	1	4	7
TOTALS	20	29	76

CINCINNATI			
WILLIAMS	1	1	3
BISHOP	2	0	4
GATES	1	0	2
VAUGHN	7	8	27
DAVIS	2	0	6
DIXON	3	5	11
WILKS	0	2	2
MILLER	0	0	0
MITCHELL	0	0	0
MCCLAIN	0	0	0
TOYLOY	5	1	11
TOTALS	21	17	66

3-PT. SHOTS: 7-19 (BROWN 2-5, RAYMOND 1-6, JACKSON 3-6, HOLLOWAY 1-1).

3-PT. SHOTS: 7-21 (VAUGHN 5-11, DAVIS 2-3).

HALFTIME: XAVIER, 39-25. ATTENDANCE: 13,176

Xavier 83, No. 19 Cincinnati 79 (2OT)
Dec. 13, 2009 – Cintas Center

CINCINNATI				XAVIER			
BISHOP	2	1	5	MCCLEAN	0	1	1
TOYLOY	0	0	0	LOVE	3	1	7
WRIGHT	1	2	4	LYONS	3	4	11
VAUGHN	6	0	13	JACKSON	2	3	9
STEPHENSON	9	2	22	HOLLOWAY	7	11	26
DIXON	0	3	3	REDFORD	0	0	0
DAVIS	2	0	4	TAYLOR	2	0	4
WILKS	3	0	8	FREASE	3	3	9
MCCLAIN	0	0	0	CRAWFORD	5	5	16
THOMAS	1	0	2	**TOTALS**	**25**	**28**	**83**
GATES	8	2	18				
PARKER	0	0	0				
TOTALS	**32**	**10**	**79**				

3-PT. SHOTS: 5-18 (LYONS 1-2, JACKSON 2-4, HOLLOWAY 1-5, CRAWFORD 1-6).

3-PT. SHOTS: 5-23 (VAUGHN 1-7, STEPHENSON 2-4, WILKS 2-4).

HALFTIME: XAVIER, 31-26.. ATTENDANCE: 10,250

No. 24 Cincinnati 66, Xavier 46
Jan. 6, 2011 – Fifth Third Arena

XAVIER				CINCINNATI			
MCLEAN	6	6	18	BISHOP	3	0	8
FREASE	4	0	8	THOMAS	1	0	2
LYONS	5	0	11	GATES	10	2	22
JACKSON	0	2	2	WRIGHT	1	8	10
HOLLOWAY	2	1	5	DIXON	6	3	16
LATHAN	0	0	0	JACKSON	0	0	0
FEENEY	0	0	0	DAVIS	2	0	8
TAYLOR	0	0	0	WILKS	0	0	0
ROBINSON	1	0	2	KILPATRICK	0	0	0
MCKENZIE	0	0	0	MCCLAIN	0	0	0
TOTALS	**18**	**9**	**46**	**TOTALS**	**23**	**15**	**66**

3-PT. SHOTS: 1-10 (LYONS 1-2).

3-PT. SHOTS: 5-16 (BISHOP 2-3, DIXON 1-4, DAVIS 2-4).

HALFTIME: CINCINNATI, 28-20. ATTENDANCE: 13,176

No. 8 Xavier 76, Cincinnati 53
Dec. 10, 2011 – Cintas Center

CINCINNATI				XAVIER			
JACKSON	0	0	0	WELLS	7	0	14
KILPATRICK	3	4	11	WALKER	1	0	2
GATES	7	4	18	FREASE	6	1	13
WRIGHT	1	2	4	LYONS	6	4	19
DIXON	4	6	14	HOLLOWAY	5	6	17
MBODJ	1	0	2	DAVIS	0	0	0
GUYN	0	0	0	TAYLOR	0	1	1
SANDERS	0	0	0	REDFORD	2	0	4
GAINES	0	0	0	MARTIN	2	0	5
PARKER	1	2	4	ROBINSON			
TOTALS	**17**	**18**	**53**	**TOTALS**	**29**	**13**	**76**

3-PT. SHOTS: 1-16 (KILPATRICK 1-8).

3-PT. SHOTS: 5-14 (LYONS 3-5, HOLLOWAY 1-5, MARTIN 1-1).

HALFTIME: XAVIER 34-25. ATTENDANCE: 10,250

No. 11 Cincinnati 60, Xavier 45
Dec. 19, 2012 – U.S. Bank Arena

XAVIER				CINCINNATI			
TAYLOR	6	0	12	JACKSON	0	0	0
MARTIN	0	0	0	MBODJ	1	1	3
PHILMORE	3	2	8	WRIGHT	5	2	15
CHRISTON	3	0	6	KILPATRICK	10	3	25
DAVIS	3	0	7	PARKER	2	7	11
FARR	0	0	0	RUBLES	1	0	2
REDFORD	2	1	6	THOMAS	1	0	2
ROBINSON	3	0	6	GUYN	1	0	2
AMOS	0	0	0	SANDERS	0	0	0
STENGER	0	0	0	NYARSUK	0	0	0
TOTALS	**20**	**3**	**45**	**TOTALS**	**21**	**13**	**60**

3-PT. SHOTS: 3-14 (PHILMORE 2-5, REDFORD 1-2).

3-PT. SHOTS: 5-24 (WRIGHT 3-7, KILPATRICK 2-10).

HALFTIME: XAVIER, 24-22. ATTENDANCE: 14,258

Xavier 64, Cincinnati 47
Dec. 14, 2013 – U.S. Bank Arena

CINCINNATI				XAVIER			
RUBLES	0	3	3	MARTIN	5	4	17
THOMAS	5	1	13	PHILMORE	2	2	6
JACKSON	0	1	1	M. STAINBROOK	2	3	11
GUYN	0	0	0	CHRISTON	3	0	8
KILPATRICK	4	8	17	D. DAVIS	1	0	3
CAUPAIN	2	0	4	REYNOLDS	0	0	0
LAWRENCE	1	1	3	FARR	4	0	10
SANDERS	0	0	0	RANDOLPH	3	0	8
JOHNSON	2	1	5	WHELAN	0	0	0
NYARSUK	0	0	0	M. DAVIS	2	0	5
TOBLER	0	0	0	T. STAINBROOK	0	0	0
TOTALS	**14**	**14**	**47**	AMOS	0	0	0
				COKER	0	0	0
				STENGER	0	0	0
				TOTALS	**22**	**9**	**64**

3-PT. SHOTS: 5-14 (THOMAS 2-3, KILPATRICK 1-3, CAUPAIN 1-3, JOHNSON 1-3).

3-PT. SHOTS: 11-16 (MARTIN 3-5, CHRISTON 2-3, DAVIS 1-2, FARR 2-2, RANDOLPH 2-3, M. DAVIS 1-1.

HALFTIME: XAVIER, 41-25. ATTENDANCE: 10,250

Xavier 59, Cincinnati 57
Feb. 18, 2015 – Fifth Third Arena

XAVIER				CINCINNATI			
BLUIETT	0	0	2	ELLIS	5	1	11
STAINBROOK	3	1	7	CLARK	7	0	14
ABELL	2	1	5	SANDERS	0	0	0
D. DAVIS	5	1	16	CAUPAIN	3	2	9
M. DAVIS	4	1	12	JOHNSON	1	0	2
REYNOLDS	2	3	7	MORMAN	0	0	0
FARR	3	1	7	THOMAS	4	0	8
MACURA	1	0	3	COBB	3	0	9
TOTALS	20	9	59	DEBERRY	2	0	4
				TOTALS	24	3	47

3-PT. SHOTS: 10-17 (D. DAVIS 5-5, M. DAVIS 3-5, FARR 1-2, MACURA 1-2).

3-PT. SHOTS: 4-16 (CAUPAIN 1-3, COBB 3-10).

HALFTIME: XAVIER, 36-24. ATTENDANCE: 13,176

No. 12 Xavier 65, No. 23 Cincinnati 55
Dec. 12, 2015 – Cintas Center

CINCINNATI				XAVIER			
ELLIS	6	1	13	REYNOLDS	4	0	8
CLARK	0	0	0	SUMNER	5	1	11
THOMAS	5	0	11	BLUIETT	1	0	3
CAUPAIN	3	2	10	ABELL	3	0	9
COBB	3	2	11	DAVIS	7	0	17
EVANS	2	0	4	AUSTIN	0	0	0
DEBERRY	1	1	3	FARR	4	1	9
JOHNSON	1	0	3	O'MARA	1	0	2
JENIFER	0	0	0	MACURA	2	2	6
TOBLER	0	0	0	TOTALS	27	5	65
TOTALS	21	6	55				

3-PT. SHOTS: 7-26 (THOMAS 1-4, CAUPAIN 2-9, COBB 3-8, JOHNSON 1-2).

3-PT. SHOTS: 6-15 (ABELL 3-5, DAVIS 3-3-4).

HALFTIME: XAVIER, 42-26. ATTENDANCE: 10,617

OVERALL SERIES
UC leads 49-34

BEFORE 1980
UC leads 34-12

FROM 1980 TO PRESENT
Xavier leads 22-15

LONGEST UC WIN STREAK
12 (1957-'67)

LONGEST XAVIER WIN STREAK
3 (three times, most recently from 2013-'16)

UC's LARGEST WINNING MARGIN
36 points, 89-53, March 7, 1961

XAVIER'S LARGEST WINNING MARGIN
26 points, 88-62 on Jan. 9, 1957

OVERTIME GAMES
Xavier leads, 5-1

GAMES DECIDED BY THREE OR FEWER POINTS
Xavier leads 15-6

GAMES DECIDED BY 10 OR MORE POINTS
UC leads, 30-8

NATIONAL CHAMPIONSHIPS
UC 2, Xavier 0

FINAL FOURS
UC 6, Xavier 0

ELITE EIGHTS
UC 8, Xavier 2

SWEET 16s
UC 13, Xavier 7

NCAA TOURNAMENTS
UC 30, Xavier 26

NIT CHAMPIONSHIPS
Xavier 1, UC 0

NIT APPEARANCES
UC 10, Xavier 5

Sources: Cincinnati and Xavier media guides

— ALL-TIME UC-XAVIER RESULTS —

March 7, 1928 – Xavier 29, UC 25 (Schmidt Fieldhouse)
March 3, 1943 – Xavier 51, UC 37 (Schmidt Fieldhouse)
Feb. 27, 1946 – UC 53, Xavier 39 (Schmidt Fieldhouse)
Feb. 26, 1947 – UC 76, Xavier 51 (Schmidt Fieldhouse)
March 3, 1948 – UC 52, Xavier 45 (Schmidt Fieldhouse)
Feb. 5, 1949 – Xavier 71, UC 64 (Schmidt Fieldhouse)
March 9, 1949 – UC 57, Xavier 46 (Cincinnati Gardens)
March 9, 1950 – Xavier 54, UC 53 (Cincinnati Gardens)
March 18, 1950 – UC 59, Xavier 48 (Cincinnati Gardens)
Dec. 28, 1950 – UC 83, Xavier 70 (Cincinnati Gardens)
March 8, 1951 – UC 81, Xavier 66 (Cincinnati Gardens)
Dec. 29, 1951 – Xavier 77, UC 70 (Cincinnati Gardens)
Feb. 13, 1952 – UC 68, Xavier 63 (Cincinnati Gardens)
Jan. 6, 1953 – Xavier 81, UC 78 (Cincinnati Gardens)
Feb. 10, 1953 – Xavier 70, UC 68 (Cincinnati Gardens)
Jan. 6, 1954 – UC 77, Xavier 58 (Cincinnati Gardens)
Feb. 10, 1954 – UC 81, Xavier 76 (Cincinnati Gardens)
Jan. 6, 1955 – Xavier 67, UC 64 (Cincinnati Gardens)
Feb. 9, 1955 – UC 70, Xavier 69 (Armory Fieldhouse)
Jan. 17, 1956 – UC 71, Xavier 66 (Cincinnati Gardens)
Feb. 8, 1956 – Xavier 79, UC 72 (OT) (Armory Fieldhouse)
Jan. 9, 1957 – Xavier 88, UC 62 (Cincinnati Gardens)
Feb. 13, 1957 – UC 69, Xavier 57 (Armory Fieldhouse)
Dec. 14, 1957 – UC 79, Xavier 68 (Armory Fieldhouse)
March 8, 1958 – UC 80, Xavier 68 (Cincinnati Gardens)
Jan. 24, 1959 – UC 92, Xavier 66 (Cincinnati Gardens)
March 7, 1960 – UC 86, Xavier 68 (Cincinnati Gardens)
March 2, 1961 – UC 89, Xavier 53 (Cincinnati Gardens)
March 1, 1962 – UC 61, Xavier 58 (Cincinnati Gardens)
Feb. 26, 1963 – UC 72, Xavier 61 (Cincinnati Gardens)
March 4, 1964 – UC 94, Xavier 92 (Cincinnati Gardens)
March 3, 1965 – UC 102, Xavier 72 (Cincinnati Gardens)
March 3, 1966 – UC 67, Xavier 62 (Cincinnati Gardens)
March 3, 1967 – UC 79, Xavier 69 (OT) Cincinnati Gardens
March 5, 1968 – Xavier 72, UC 71 (Cincinnati Gardens)
Jan. 8, 1969 – UC 52, Xavier 50 (Cincinnati Gardens)
Feb. 17, 1970 – UC 85, Xavier 72 (Cincinnati Gardens)
Feb. 17, 1971 – Xavier 66, UC 65 (Cincinnati Gardens)
Feb. 16, 1972 – UC 76, Xavier 71 (Cincinnati Gardens)
Feb. 21, 1973 – UC 78, Xavier 68 (Cincinnati Gardens)
Feb. 20, 1974 – UC 68, Xavier 56 (Cincinnati Gardens)
Feb. 26, 1975 – UC 66, Xavier 57 (Cincinnati Gardens)

Feb. 18, 1976 – UC 81, Xavier 74 (Riverfront Coliseum)
Feb. 16, 1977 – UC 77, Xavier 68 (Riverfront Coliseum)
Feb. 13, 1978 – UC 59, Xavier 54 (Riverfront Coliseum)
Feb. 12, 1979 – UC 60, Xavier 58 (Riverfront Coliseum)
Feb. 4, 1980 – Xavier 77, UC 69 (Riverfront Coliseum)
Feb. 18, 1981 – UC 79, Xavier 72 (Riverfront Coliseum)
Jan. 27, 1982 – Xavier 53, UC 51 (Riverfront Coliseum)
Jan. 26, 1983 – UC 73, Xavier 58 (Riverfront Coliseum)
Jan. 26, 1984 – Xavier 72, UC 63 (Cincinnati Gardens)
Jan. 30, 1985 – Xavier 55, UC 52 (Riverfront Coliseum)
Jan. 23, 1986 – Xavier 80, UC 76 (Cincinnati Gardens)
Jan. 29, 1987 – UC 75, Xavier 73 (Riverfront Coliseum)
Jan. 12, 1988 – Xavier 98, UC 80 (Cincinnati Gardens)
Feb. 1, 1989 – UC 86, Xavier 76 (Cincinnati Gardens)
Jan. 31, 1990 – Xavier 90, UC 88 (OT) (Cincinnati Gardens)
Jan. 30, 1991 – UC 69, Xavier 56 (Shoemaker Center)
Jan. 29, 1992 – UC 93, Xavier 75 (Cincinnati Gardens)
Jan. 27, 1993 – UC 78, Xavier 67 (Shoemaker Center)
Jan. 19, 1994 – Xavier 82, UC 76 (OT) (Cincinnati Gardens)
Jan. 9, 1995 – UC 87, Xavier 80 (Shoemaker Center)
Jan. 17, 1996 – UC 99, Xavier 90 (Cincinnati Gardens)
Nov. 26, 1996 – Xavier 71, UC 69 (Shoemaker Center)
Dec. 13, 1997 – Xavier 88, UC 68 (Cincinnati Gardens)
Jan. 28, 1999 – UC 87, Xavier 77 (Shoemaker Center)
Dec. 18, 1999 – Xavier 66, UC 64 (Cincinnati Gardens)
Dec. 14, 2000 – Xavier 69, UC 67 (Shoemaker Center)
Dec. 14, 2001 – UC 75, Xavier 55 (Cintas Center)
Dec. 7, 2002 – Xavier 50, UC 44 (Shoemaker Center)
Feb. 3, 2004 – Xavier 71, UC 69 (Cintas Center)
Feb. 10, 2005 – UC 65, Xavier 54 (Shoemaker Center)
Jan. 19, 2006 – Xavier 73, UC 71 (OT) (Cintas Center)
Dec. 13, 2006 – UC 67, Xavier 57 (Shoemaker Center)
Dec. 12, 2007 – Xavier 64, UC 59 (Cintas Center)
Dec. 13, 2008 – Xavier 76, UC 66 (Shoemaker Center)
Feb. 13, 2009 – Xavier 83, UC 79 (2OT) (Cintas Center)
Jan. 6, 2011 – UC 66, Xavier 46 (Shoemaker Center)
Dec. 10, 2011 – Xavier 76, UC 53 (Cintas Center)
Dec. 19, 2012 – UC 60, Xavier 45 (U.S. Bank Arena/Coliseum)
Dec. 14, 2013 – Xavier 64, UC 47 (U.S. Bank Arena/Coliseum)
Feb. 18, 2015 – Xavier 59, UC 57 (Shoemaker Center)
Dec. 12, 2015 – Xavier 65, UC 55 (Cintas Center)

Sources: Cincinnati and Xavier media guides

PHOTO CREDITS

COACHES SECTION

Page 18 – Photo courtesy of the Cincinnati Enquirer.

Page 25 – Photo courtesy of the University of Cincinnati.

Page 28 – Photo courtesy of the Cincinnati Enquirer.

Page 33 – Photo courtesy of the Cincinnati Enquirer.

Page 36 – Photo courtesy of the Cincinnati Enquirer/Craig Ruttle.

Page 42 – Photo courtesy of the Cincinnati Enquirer/Jeff Swinger.

Page 49 – Photo courtesy of the Cincinnati Enquirer/Stephen M. Herppich.

Page 53 – Photo courtesy of the University of Cincinnati.

Page 56 – Photo courtesy of the Cincinnati Enquirer/Jeff Swinger.

Page 62 – Photo courtesy of the Cincinnati Enquirer/Sam Greene.

Page 70 – Photo courtesy of the Cincinnati Enquirer/Ernest Coleman.

Page 76 – Photo courtesy of the University of Cincinnati.

Page 82 – Photo courtesy of the Cincinnati Enquirer.

XAVIER PLAYERS SECTION

Page 88 – Photo courtesy of the Cincinnati Enquirer.

Page 95 – Photo courtesy of the Cincinnati Enquirer.

Page 98 – Photo courtesy of the Cincinnati Enquirer.

Page 104 – Photo courtesy of the Cincinnati Enquirer.

Page 108 – Photo courtesy of the Cincinnati Enquirer.

Page 112 – Photo courtesy of the Cincinnati Enquirer/Ernest Coleman.

Page 118 – Photo courtesy of the Cincinnati Enquirer/Tony Jones.

Page 123 – Photo courtesy of the Cincinnati Enquirer/Craig Ruttle.

Page 126 – Photo courtesy of the Cincinnati Enquirer/Joseph Fuqua II.

Page 133 – Photo courtesy of the Cincinnati Enquirer/Stephen M. Herppich.

Page 137 – Photo courtesy of the Cincinnati Enquirer/Brandi Stafford.

Page 140 – Photo courtesy of the Cincinnati Enquirer/Ernest Coleman.

Page 144 – Photo courtesy of the Cincinnati Enquirer/Ernest Coleman.

Page 148 – Photo courtesy of the Cincinnati Enquirer/Jeff Swinger.

Page 154 – Photo courtesy of the Cincinnati Enquirer/Frank Victores.

PHOTO GALLERY SECTION

From left to right, top to bottom.

Page 162 – Photo courtesy of the Cincinnati Enquirer.

Page 163 – Photo courtesy of the Cincinnati Enquirer/Leigh Taylor.

Page 163 – Photo courtesy of the Cincinnati Enquirer/Glenn Hartong.

Page 164 – Photo courtesy of the University of Cincinnati.

Page 164 – Photo courtesy of the University of Cincinnati.

Page 164 – Photo courtesy of the Cincinnati Enquirer/Jeff Swinger.

Page 165 – Photo courtesy of the Cincinnati Enquirer/Ernest Coleman.

Page 165 – Photo courtesy of the Cincinnati Enquirer/Jeff Swinger.

Page 165 – Photo courtesy of the Cincinnati Enquirer/Ernest Coleman.

Page 166 – Photo courtesy of the Cincinnati Enquirer/Brandi Stafford.

Page 166 – Photo courtesy of the Cincinnati Enquirer/Ernest Coleman.

Page 166 – Photo courtesy of the Cincinnati Enquirer/Cameron Knight.

Page 166 – Photo courtesy of the Cincinnati Enquirer.

Page 167 – Photo courtesy of the Cincinnati Enquirer.

Page 167 – Photo courtesy of the Cincinnati Enquirer/Ernest Coleman.

Page 167 – Photo courtesy of the Cincinnati Enquirer/Jason Clark.

Page 168 – Photo courtesy of the Cincinnati Enquirer.

Page 168 – Photo courtesy of the Cincinnati Enquirer.

Page 168 – Photo courtesy of the Cincinnati Enquirer.

Page 169 – Photo courtesy of the Cincinnati Enquirer.

Page 169 – Photo courtesy of the University of Cincinnati.

Page 170 – Photo courtesy of the Cincinnati Enquirer/Kareem Elgazzas.

Page 170 – Photo courtesy of the Cincinnati Enquirer/Ernst Coleman.

Page 170 – Photo courtesy of the Cincinnati Enquirer/Sam Greene.

Page 171 – Photo courtesy of the Cincinnati Enquirer/Saed Hindash.

Page 171 – Photo courtesy of the Cincinnati Enquirer/Jeff Swinger.

Page 171 – Photo courtesy of the Cincinnati Enquirer/Saed Hindash.

Page 171 – Photo courtesy of the Cincinnati Enquirer/Steven M. Herppich.

UC PLAYERS SECTION

Page 174 – Photo courtesy of the Cincinnati Enquirer.
Page 181 – Photo courtesy of the University of Cincinnati.
Page 184 – Photo courtesy of the University of Cincinnati.
Page 190 – Photo courtesy of the University of Cincinnati.
Page 194 – Photo courtesy of the University of Cincinnati.
Page 201 – Photo courtesy of the University of Cincinnati.
Page 204 – Photo courtesy of the University of Cincinnati.
Page 210 – Photo courtesy of the University of Cincinnati.
Page 217 – Photo courtesy of the University of Cincinnati.
Page 220 – Photo courtesy of the University of Cincinnati.
Page 224 – Photo courtesy of the University of Cincinnati.
Page 228 – Photo courtesy of the University of Cincinnati.
Page 234 – Photo courtesy of the University of Cincinnati/Ernest Coleman.
Page 238 – Photo courtesy of the Cincinnati Enquirer/Jeff Swinger.
Page 244 – Photo courtesy of the University of Cincinnati.
Page 248 – Photo courtesy of the University of Cincinnati.
Page 255 – Photo courtesy of the Cincinnati Enquirer.

MEDIA SECTION

Page 258 – Photo courtesy of the Cincinnati Enquirer/Glenn Hartong.
Page 265 – Photo courtesy of the Cincinnati Enquirer.
Page 268 – Photo courtesy of Dan Hoard.
Page 274 – Photo courtesy of the University of Cincinnati.
Page 278 – Photo courtesy of Mike DeCourcy.

ABOUT THE AUTHOR

*B*ill Koch grew up in Cincinnati, attended the University of Dayton and earned his bachelor of arts degree from the University of Cincinnati in English in 1977. He worked as a reporter at the *Community Press* from 1976 to 1978, the *Chillicothe Gazette* in 1978, the *Cincinnati Post* from 1978 to 2001, and the *Cincinnati Enquirer* from 2002 to 2014. He has covered everything from high school sports to Xavier University basketball, UC basketball and football, the Cincinnati Bengals, the Cincinnati Reds and professional tennis. He was the sports columnist at The Post from 1997 to 2001. Koch is the author of three previous books on high school sports plus a memoir, *I Can't Believe I Got Paid For This*, published in 2015. He has covered over 30 Crosstown Shootouts and as a beat reporter has seen the rivalry up close from the vantage of both UC and Xavier. He currently writes for GoBearcats.com, UC's athletics web site.

CPSIA information can be obtained
at www.ICGtesting.com
Printed in the USA
LVOW04s2207111216
516840LV00022B/1748/P

9 780998 277103